Pr

"Many companies and leaders have a compulsion to grow, which leads them to create workplaces filled with striving and stress. But there is a far better, healthier approach to growing a business, one that is about the emotional and spiritual growth of its leaders and employees. Such companies become sources of healing, and the more they grow, the better it is for the world and all the lives they touch. BIGGBY COFFEE is one such company. In this important and inspiring book, Michael McFall shares how he acquired and applied the wisdom to become a healing leader."

–RAJ SISODIA, FEMSA Distinguished University Professor of Conscious Enterprise, Tecnológico de Monterrey, co-founder and chairman emeritus, Conscious Capitalism, Inc.

"Any book that uses four pages to cover the work of a beer league hockey team manager in relationship to leadership is a book I want to read."

–STEVE YZERMAN, general manager and longest-serving captain in NHL history, Detroit Red Wings (1986–2006)

"Entrepreneurs are the backbone of our economy. I meet them every day in my work and commend those like Michael McFall who are willing to share their experiences and insights to help future generations follow in their footsteps."

–JOHN TUTTLE, vice chairman, New York Stock Exchange

"This book is like a look inside the heart and soul of a leader who has traversed the landscape from bootstrapping entrepreneur to bonified leader of a powerful company. It is down to earth and practical with sage advice for anyone looking to go on the same journey."

—JOSH LINKNER, co-founder and managing partner, Muditā Venture Partners, *New York Times* best-selling author of *Big Little Breakthroughs* and *Disciplined Dreaming*

"This is a powerful work that outlines the importance of putting human beings and healthy relationships at the center of one's organizational philosophy. We need more business leaders like Michael McFall, who takes a strong stand on JEDI (Justice, Equity, Diversity, and Inclusion) while understanding his own positionality. I am proud of him for writing this book, but—as I know he would expect—I would urge him to keep going further and deeper along the JEDI path."

—LISA BROCK, PHD, professor emeritus and former academic director, Kalamazoo College, JEDI (Justice, Equity, Diversity, and Inclusion) consultant

"I spent the last two decades moving the software industry from chaos to joy. Now my friend Michael McFall is helping me—with his hard-won wisdom in *GROW*—to move from chaos to calm. The lessons in the book are simple and practical and require personal change that is both hard and uplifting. This timeless book will be a staple in the Menlo Innovations library."

—RICHARD SHERIDAN, CEO and chief storyteller, Menlo Innovations at Ann Arbor, author of *Joy, Inc.* and *Chief Joy Officer*

"To transition from being a successful entrepreneur to an inspiring leader, one must recognize that culture is the secret sauce of the most successful organizations. With self-effacing humor and candor, this book provides a roadmap for this transformation."

—JORGE G. GONZALEZ, PHD, president, Kalamazoo College

"If you read only one book this year on business leadership, *GROW* by Michael McFall is *the* book to read. Based upon his deeply ingrained leadership principle that all (business) success is based upon the ability to create, nurture, and *grow* healthy relationships, he has grown his company BIGGBY COFFEE from zero to over $100 million in revenue. Michael McFall understands that a true leader seeks to acknowledge both the personal and professional lives of his employees and how they impact each other. He describes the importance of using active listening to ensure all employees feel valued and heard. Thank you, Michael McFall, for sharing your wisdom and insight in *GROW*—the leadership book every leader must read."

—DR. PATTY ANN TUBLIN, CEO and founder, Relationship Toolbox, LLC

"Leading an organization to sustainability and scale requires a completely different approach than leading a startup from zero to profitability. In his new book, Michael McFall provides a compelling roadmap for leaders looking to *grow* into success at scale."

—KURT SKIFSTAD, PHD, Dixon and Carol Doll executive director, University of Michigan Center for Entrepreneurship

"The most important topic for any manager today relates to people. This book provides many valuable insights and suggestions on how to better engage your people and create a healthy environment."

—**LANCE KEZIAH,** CEO, Crypton

"*Zing!* The leader as a chameleon is so simple yet so powerful. Michael McFall does a nice job of explaining how adaptability both is important and can be exhausting at the same time. Read on for more simple yet powerful nuggets you can carry forward in your role as a leader."

—**STUART SHULMAN,** CEO, Omni Holding Company, LLC

"This is next-gen content on leadership. I am excited to see the messages in this book land in the world and their positive impact proliferate."

—**JOE SAAD,** managing partner, Diag Partners

"This book opened my eyes to quite a few different concepts. I love learning new and different ways to think. Take the time to read it, and I promise you will walk away with value."

—**CHRIS MCCUISTON,** CEO,
Goldfish Swim School Franchising, LLC

GROW

MICHAEL J. McFALL

TAKE

[YOUR BUSINESS]

FROM CHAOS

TO CALM

GROW

AN INC.
ORIGINAL

An Inc. Original
New York, New York

www.anincoriginal.com

Distributed by Greenleaf Book Group

For ordering information or special discounts for bulk purchases, please contact Greenleaf Book Group at PO Box 91869, Austin, TX 78709, 512.891.6100.

Design and composition by Greenleaf Book Group
Cover design by Greenleaf Book Group
Cover images copyright Anneka, 2022; Ian 2010, 2022.
Used under license from Shutterstock.com

Publisher's Cataloging-in-Publication data is available.

Print ISBN: 978-1-63909-010-5

eBook ISBN: 978-1-63909-011-2

To offset the number of trees consumed in the printing of our books, Greenleaf donates a portion of the proceeds from each printing to the Arbor Day Foundation. Greenleaf Book Group has replaced over 50,000 trees since 2007.

Printed in the United States of America on acid-free paper

23 24 25 26 27 28 29 30 10 9 8 7 6 5 4 3 2 1

First Edition

GROW is dedicated to my parents, Jim and JoAnn McFall, who have provided me with unwavering support through all the twists and turns life has presented. They taught me the value of staying focused on growing and learning, and countless lessons in this book were a product of my relationship with them—I am eternally grateful

[CONTENTS]

Foreword

IT WAS SPRING OF 2017, and I remember sitting in our large classroom at the BIGGBY COFFEE Home Office, listening to our co-CEOs share the results of a cultural survey/assessment. I was cemented to my chair. I felt like I weighed five thousand pounds, and I could not budge. I heard my own words read back to me through Mike's mouth, and I was stunned to hear his voice quiver. Mike's voice never shook. I always viewed him as unshakable. Unbreakable. Unchangeable. Larger than life. Something more than human. That is what we do with CEOs, isn't it? We expect them to be more than human, larger than life. The problem is, if you are more than human, you need little growth. That makes you a lifeless stone pillar. Strong? Yes. But growing? Nope.

Everything changed that day for BIGGBY COFFEE, for me, and I believe for Mike McFall. I was an entry-level employee when the cultural survey/assessment was shared with our Home Office staff. Upon listening to how our company was described at that moment—with happiness as a cultural expectation but not a personal reality—and with genuine concern about this dynamic, I settled in, prepared for and wanting to be part of what was to come next. Bob and Mike finished reporting and solemnly committed to changing and improving the culture of the company. Nobody knew what it was going to look like or feel like, but we believed it was going to be powerful. Our leaders, who had tirelessly worked for over twenty years to build a remarkably successful company, were onstage apologizing for our unhealthy culture and committing to doing whatever it took to have our culture close the gap between cultural expectation and the personal reality for everyone in the room. A place where genuine happiness was not a cultural expectation but a cultural norm.

The following year, with cultural work well underway, Mike and Bob introduced a plan to change up leadership and our organizational structure to better suit our new reality. I had been with the company only four years, but I threw my hat in the ring and found myself sitting at the senior leadership table. Cue overwhelming imposter syndrome.

We had critically important work to do—to find our company's Purpose and Vision. It took two years of painstaking effort, commitment, and dedication to develop it. We struggled through personal vulnerability, philosophical disagreements, and our own biases, so we made friendly amendments to get on the same page. The Purpose and Vision we landed on read, "BIGGBY COFFEE exists to support you in building a life you love." During this time, I found myself sitting around the table with Mike, disagreeing more often than was comfortable. For those personality type nerds, I feel like I should mention that I am a DiSC style S, Enneagram 9, and Meyers-Briggs type ISFJ. Peacekeeping is my gift, over debate and disagreement. All voices on that committee were critical, including mine, so I powered through and brought everything I had to the group. In the end, we were in love with and committed to our purpose.

During those painstaking yet powerful two years, I grew quickly on the steepest trajectory of my life, and Mike was there adding rocket fuel to my tank. Two stories will be recounted in *GROW*, but Mike's impact goes beyond a few stories; I am the person I am today because of his unrelenting care and support. Make no mistake, when Mike cares about your growth, watch out, as you will be forced off the easy path of comfort and consistency and launched into the land of discovery and questioning. I have been hit with his straightforward feedback (as Brené Brown would say, "Clear is kind,") and experienced frustration in falling short of a challenge but also absolute joy in meeting a different challenge. Throughout, I struggled with unforeseen setbacks in my own development and experienced the joy that comes with new realizations and understanding. Mike has been with me through it all, and after this many years, I can attest that he won't quit. I would only worry if he stopped bringing me the tough stuff.

My hope is that this book and our stories can help other leaders have the courage to start their own quest for purpose while finding their stride with their people so they can become the leaders their organizations require. That is my journey. Now, let us talk about Mike's journey from my vantage (even though I am quite sure he is going blush).

In *GROW*, you will hear a slight change in tone from his first book, *GRIND* (and if you have not read it yet, trust me, you *want* to). This is due to his evolution from the stone pillar I described at the beginning of this section into a tree: still powerful and strong, but vulnerable, flexible, alive, and growing. During the first 20 years of

BIGGBY COFFEE, Mike and Bob bootstrapped our company to stability, and while I am thankful for the position that Mike and Bob put us in today, it required a hard-edged leadership style that produced an unhealthy culture—one that led to unpredictability and "spicy" conversations between Mike and people all around our organization. Maniacal day in and day out. This is simply not the same person who you will hear from in *GROW*, who describes the importance of consistency, emotional stability, and a persistent focus on nurturing people.

Mike and I have talked about whether mania is critical to the success of a start-up, but that topic is too much for us to take on. We will leave that question for a research team at some university to drill into.

I had a front-row seat to see Mike's hardness and unpredictability melt away as he grew. It started at the fateful all-staff meeting I described, but I also vividly remember pivotal some moments from a particularly influential conference that Mike and I attended, the Conscious Leadership Group Forum. Mike and I felt like frauds when we got there: People were having conversations about going all-in on Purpose and Vision while we had only scratched the surface within our company. They chewed on the power and responsibility of corporations to do what governments can't—caring for people, all people. They discussed how to disassemble the patriarchal system and become truly inclusive. These were powerful conversations. In addition, the group did breathing exercises to start each session and stressed the power of meditation. They even had a gong!

While I treaded through the philosophical and metaphysical mud cautiously, Mike leaned all the way in. I watched him sort through a particularly difficult assessment of his own involvement in perpetuating patriarchal stereotypes with one of the hosts, who was an out-and-proud, female member of the LGBTQIA+ community. Later, I watched Mike admit onstage how much we didn't know about business and organizational health. It was an important display of vulnerability. And when we were all invited to effectively mosh to electric dance music with a spoken word performing artist, Mike didn't hesitate. He *went for it.* Mike can mosh. Trust me. It was amazing to see.

This is what Mike does. When confronted with an opportunity to grow, he leans all in and goes for it. Once he has a solid understanding of something, he has this deep calling to share it with others. I am confident that this is how he ended up as a professor at the University of Michigan. He wants to share what he has learned so others can synthesize and improve their understanding. That is how my team came to exist. The Life You Love Laboratory at BIGGBY COFFEE is the practical idea incubator for putting love into leadership through systematic practice and continual learning. We are first working within BIGGBY, and then we are looking to take it to America and beyond. Our job is to collect, systematize, and share what we know about purpose- and people-forward practices. The creation of LifeLab is how Mike instinctively both impacted our organization and committed to helping others grow.

That nuanced shift in tone from *GRIND* to *GROW* is the result of a massive shift in attitude and perspective from the Mike of his bootstrapping years to the Mike I know today.

This book is a gift because it cuts straight through to what truly matters in the pursuit of growing people by building a loving, nurturing, and supportive environment within companies, which propels people to build a life they love.

There is nothing in this book that Mike has not learned firsthand by trying it himself, failing, learning, trying again, growing, learning, trying again, and finally teaching others what he learned. That is the magic of it.

This book is not a complex series of abstract ideas that have to be carried out in their entirety in order to make a difference in people's lives. Rather, it is a series of simple, human ideas that should be treated more like a toolbox from which you are able to carefully choose the right tool for what is needed to support the individual you are working with directly.

I described Mike as having changed from a stone pillar into a living and growing tree, but the more remarkable thing is that he is not satisfied with his own growth. He is busy propagating a forest.

Grab a pen—you are going to need to jot things down. He is starting with you. Enjoy this read, and learn about how to love people and create an environment for them to thrive and turn into their most beautiful, powerful, and ever-growing selves.

Listen, learn, lead!

Laura

Introduction

MY BUSINESS PARTNER AND I have beaten the 1-in-37,000 odds that a start-up can reach $100M in revenue. I want the same for you!!

I started out as a barista in the very first BIGGBY COFFEE location in East Lansing, Michigan, in the mid-1990s, and joined with the owners of that store, Bob Fish and Mary Roszel, to develop what has become the BIGGBY COFFEE phenomenon with more than 300 stores. We surpassed the $100M benchmark some time ago.

The journey from concept/idea to profitable enterprise was covered in my first book, GRIND. If you've met that first major milestone of generating positive cash flow from your start-up, congratulations! You have beaten those odds. (Only 40 percent of start-up businesses ever reach this threshold.)

But if you are like me and Bob, you're always ready to chase the next milestone. For our entrepreneurial journey, there were many along the way, but the grandest milestone of all was this—sustainability. Where you, the entrepreneur, can get trucked by a bus, end up six feet under sucking tulip roots, but your company will continue to thrive. I am defining that as $100 million in revenue. Yes, this numerical hurdle is debatable, but I ask for leeway on specifics because it's a good, clean, round number.

The fact is most entrepreneurs exit before reaching sustainability, and more often than not, it's no peaceful swan song, no tiptoeing through the tulip garden in a graceful exit. Instead, they end up with a valuation considerably less than their aspiration, or they wind down their business in a less-than-gratifying way. Even worse, they might lose the business or crash and burn headlong into bankruptcy. Why? It's mainly because they can't get out of their own way.

Here's the rub: Everything you learned to become successful as an entrepreneur, what got you through the GRIND phase and to positive cash flow, needs to be chucked out the window and forgotten. You need to evolve into a completely different person to lead a sustainable enterprise. Most entrepreneurs can't make the transition, even the very "successful" who are selling for tens of millions—who cash out, take their chips off the table, because they don't believe they can elevate as a leader and take the company where it needs to go to become sustainable. They sell to a private equity firm or a strategic buyer who has the expertise and know-how to grow the business into perpetuity. Frankly, they give up and miss out on the absolute joy of growing their company into a jewel to be proud of. For so many entrepreneurs, everything focuses on the "exit." But is it really only about the size of the check at the end of the day?

Cashing out, for many, is not a spiritually enriching event. Sure, they walk away wealthy, but more often than not, they don't feel good about the experience, and they are left wanting. The process beats them down.

Let me be clear: There is nothing wrong with cashing out. But I advocate doing it on your terms. If you build your business to the point of sustainability, you have ultimate freedom to do it on your terms. There is a different and better way than making the exit your obsession.

There is a better way, and that is the premise of this book. There is an outcome that is more powerful than cashing out early and becoming another fat cat at the country club playing the game, "Who's richer?"

What does that outcome look like? Retaining ownership of your company and building the same company the professionals (private equity investors or strategic buyers) would. Let's get you to sustainability. Let's get you to $100M and beyond. Let's build your organization from wherever it is today to one that is rock solid, with a strong culture and a strong leadership team in place. A place where you are an owner of an asset that you spent your life building and take great pride in. This path will not only give you more options in the long run, but it will also put you in an incredibly strong position to cash out if and when you choose to do so. If you have built a sustainable company, you will be more powerful in the process of selling and get a much more desirable—financial and nonfinancial—outcome from the final deal you strike.

This is what Bob and I aspire to accomplish. We want the legacy of growing and managing something from the beginning all the way to the end. Years ago, we realized that if we sold BIGGBY and had a piggy bank full of money but were not proud of the outcome, we would have failed. If all stakeholders in the business weren't taken care of, we knew we would have been ashamed of our work. If BIGGBY ended up in the hands of some devotee of Milton Friedman who was solely in the business of maximizing shareholder value, we would feel like our life's work was at best compromised and at worst gutted. That was not going to be our outcome.

Our ideal outcome is to be 80ish (still decades from now!) and retiring from a leadership role in the business, with ultimate flexibility of what we want to do with our asset—our baby. We wanted to take on the challenge of transforming and growing the company by growing as people and becoming the leaders the company needed in order to reach sustainability.

We knew we might screw it up if we couldn't grow and transition from bootstrapping entrepreneurs to leaders, but we knew that process would be more intriguing, more interesting, and more fulfilling than sitting in a rocking chair stroking our overflowing piggy bank.

We believe we are 85 percent of the way to full sustainability. We believe BIGGBY would continue to thrive even if one or both of us went tits up today, but we have some things we are still working on and we are extremely confident we will make the full transition.

This book is about the growth and transition we had to go through as individuals to make our sustainability goal achievable. My hope is that this book will encourage your thinking and guide you to a place where you can beat the 1-in-37,000 odds as well, where you are leading an incredibly powerful company and where you as the founder/entrepreneur have many options as you move into the twilight of your career.

Manage and Lead with Love

Ask anyone I work with. I am a hard-core pragmatist who loves to grind numbers and crush strategy with anyone. I am as hard nosed and hard charging as anyone you know. I started as a minimum wage barista 26 years ago, and I am now selling over $250M a year in coffee. If street credibility is important to you, I hope I have earned enough to push you into a few areas that make most people uncomfortable. Do I have your permission?

I hope you'll believe me when I say that to continue to grow your business, you need to become 100 percent focused on people and the relationships within your organization. They are all that matter; they are everything. You need to make love the glue that holds your organization together. Yep, I did it! I used the word "love" in the context of management and leadership. Some will shut down when they read those four letters. I am here to tell you the organization of the future is going to make love the cornerstone of what they do. Get with it or get left behind.

Yes, I know that the traditional mindset is to hit your numbers, accomplish your tasks, keep your nose clean, and hopefully everything works. Miss your numbers, fall short on your work, or engage in unhealthy behavior, and bam, you are sent packing. It's on you, the employee. Be accountable or be gone with you.

But times are a-changing. Being a good manager/leader is about relationships. Relationships are a two-way street. You are as accountable for your people's success as they are. You must constantly bring value to them, and when that is your focus, you will find people falling all over themselves to support you too. The relationship will be mutually beneficial, a two-way street. Your people will be in love with you and vice versa because you are both committed to the personal growth and development of one another. To me that is the definition of love.

Here is what I know to be true: Great organizations, great teams throughout history were overflowing with love; we just didn't call it that. I share examples later. This book is written to attempt to unlock the power of love. I promise you this isn't some bullshit, smarmy book written by a dope-smoking hippie who lives in the land of Oompa Loompas riding a unicorn through a tulip field. Love isn't only about making people warm and fuzzy. Love is so much more. It is about engaging somebody and supporting them in their own growth so they can have the life of their dreams, a life they love. You can't do this with only gratitude and platitudes. Often it entails having hard conversations. It is holding a mirror up and reflecting unacceptable behavior. It is reminding people of their commitments, and yes, it is ultimately about telling people they are amazing when, well, they are amazing.

This book is not soft, and love most definitely doesn't let anyone off the hook. Having an environment that is loving is often much harder than running one that isn't. Solutions to problems can become more complicated when love is the baseline.

When you manage from a position of love, you are obligated to know your people intimately, to know them better than they know themselves. You are coaching and mentoring them daily; you get to be a part of the inner sanctum. If somebody is falling short, it is as much on you as their manager as on them to course-correct and get things moving in a healthy direction as it is on them. If you work with them and don't see progress, you have an obligation to move the person into a more suitable role. Here we go with another primary theme of this book, the responsibility starts with you. It is on you to make sure you are building healthy teams, and that starts by having healthy members. Your job is to lead each member of your team, to coach and teach them so they reach their potential specifically at work and more generally in life. The responsibility is immense.

Not for the Faint of Heart

Be prepared for the transition from bootstrapping entrepreneur to leader to be a winding journey and excruciatingly painful. I am proposing you first completely overhaul your personality to become a great leader and then ultimately strive to make yourself irrelevant in your business. Once you are irrelevant, you have completed the grow phase of your business journey. It's unsettling to go from knuckle-grinding, spit-flying, maniacal control freak of the start-up phase to the loving, tender, nurturing leader of the growth phase to one who is finally unnecessary once the business is sustainable. And as hard as that first transition is, from entrepreneur to leader, the second, from leader to irrelevant, is even harder.

Most entrepreneurs, most people, want to feel needed. It makes them feel worthy. It gives them identity; it gives them a reason for being. When you are unnecessary, your phone doesn't ring, and your calendar is pretty open. You will be left feeling dumb because you aren't aware of something pivotal happening in the organization. Your temper will flair as your team tells you an interaction with a middle manager was unhealthy and way too "micro." You were just trying to be helpful. People in the organization will still copy you on things but more to be polite than because they need you and/or want your approval. Being irrelevant is gut wrenching, infuriating, lonely, and unsettling.

You are going to screw up constantly. The learning curve is going to feel like a sheer rock face. You have no ropes, no guides, nobody at the top shouting words of encouragement because so few have been able to make the transition. Your hands will feel like they are on wet rocks with loose foundations. You will feel like you can fall at any time. Sound dramatic? It is! Remember, 1 in 37,000.

Not only is feeling irrelevant hard, but watching your baby—your business—go off to college to be raised by others—your management team—is like taking a heavy body blow. Your team will do things with which you disagree, and you must support them and even encourage them anyway. You must believe in them with all your soul—not because you must let them make mistakes and learn, which is often how this process is framed by many leaders, but because you hired them, and they are smarter than you. Now, you have to let them work. Eeecckk! What? Yep, they are smarter than you. It is a hard pill to swallow.

I always know I am in the presence of a simplistic, unsophisticated leader when I hear "let them fall, skin their knees, and learn," because the assumption in that line of thinking is that the manager knows the one and only "right" answer and is letting them go down a different path. If this is your mindset—and it is the thinking of many managers/leaders—you need this book deeply. If you are doing your job appropriately and assembling a team to run the business for you by hiring and developing leaders who are better in their discipline than you, then that collective group is going to be infinitely smarter than you and their decisions will be better than yours. It is a psychological chasm most entrepreneurs can't get over. Most want to stay in the space of skinning knees, as it allows them to continue to be the smartest person in the room.

In the end what I am talking about is ego management. Ego is a beast with big hairy fangs, dripping with blood. Everyone has one. When I hear somebody say they don't have an ego, I automatically understand that they lack emotional intelligence. Strong management/leadership isn't about eliminating ego, it is about being mindful and making sure we know how it is impacting our behavior and how that behavior is impacting our team and business. Those who understand their ego have a chance at becoming powerful leaders, and those that can't will run middling enterprises that never reach the promised land of sustainability.

You will grow accustomed to hearing and understanding the voice of your ego. You will begin to evaluate it while breathing deeply and treading lightly as it drives spikes into your heart and soul. The conflict between you and your ego will be intense. Understanding that your ego is not you and that it can be coached and understood is pivotal to your growth and development as a leader. Managing your ego will become a huge part of your life and be one of the hardest management challenges you face.

As I said, this is not for the faint of heart.

Defining the New You

To help you understand the priorities and responsibilities as you take a business from bootstrapping profitability to the promised land of sustainability, I talk about the following five topics in this book:

- Part 1: Due Diligence on You describes the traits you will need to develop as you and your business grow and develop. I don't offer a comprehensive list; rather, I describe what I think are the most important traits if you want to be a solid leader whose business will continue to grow.
- Part 2: Beyond Bean Bag Chairs and Kegerators—Building a Better Workplace covers the attributes of a workplace where employees can lead their fullest lives (both inside and outside of work) and will put in their best efforts to help you build a sustainable business.

- Part 3: Welcoming All Voices reviews what you need to do to build a workplace where communication is healthy and respectful, rather than destructive and divisive.
- Part 4: The Power of Learning and New Perspectives provides general tips for broadening your horizons and keeping you attuned to worthy new ideas, along with specific tools that will help your business stay ahead in a rapidly changing marketplace.
- Part 5: Organizations of Tomorrow describes the four things you must do if you want to create a modern organization that thrives well beyond your involvement.

Take a Deep Breath

Rest assured that the journey from hard-driving entrepreneur to inspiring leader of a growing business is not linear—and you shouldn't expect it to be. It will ebb and flow; you will get sucked back into your entrepreneurial role regularly—more so in the early part of your journey, but over time (it took Bob and me 20 years), you will begin to understand the new dynamic you need to build more and more. The more you become aware of your impact and cede control to your team and grow comfortable with the results, the more confidence you will have that you are doing the right things.

Again, the goal is to get the business to the point where you are irrelevant to the day-to-day operations, meaning that you are only involved in the things you want to be and that your team agrees are healthy for you to engage. This provides you ultimate flexibility once established. You can continue to own the business but not manage, you can sell the business, you can bring in strategic partners who can aid your growth, you can do an IPO, you can pass it on to your children, you can keep managing and go out with your boots on. Whatever your goal, you will be well prepared to guide the business and see it through to the best possible outcome for everyone involved, yourself included.

Godspeed!

PART 1

DUE DILIGENCE ON YOU

As you and your business begin the metamorphosis needed to go from bootstrapping upstart to sustainable enterprise, the demands on you as a leader change dramatically. As I talked about in GRIND, too many entrepreneurs spend too much time doing traditional due diligence, investigating issues such as capital structure, real estate, financial projections, market and demographics, consumer behavior, and so on. Yes, it is important that you understand all those factors.

But what I said in GRIND holds true here as well: the single most important factor that will determine whether your business will successfully traverse the GROW phase and reach sustainability is you and how you choose to interact with your business—or, better said, how you choose to interact with the people in your business. With your business growing, you can't be the only leader anymore. You need to be creating an environment where people thrive. You need to be growing leaders.

Are you prepared? You won't know unless you do the appropriate due diligence on yourself. You must understand your strengths and weaknesses to determine where you thrive and where you need support.

Self-awareness and emotional intelligence have become buzzwords. Though they're often used, I think they're rarely understood. In my mind, both can be summed up in one simple concept: Do you understand the impact you and your behavior are having on those around you? It is the rare bird that does. Showing you how to become one of these rare birds is the topic of part 1.

We all have an impact on the people around us, for better or worse. Getting grips on this magical power is an enormous challenge. Even well-meaning, nice people have an impact on others, the nature of which is often news to them. It is complicated because our impact on one person is different from our impact on another. That's why self-awareness is the first step in becoming an effective leader.

Leading people is about having an intimate enough relationship with those you are leading to know individually how people react to you and your impact on them. There is much more on this subject later in the book, but the chapters here in part 1 contain principles you should consider as you dive into the GROW phase and develop the skills of solid leadership and management. As always, it is not a comprehensive list; it is a list of the most important traits needed to be a solid leader.

- Chapter 1: Getting Relationships Right—The Importance of Fluidability talks about how you will be tested regularly on your ability to stay fluid and adaptable (i.e., fluidability) in the GROW phase. There is no one-size-fits-all management style or strategy here. You will need to engage differently with each person and situation to achieve positive and healthy outcomes. To do this, you will have to become chameleonlike, shifting your own mentality and the type of engagement from moment to moment, person to person as you go about your days. It is on you to learn and understand who you need to be in a given moment. It is one of the great challenges of leadership.
- Chapter 2: Emotional Stability—Creating a Thriving Home for Your Team is about the counterpoint to fluidability. While you need to be like a chameleon and behave differently in different moments, you also need to be perfectly stable emotionally. Your team members need to feel safe when coming to you to discuss difficult business or personal issues. They can't get a calm, level-headed leader one day and a frenetic, hyperactive gerbil the next.

Being consistent and even keeled is paramount to allowing your team to grow into their roles as leaders, and knowing how you are going to react provides them with a feeling of safety.

- Chapter 3: Optimism—Where Dreams Turn into Reality promotes the need for optimism as the leader. From the moment your business is conceived to its getting through the GROW phase, you are the energy source to your team. You have to bring the juice or magic pixie dust to the room. People need to see from you that it is all under control and you believe in what is happening and have full faith and confidence in the direction of the company—because if you don't nobody will.
- Chapter 4: Integrity—The Superpower to Gaining Trust expresses the critical need for integrity. You can't lead properly if you are not a person of integrity. Everyone needs to believe in you and your actions. If you lose integrity in the eyes of your team, you will create a debilitating environment that is insurmountable to overcome.

These chapters take on a critical aspect of leadership that is often overlooked. It is mission critical you show up in your business in the way that it and your team need you to show up at any given time. This will feel amorphous because you will need to adapt depending on where your business and leadership team are in any given moment. It will vary from day to day, and that can be exhausting. Worse, there is no guidebook for leading your particular team. It is on you to become powerful in your role, and these chapters describe the principles you'll need to be able to live out. If you can do that, congratulations! You have a fighting chance to reach sustainability. If not, you must accept that you will struggle to GROW your business.

CHAPTER 1

Getting Relationships Right–The Importance of Fluidability

IN *THE NEW ECONOMICS FOR INDUSTRY, GOVERNMENT, EDUCATION,* W. Edwards Deming says, "An important job of management is to recognize and manage the interdependence between components. Resolution of conflicts, and removal of barriers to cooperation, are responsibilities of management."[1] Most managers don't understand these important concepts about managing the relationships between people. If you aren't making this a priority, dysfunction will be what thrives in your organization.

Let's do a little math so I can illustrate why managing relationships is so difficult and so critical. Let's say each member of your team has nine different variables that affect their personality, work style, and general demeanor. What could these be? Randomly, I'll point out self-awareness, extroversion vs. introversion, verbosity, humility, cultural bias, experience, independence, sociability, health, relational status, and the weather. (Yes, I included the weather because rainy days are extraordinarily productive days for me, whereas a colleague of mine gets depressed on rainy days because she knows she is going to miss time in her garden that evening.)

In case you are counting, I purposely offered eleven possible variables in order to make the point that nine is an absurdly low number. In reality, the internal and external factors that affect people and their ability to healthily perform/engage in the workplace is verging on infinite. In the business environment, maybe someone is taking night classes on management and is eager to try out new knowledge. Maybe someone else has a coworker who just quit, causing their own workload to double. On the personal side, maybe someone just learned a good friend from high school passed away. They may have missed breakfast because their dog got loose, and they spent 30 minutes tracking Spot. Maybe the song they heard on the way to work reminded them of an ex-lover and they miss this person terribly. I could go on, but since I had to pick a number for this illustration, I picked nine for the sake of my argument.

If you have seven team members with nine different variables impacting how they are showing up to work on any given day, the interaction of those variables is seven to the ninth power. That means there are 40,353,607 different dynamics playing out in the bubble of your team. Take that number to 12 variables with eight team members and you have 68.7 billion potential interpersonal dynamics. Even if you just had three people on your team, there are nearly 20,000 different potential dynamics at play.

Do you see why it's a problem that many leaders believe they understand the dynamics within their team and have the answers to all conflicts and challenges? Or that they try to analyze the dynamics and bring solutions? It is impossible, simply impossible. There is no way for you to hold all of that inside, do the analysis, and bring answers to your team.

This is why fluidability is critical: You as the leader need to be attuned to the complexity of your leadership team and remain fluid and adaptable in order to hold that team in a place of trust. Doing so gives them the ability to work through their individual and collective issues—to be loving, caring, and hold each other in a place of respect. As a result, they will naturally resolve the day-to-day, minute-by-minute stuff smoothly, easily, and on their own.

What does it take to develop fluidability? I talk about some key factors in this chapter. As you read through, ask yourself how much these behaviors sound like you. If they don't apply to how you conduct yourself in the workplace, I propose reflection and consideration of how to support yourself in professional growth in these areas specifically.

Meeting People Where They Are

Life is complex. Each team member shows up with their own stuff. Your job is to make sure the group is prepared to take on that complexity and to help everyone bring everything they have to the moment. Some days will be amazing and dynamic for some people and middling for others. This is healthy, but to get the best out of our team, we need to be prepared as leaders to support each member where they are.

Not only do you have the innerworkings of the personality variables of each member of your team, you also have the fact that each member of your team is developing and growing differently and at different paces. It is not their job to grow and learn at the same pace. It is your job to meet each individual member where they are and coach and support them as they learn and grow independently and as a unit.

Once again, let me quote from *The New Economics* by W. Edwards Deming: "People are different from one another. A manager of people must be aware of these differences, and use them for optimization of everybody's abilities and inclinations. This is not ranking people. Management of industry, education, and government operate today under the supposition that all people are alike."[2]

Managers acting as if all people are alike? Nothing could be further from the truth. One person might be very good at analytical thinking; she gets the budget process down cold on day two. Someone else might have four years under their belt, but when the budget is mentioned, he turns into a third grader, slinking down in his chair and avoiding eye contact. You, as leader, have to fully understand that remaining fluid and bringing people along in all areas of the business must be based on where they are in the moment, not on where you think they should be or even where you need them to be.

Also, somebody who six months ago was a train wreck and is now starting to hit their stride and is needing less and less attention will be counterbalanced by a manager who for years has been a rock but just lost five of eight staff and is beginning to realize the weakness of his management style and is going to need a ton of your attention immediately. This is how it goes. As you start to feel more comfortable with one person on your team, yet another will need you to engage more aggressively. It is like being prepared to push all the rocks uphill simultaneously.

Your leadership team as it develops should become one of the most fun-loving, challenging, quirky, idiosyncratic puzzles you have ever enjoyed. Members are different people, performing different roles, at different paces, coming together around one "table" to effectively manage your organization.

You will need to understand the intricate wiring in each of your people. Some have pink, purple, blue, and yellow wires that are all crisscrossed and frayed, with sparks streaking and exploding, like an old-fashioned foundry. Other people have black, white, light gray, and dark gray wires that are all orderly, buttoned down, and running in parallel. If one wire gets out of line or any copper is showing, their system will melt down, and shutdown is imminent.

Keep in mind people's wiring is situational. One person thrives on speaking in front of a group of 600 while somebody else is in the bathroom with a tight bear hug on porcelain before speaking in front of 20. Some love to text first thing in the morning while others need an hour and two cups of coffee to engage. Another team member does her best thinking after midnight, so 2:00 a.m. emails are common. Your team is a mixed bag, and it is up to you to deeply understand the nuances.

Be the Chameleon

Because of the need to constantly match the individual people you lead, the best analogy I've come up with is to tell you to be the chameleon. Depending on the day or even the conversation within the day, you will have to be a different leader.

continued

> You might have to be bright pink with light-blue polka dots in your sales meeting first thing in the morning and then gray flannel with pinstripes at lunch with the bankers and then green camouflage in the afternoon with operations. The problem is, if you walk into the sales meeting in the morning in the gray flannel pinstripes, you are going to botch that meeting, and of course the bankers will run for the hills if you walk in with a pink suit sporting light-blue polka dots. A chameleon's appearance naturally changes to reflect its environment, and you must do the same.

Three Tests of Your Fluidability

There are three aspects of every organizational puzzle that are especially challenging to fluidability.

First is the group dynamic. The dynamics of any group are exponentially more complex than the interactions between independent members of the group. You will need to understand factors such as the following:

- What is the trust level?
- Does the team have a sense of playfulness?
- How does leadership play out on the team? Who is the appointed leader? Do people follow that leader, or is there an informal leader who has more influence?
- What is the methodology for resolving conflict?
- Is the group resolute and decisive, or half-hearted and uncertain, or does it change depending on the topic?

In addition, unseen undercurrents can influence how a group behaves, including everything from two members of the group who are lovers to several members having a feud with another member to a handful of members who are amused by another manager's fixation on the company fantasy football league. There are countless possibilities to consider within the group dynamic.

The second test of your fluidability is the experience level and emotional intelligence of each individual. You may have leaders who have been doing their job for decades and know everything there is to know about their role, but they are relatively new to the company. You may have a leader who is new to leadership but has been with the company for 15 years. You may have a leader who is young and has advanced very quickly to join the leadership team. You may have leaders who are wise old birds and others who are bright and good at their jobs but lack some emotional intelligence.

A third test is to make sure you are prepared for and understand the nuances of conflict between members of the group. There is no way to stay in front of the conflict, but you have to be prepared for it and be fluid enough to understand that it is natural. Your job is not to solve the conflict but to nurture a trusting environment so that your team works through its own issues. Thus, it is imperative that you remain fluid and adaptable because there is no one right answer for how to engage the inner workings of your team and the conflict naturally arising within dynamic, high-functioning teams.

Staffing Challenges Require Fluidability

Some of the most shocking moments of my managerial career involve people and how suddenly their personal and professional lives can throw a wrench into the best-laid plans. Things can be moving along swimmingly and BAM! a bomb is set off in your world. The manager in operations approaches you with tear-filled eyes because her girlfriend got into law school in Boston, and she will be moving in the fall to be with her. There doesn't appear to be a candidate internally who can slide in and take over. You have a huge void on your team. All the while the controller position you have been trying to fill for over 15 months remains unfilled, and you haven't had a reasonable candidate for 3 months. Your director of IT, who has been with you for seven years, has been given an offer from the company up on the fifth floor for a 25 percent raise, and you now regret scraping by for two to three years knowing he was underpaid. Situations like these provide constant challenges to your fluidability, and a huge part of managing is rolling with these punches and limiting the impact on the organization. Your expectation needs to be constant change. I love the phrases, "The only constant in the world is change" and "People and their lives don't give a shit about your plan."

Are You a Multiplier or Diminisher?

From Liz Wiseman's book *Multipliers*, I learned about the concept of leadership as either multiplying or diminishing. (The book is a must-read for any aspiring manager.) Ms. Wiseman suggests that most entrepreneurs believe they were able to get their company beyond the start-up phase because of their own capability, cunning, courage, and, frankly, genius.[3] Often there is some truth to this.

Then, once the company has continued success, this mentality is confirmed day in and day out through constant reinforcement of the CEO and their genius. This dynamic works short term, but over time the environment gets ugly as people feel their role in the organization is continuously diminished by the overbearing, genius CEO. The job becomes more about supporting and looking good to the CEO, so people tell the budding tyrant exactly what they think she wants to hear. This is the germ that spreads the "CEO disease." The CEO disease is responsible for many dysfunctional management teams in the world. When everyone is complimenting your ideas constantly, the ego runs amok and exercises control. The result is an environment where there is little room for others, one which leaves decision-making in the hands of the CEO, and which Liz Wiseman calls a diminishing environment.

It is a vicious circle. In the diminishing environment members of the team spend their time trying to figure out what the leader wants, rather than trying to solve the problem. In this environment ideas typically come from the leader and the team operates well below full capacity, probably something like half throttle.

In contrast, in a multiplying environment, the leader is engaged, encouraging, supportive, and demanding without having to be the star, the center of the universe, the be-all and end-all. The leader must remain fluid and adaptable, having the patience for the group to come forward with their own ideas. This last point is a staggering nuance you need to master. You need to slowly step back so others can step forward.

You are the leader who brought the company out of the start-up, GRIND phase and into the bootstrapping phase where it is gaining stability. You need to be aware that you will need to encourage, support, and coach people to step in and begin to fill your shoes. It is imperative you become aware of how bright your star shines and that your engagement can diminish others' growth and development. Be patient with people—it is intimidating to take over from the hard-charging CEO; people need time to fill the new role. People need to be supported when stepping forward and taking charge.

If it exists in an organization, what is the number one thing a CEO can do to start to cure the CEO disease? Shut up! It really is that simple.

A close personal friend was CEO of a Fortune 500 company, one of the storied brands in America. He had assembled his team of amazing people who were deep on experience and who dwarfed his capability in their area of expertise. His team doubled the value of the company in four years. I remember calling him some random weekday afternoon, and he was at Pottery Barn. He complained about being bored. He was very much of the mindset that he needed to let his team make the decisions, to let them own their work and ultimately allow them to succeed. His idea was that as the CEO he was there to facilitate a healthy group dynamic, hold the culture of the company, and to answer anywhere from two to four questions a year. Otherwise, he went with their flow. Ultimately his guidance and tutelage culminated in a wonderful success story.

As a leader, and especially as an entrepreneur, the ability to step back and let others have control takes extraordinary discipline. Our inclination as leaders is to engage, to charge the hill, to be the smartest person in the room, and to manipulate the group to agree with our way of thinking. Cajoling people to think that our idea was really their idea is common practice and simple manipulation and very unhealthy.

What I'm recommending instead is that you rely on fluidability: be fluid and adaptable since most events in the company will happen differently than you expect. Give up the notion that you are the smartest person in the room and support your people in blowing forward with their decisions. You have hired people in their discipline who are better at what they do than you. Let them own their work and bring powerful results.

The hardest transition is when you promote people from within to positions of authority. Often, they have learned much of what they know from you. You have to step aside and let them run. The only way they will ever be effective in their position is if they are allowed to make decisions and execute. They are better at the job than you—and if they are not, you shouldn't have them in the position. Traditionally, growth from within is preferred by hard-charging CEOs because they can still have a firm grasp on the inner workings because they have their protégé in place. The protégé can't do a thing without the input and consent of the CEO. Dysfunction at the highest level. Put people in place because you trust they can do an amazing job. Let them make decisions and execute and own their work, and you will find the business will perform at a higher level than when you were in charge. This is a tough pill for most entrepreneurs to swallow.

How's Your Fluidability?

Getting each relationship right all of the time is nearly impossible, but how well you balance the complexity of each relationship determines whether you are successful in building a team and therefore a long-term sustainable business. This is why fluidity and adaptability are an essential element in the management of people. In *The Breakthrough Company*, Keith McFarland includes an important quote from Charles Darwin: "It is not the strongest of the species that survive, nor the most intelligent, but the ones most responsive to change."[4] If there is one thing we know, it is that one human being interacting with another human being will bring new and different challenges every single time.

Pressure to get managing people right? Of course, there is pressure. Few people are naturally good at managing and even fewer entrepreneurs manage well because the things that made them a good entrepreneur are exactly the things that will get in the way of being a successful manager. Managing is not about grabbing the bull by the horns and wrestling it to the ground. You have to engage people where they need to be met. You have to figure out who you need to be right now. You have to be fluid. You have to be adaptable. A rigid belief that you have all the answers—a common mindset among entrepreneurs—is going to be a massive roadblock in the development of your team and therefore the development of your company. This is the curse of the entrepreneur. Don't let it be yours.

Due Diligence on Your Fluidability

Are you ready to be fluid and adaptable to support your team and their development? Ask yourself these questions:

- Can you acknowledge that your team is one of the most complex organisms on the planet?
- Are you prepared to meet each team member where they are in their development and to provide them what they need?
- If you were an animal, what animal would you be as a leader? A lion? A chameleon?
- As a leader, are you responsible for solving conflict in the room or within the leadership team?
- What is the first thing you can do to counter the CEO disease, if present?
- How often do you believe you are the smartest person in the room?
- Is change something that scares you or excites you?
- How big is your ego? How much control does it have? How loud is its voice?
- Do you think you can support people's decisions even when you disagree with their course?

CHAPTER 2

Emotional Stability—Creating a Thriving Home for Your Team

I WISH IT WEREN'T TRUE, but I am an emotional person and I project my emotion. I am an open book. This behavior impacts people, sometimes for the better but often for the worse.

An example: One day, a BIGGBY staffer named Gordie approached me. My feet were up on the table, and we had a pleasant exchange. He asked a short question, got what he needed, and glided off. Two days later Gordie saw me walking with my brow furrowed. He needed my opinion on something so he approached me, lighthearted and confident, and spoke his piece. I rested my head in the palm of my hand as I massaged my temples and said, "Tell me you're kidding! We have talked about this thirty times. You are more than qualified to make this call. Just make it."

Two very different responses from me to a similar behavior on Gordie's part. These types of exchanges have a lasting impact. The problem wasn't that I was short and pointed the second time. If I were short and pointed all of the time, Gordie would be fine. He would approach me with that understanding and expect some kind of terse reply. He would get his answer and move on.

No, the problem was the inconsistency of my reactions based on my emotions. This has been one of the struggles I have had in my career and one of the topics I work on regularly. It is one of my bogies. It forces Gordie (and all other BIGGBY staff) to figure me out, to solve the puzzle that is me: Is this the right time, or should I wait till tomorrow morning to talk to Mike? Maybe I should come back later today? Should I keep my distance? What's Mike's mood?

Gordie is not simply considering the topic at hand—he is forced to read the tea leaves to determine my mood and state of mind. Boil into that pot of stew that Gordie may be in a gregarious mood ready to take on the world, or he may be coming off a fight with his partner that morning and feeling emotionally frail.

Gordie shouldn't have to worry about my mood; Gordie has enough to worry about. He should be able to depend on me, his leader, to be consistent, available, and able to guide him without repercussions. If and when your leader cuts into you, the impact can last for days, weeks, and months. As the leader, you can't let this happen. Consistency and stability are the answer, as I'll talk about in this chapter.

Stability Brings Security; Security Brings Your Volunteers Back

We work with a leadership consultant who used to come to our office on a monthly basis always wearing the same coat, the same tie, the same cuff links, etc. One time a few years into the relationship I made some comment about his tie being the same as last month. He chuckled and replied, "You are just now noticing? I have worn this tie to every one of our engagements." What amazes me is not that I never noticed; it was his rationale for this consistency. He told me he does this because he doesn't want what he is wearing to be a thing. He doesn't want someone thinking about whether his shirt and tie match. He takes those variables right out of the equation. His commitment to stability is inspiring. I found this fascinating—a little extreme maybe, but fascinating.

There is a great deal of security in stability. An environment should be ready to hold and support you no matter what state of mind you have when you enter. I have a powerful example. I belong to one of the greatest sporting franchises in history. My beer league hockey team, the BIGGBY Bombers, has been in existence for 26 years. There is a core group of seven or eight guys who have been around from the beginning. We have been showing up together to play in a weekly hockey game like clockwork for more than half of our lives. There is no bond holding us together other than the camaraderie we get out of showing up, the love of showing up, and frankly the love of each other. None of us have to show up; we could easily have disbanded multiple times over the years, and nobody would have noticed. But we have stuck with it for a quarter century. Why?

The most powerful factor has been the stability in leadership. Our manager, Rick "Tricky" Slaght, has been a remarkably steady force. We owe our stickiness to Ricky. His challenge is immense. It is one thing to manage people who, like employees, have to show up and have to listen to you because they are getting paid to do so. Managing a bunch of harebrained adult men who are half-cocked most of the time is a management case study that should be used in every business school in the world. How does he do it? By being consistent, by being stable, showing up, and being Ricky over and over and over.

One part of his magic is tangible: He shows up and things are handled. The experience I am expecting to have is the experience I actually have. Ricky is sitting in the back right corner of the locker room every time. The beer is iced and sitting in the middle of the room. The water bottles are filled and set by the door, and our hockey playlist is bumping in the background. Every time without fail.

The other part of Ricky's magic is harder to define. Somehow, and more importantly than the consistency of the environment, Ricky has been able to navigate this group through countless dramatic events over the years, avoiding peril. Whenever I have the opportunity to introduce Ricky, I refer to him as the nicest guy in the world. I have only ever seen Ricky get mad one time. It was at a friend's bachelor party, and we were golfing. He was playing in the group behind mine and my behavior impacted his round of golf. I don't think he has forgiven me to this day. Mostly, though, he takes everything that comes at him, absorbs it, and comes back with solutions/decisions that are generally acceptable to everyone. He remains pleasant through it all.

For example, most recently we put our roster together for a tournament in Indianapolis. We usually invite former Bombers too, because often the regulars can't make the weekend and we want to have a full team (important as we could play four to five games in 48 hours). As it turned out, for this tournament, everyone accepted the invitation, and our roster was huge. Typically, we would have three lines of forwards (nine players), three sets of defensemen (six players), and a goalie. Total: 16 players. This time, we had 19 signed up to go. We decided to go with three sets of forwards, three sets of defensemen on the ice, and three guys would be healthy scratches and sit out a game. This surely wasn't ideal, but Ricky's thinking was that it is more about the social event and the party than it was about any individual's playing time. This made sense to most of us, but there were a couple of guys who weren't particularly happy. Tricky, being Tricky, took the phone calls from the disgruntled players and remained on an even keel as he explained the situation and his decision. Ultimately, all 19 of us were content with the plan and excited to go.

This example is tame. Over the 26 years of the Bombers' history, we have had some real doozies. Ricky has navigated us through full-on fist fights between brothers in the locker room . . . the financial destruction of a league we were running that until then had been ongoing for 30+ years . . . the crumbling of the team to the point we went 2–24 one season and were forced to move cities because many of our players weren't interested in playing with the assemblage of players in the old league. We created a movie without anyone getting their feelings hurt. We had our original goalie die in a motorcycle accident. We have been through divorces, weddings, and the births of 20+ kids. We have won six championships and lost heartbreaking games that meant the world to us. We have been there in times of celebration and times of mourning.

What I've taken from this experience is that a key factor in having a healthy environment that embraces and takes care of people is the stability of the leader. Tricky has been Tricky for 26 years. He has contributed more than anybody to the foundation of love and support that has been created by a bunch of knuckleheaded, beer league hockey players. The leader must build a home for the team that allows love to germinate, sprout, and grow from within. This happens when the team feels secure in the environment, and the stability of the leader is the critical foundation to building a thriving home for the team.

Here's what most managers don't appreciate until it's too late: Just like the team Ricky is managing, you are managing a bunch of volunteers. Most managers don't think this way or want to admit it. If you have done your job assembling a strong team and your organization is performing at a high level, then you have strong people around you. Any one of them could leave to work elsewhere. Therefore, they are choosing to show up to your company tomorrow instead of volunteering their time somewhere else—and that, my friend, is a cold hard truth. Are you treating your people like you would somebody who is volunteering their time to further your cause? If not, you need to rethink your mentality.

The Human Condition Is Unstable

Your business is a microcosm of your broader community. The only constant is change. Chaos, drama, rhetoric, and bombast are all around us. People are starved for attention, for adulation, for security and love. They are living out stories they have created that are based on their own interpretation of reality. The biggest problem is that the stories are fungible. There are no facts; it is not reality, and everything can change on a dime. It is amazing to watch somebody rewrite their story in real time, and as a leader you need to be prepared for this to happen in an instant and on a regular basis. It is human. People's emotions are not controlled by facts and reality, but rather are governed by their interpretation of those facts, or their story. People's stories are volatile. Volatility is tough to manage and is the root of why "people" are the hardest part of business. Let me be clear: This concept applies to everyone, even the most seasoned leader. People live within their own reality. Their story is their reality, but the problem is that it is fiction, and very few people recognize that about themselves.

This is obtuse. People's reality is their truth. But because it is their truth does not mean it is the truth. We as leaders have to fight our prejudice and our pretending that our truth is the truth. For example, for hundreds of years, conductors of orchestras thought women didn't have the lung strength to play instruments as well as men. But then the Berlin Symphony Orchestra in the late stages of the 20th century did a blind audition due to a family member of the conductor wanting to try out. The winner was a woman. That was an eye-opening moment when people realized their "truth" about women being not fit to play in orchestras was totally "jacked." Today, 50 percent of orchestras are made up of women. Throughout history, when a man watched a woman play, his prejudice or bias told him she wasn't up to par, and that was his reality. Blind auditions taught him this wasn't true. His truth was fungible when he was presented with new and powerful information.

Your most well-put-together employee, who is a rock, is also emotionally attached to her story and constantly being guided by her commitment to making her story true. Confirmation bias is a powerful force. You constantly are searching for evidence that supports your truth. In my experience, it is rare to find a person who has awareness of their own story, prejudice, and bias, and even more rare that somebody is aware of how these factors impact their life.

It has always fascinated me, as my company has grown—the number of "issues" people employed in my organization are dealing with at any given moment. My point is that the human condition is one of complete instability. Few people have built lives that are solid and stable. Most people are searching for the security of friendship. They desire unconditional love, they want the stability of a job and boss they can depend on, they want the opportunity to give, and they need the space to be themselves. The fact that they are starved for these things can make them behave in peculiar ways. As the leader, it is your job to be engaged in this quagmire, this puzzle. It is by many accounts the most challenging part of being a leader. How you react in the moment will be a primary factor in your success as a leader. You need to be a rock, unwavering for your people. They will love you for it and respond with loyalty and healthy behavior.

"Stable" Is Not "Soft"

Let me be crystal clear on one final point. Being a stable leader does not mean you are a soft leader or you don't have extraordinary expectations of your people and your teams. To the contrary, being a good leader means demanding that your people are growing and improving. It means holding everyone to the highest standards. It means requiring the exceptional performance of each individual, within each team in your organization. The point of this chapter is not to say you aren't a demanding leader or that you aren't challenging. The point is that you have to be stable and consistent in who you are so your people can orient themselves to you. That way, they aren't left guessing or spending time trying to figure out your puzzle before they grant you the ability to lead them. Major point: People need to grant you the ability to lead them. You have to earn it, and stability is one of the key factors in making it happen.

Due Diligence on Your Emotional Stability

Are you ready to be a rock? Ready to be the foundation by being an incredibly stable force within your organization? Ask yourself these questions:

- How does it make you feel to think about your people as volunteers? How would you treat them differently if they were volunteers?
- What are things you do or should do to encourage stability within your group?
- What is it that makes people believe their reality is the truth? What prominent bias do you carry with you as a leader?
- How often do your people fear coming to you or are concerned they are going to get the wrong you when they approach?
- On a scale of 1–10, how stable would your people rate you, 10 being stable as a rock?
- Why are people usually considered to be the hardest part of business? How do you counter volatility as a leader?

CHAPTER 3

Optimism—Where Dreams Turn into Reality

IF THERE IS ONE CHARACTERISTIC THAT STANDS OUT in successful entrepreneurs and leaders with whom I have been associated, it is optimism. The great managers I have known have been optimists. Optimism is what got you through the tough-going as you launched your business, and it's optimism that can carry you—and now your team as well—through to sustainability. Let's explore what optimism can bring to the sustainability journey.

Optimism Is a Choice

The amazing thing about optimism is that you can control it. You can control how your brain works, and you can choose to be positive and optimistic rather than negative and pessimistic—each moment of every day.

It is not always easy, and nobody is the perfect optimist, but as leaders it is incredibly important to keep trying to stay in an optimistic space. Life can kick you in the teeth, and it is horrible when it happens. Everyone at one point or another has been taken down on a knee or even put flat on their back. We have all chosen how we were going to respond after taking a heavy blow. Are we going to curl up in the fetal position and complain, or are we going to assess our circumstances and look for the quickest way to get back on track?

The major blows are one thing, but there are also the day-in, day-out moments that can bring us down. Typically, there are patterns in our lives that trigger negativity. We need to have the self-awareness in these moments to yank ourselves off of the negativity bus and jump on the back of optimism and keep riding.

Simple to state, really, really hard to do. What are some methods to do this?

1. Express gratitude for the people involved in any given situation. What are the things you love about them? What are the things you appreciate about their work?

2. Put yourself in time-out. If possible, take a break from the dynamics occurring for you in the present moment. Go for a walk, take a nap, meditate, exercise, whatever works.

3. Here comes a crazy one . . . Water in, water on, water out. Drink a bunch of water (in), take a long shower (on), do something to make yourself sweat (out), and get back to it.

This idea of attitude being a choice is one of life's great secrets. When we approach any situation, our attitude will impact the outcome dramatically. If you are negative, you learn to accept negative outcomes because it is what you expect. If you are positive, you typically get positive outcomes, or you find a way to think about and turn a negative into a positive outcome. How you approach the world—and the people around you—is how the world will reciprocate.

There was a middle-aged man who was sentenced to 18 months in prison for a white-collar crime. His demeanor was remarkable. He was generally relieved to be out from under the pressure of illegal activity, and he promised his two young daughters he would write a book telling them the story of their grandmother. He could have been dwelling on not seeing his girls for the length of his prison term, which of course was weighing on him, but he chose to focus on the positives of the event. He would have time to think and write. He told his girls he would send them chapters as he completed them, and he couldn't wait for them to learn about their family history. The difference this made for everyone involved was remarkable. Imagine the power of positivity and optimism in your daily life and how much easier it would be for you to choose the positive route than it was for this guy going to prison. If he can do it, you can too.

Find a Positive Yin to Your Negative Yang

If you are not a naturally optimistic person, you may want to follow the example of Scotty Bowman, one of the great hockey coaches of all time. No one would describe Mr. Bowman as cheery, uplifting, or optimistic. He was more likely to focus on the negative aspects of the team and the weaknesses that were going to be exposed with an

continued

upcoming opponent. This made him a strategy genius and gave him amazing insight into what needed to occur in preparation for an upcoming contest.

But Mr. Bowman also understood there needed to be a balance to his approach, and he always had a coaching assistant who was responsible for checking in on the players, who had a positive, uplifting demeanor, and who would inject life and warmth into the locker room. This awareness is most likely one of the things that propelled Mr. Bowman to becoming one of the greatest coaches of all time. You can't be grumpy and critical all of the time–it won't work. If this is your demeanor, get support around you to offset you and your natural way.

Impact of Negative vs. Positive Leaders

Your team will feed off of your position, and the optimism (or pessimism) will multiply. If you are positive and optimistic, your team will follow that lead. They will be filled with excitement and energy to bring the positive outcome into reality. Conversely, if you are negative and pessimistic, they will be filled with fear and anxiety. The difficulty and challenges they face will seem insurmountable, and therefore there will likely be a negative outcome.

OK yes, sometimes things just aren't going to work. Of course, optimism isn't the all-powerful tool that paves a smooth path toward accomplishing anything and everything you desire. There will be times when you and your team will have to agree that something isn't going to happen; you lose a big account or a team member takes a job with a competitor. You as the leader will need to stay positive. Lean into and learn whatever lesson you can from the experience. The lesson learned becomes the victory. It is then that you can chalk it up as a win for you and your team. You all vow that you won't make the same mistake in the future. Leaders often say the loss was more valuable than the win because we learned so much. The loss allowed us to improve and get better so we could come out the other side whole and ready to get back at it.

Healthy teams are positive, supportive groups that help each other through the thick and thin of the work they tackle. It is your job as the leader to be the optimistic beacon for the group. If you are, everyone in your organization will aim to follow your lead.

What happens if a negative, pessimistic leader is in charge? You as the leader control the fate and destiny of everyone in the room. If you are pissed, everyone is spending time trying to figure out why you are pissed and, worse, whether you are pissed at them. Once your team knows you are negative, what are the chances anyone challenges you or offers an opposing opinion? Filters engage to make sure everything is in line with you and your thinking. Nobody in the room is trying to find the dynamic solution or an innovative idea. Therefore, all you get as a leader are talented folks sitting around the table confirming your position and trying to make you feel better. This is more common in organizations than any leader would dare to imagine.

In positive, optimistic environments where people are taking risks, they are challenging you and each other to come up with the best solution. They are comfortable because you love their crazy ideas. They are engaged in a vigorous conversation to arrive at the very best outcome possible. They know ideas will be received with warmth and a sincere thank you for their effort. Everyone is aware you may not agree with everything. People love to engage and be involved at this level. You will get great input and insight from your team. The team will move forward in a healthy and strong direction.

Positivity and optimism are key to being a strong leader who can develop a powerful management team. You must always be supportive of your team if you want them to grow into an innovative, creative group that is up for taking on any and all challenges. If you can't, you will stifle their growth—and the growth of your organization.

Fighting Negativity

People who are optimists do have stretches of time or certain topics that cause a flood of pessimism and negativity. (At BIGGBY, we call this the "cortisol bath" because cortisol is the hormone that's released when we're under stress. See p. 140 for more.) We shouldn't worry too much when this occurs, as I liken it to body odor: no matter what, under certain circumstances it is going to occur. The trick is to recognize it and make the choice to go jump in the shower. With pessimism, you need to create your positivity shower. What can you do that will rinse away the negativity? There is no single answer, but I think it is important to come up with a personal option or two.

Most often for me, I just need a quick reset to change gears and get my brain refocused on all the things that are right in my world. Golf has always been one of the key ways I reset. I play by myself. It is three or four hours of time to "think without thinking." I force myself to play one ball, follow all the rules, and post a score. It makes me stay focused on the golf, as opposed to going out and knocking balls around. I have music playing, a cooler with a few cold beers, and I enjoy a cigar or two. It is pretty much the same routine as when I play with my buddies, but there are no distractions. I am immersed in my stuff and my stuff alone. I always walk away in a better place than when I arrived.

A few years back, when I was in the middle of a custody battle for my son, I would get consumed by the negative "what-ifs." I had never been in a situation with higher stakes. Throughout the four-month process, I would start to obsess over the proceedings as I was fighting an uphill battle. A father winning full custody in a rural conservative county is not common, especially with no drug use or flagrant abuse from the opposing party. My odds were marginal at best. It was critical that I stayed in a positive headspace and remained productive. Fortunately, I lived on a golf course and owned my own golf cart. On a regular basis I would put a few beers in a cooler, grab two cigars, and head out. After a few hours alone on the golf course, I had left all my negativity and worries in the bottom of the cup into which I just rolled a ten-foot putt.

In the end I prevailed and was granted full custody of my son. My lawyer became a friend, and she attributed much of our success to my full engagement and positive, can-do attitude. I attribute this to taking regular positivity showers, which were my trips to the golf course to let go and reset.

Negativity slows you down. It makes you think unhealthy thoughts; it is like dragging an anchor around as you go about your business. You have to figure out your positivity shower and take one whenever you feel yourself slipping into the abyss. The reason mine worked so well is that I always knew that no matter what happened, in the end I could jump on a golf cart, grab a few beers, light up a cigar, and go out and play a round of golf. This settled me and put me in a positive space.

Exercise is a common form of positivity shower. When stress mounts and you are dragging around the anxiety and negativity anchor, many people throw on their joggers and pound out a few miles on the asphalt. This never worked for me; it was good at dispelling anxiety and stress but didn't take me to a positive space. I never felt joy from the practice. Going out, playing a round of golf strictly by the rules, and posting a score has always brought me joy. I look forward to the outcome every time.

One of the more extreme examples of reset behavior is a story from an executive I know. He runs a large company and has been in high-growth mode for many years. He is involved in just about every detail of the business. He runs a beautiful, tight, and efficient operation. He travels a fair amount for work and when things get rough, he schedules meetings in Miami for two or three days. He actually puts appointments in his calendar so people in his office and his wife think he is working, but in reality he schedules spa appointments and visits his favorite restaurants. He goes for long runs on the beach, and while he does work, it is only on the stuff that he is excited about. These "workations," as he calls them, get him away from the rat race of his team and his personal life. He comes home in a great mind space and is energetic and optimistic. He does this three or four times per year. He is managing himself by making sure he is maintaining a positive outlook.

What is going to be your positivity shower? Will you give yourself permission to actually take the time to reset and pull yourself out of the abyss? For those more prone to pessimism and negativity, this practice is even more crucial. Not every effective leader is optimistic, but the good ones figure out how to bring energy and positivity to the job even while carrying around pessimism and negativity.

Bringing Optimism to Your Team

One last example that I love stems from a conversation with a friend who has been successful in growing a huge logistics business here in Detroit. It started as a small enterprise, but in the 15 years after purchasing it, my friend has grown it into a massive organization. He was kind enough to spend an afternoon taking me on a tour of his facility. We didn't talk to everyone as there were hundreds of people employed in the headquarters building, but I will never forget his approach to the tour. We would pop into someone's office or stand just inside a cube, and he would talk about the person's positive traits. He referred to everyone, and I mean everyone, in some kind of powerfully positive light. He would say: "Mike, meet Trish. She is our resident genius when it comes to______"; or "Mike, this is Tom. Tom has proven to be a rock star when it comes to scheduling"; or "Mike, this is Harry. Everyone who meets Harry loves Harry. He is our office manager, and my friends are always trying to hire Harry. You have never met someone better at managing an office environment"; or "Mike, this is Sarah. She is in charge of security, and you better walk a straight line because she is a franchise player when it comes to sniffing out a fraud."

That tour was powerful, and I asked him about his approach. He looked away and then told me his simple story of the baby learning how to walk. The first 50 times they try, they end up falling down. We tell them they are amazing, and then we encourage them to get back up and try again. We are always positive and encouraging. Imagine if on the first three attempts we told the baby they were terrible walkers, forced a write up of their poor job performance, and walked away in disgust. How motivated would the baby be to get up and try again?

Optimism and positivity are clearly an important choice. You must believe in the premise that where you put your focus and where you apply your energy gets your best attention and therefore will come to fruition. What you think about is what you bring to yourself. This happens because when you believe something positive (or negative), you are constantly searching for evidence to reinforce your position. Known as confirmation bias, this evidence ultimately compounds and you become increasingly convinced of the outcome with the cycle continuing until it eventually manifests. Winners believe they are going to win and then they find the evidence to prove it out.

Due Diligence on Your Optimism

Are you ready to be an optimistic force within the new world you are creating?

- What amount of time do you spend in the optimistic spectrum?
- What is your "positivity shower"? What do you do to reset when the negativity threatens to draw you down? If you don't have a positivity shower, what do you think could work?
- Why is optimism so important to your group dynamic? Pessimism and negativity cramp down engagement and

innovative, creative thinking. How will you bring positive energy and optimism to your group?

- How often do you choose to pull yourself out of the negative mind space?
- Are you aware of the things in your daily routine that cause negativity? If so, what are they?
- Why is optimism compounding?

CHAPTER 4

Integrity–The Superpower to Gaining Trust

THE OTHER DAY I WAS COMPELLED to explain to my son the concept of earning people's respect after he quipped that I could be late for a Zoom appointment because I was the boss. Well, it didn't help that I was in the middle of writing this chapter, but even had I not been, my response came like a bolt of lightning from the heavens. He wasn't ready for it. "If I am late, I am letting everyone know that I believe my time is more important than theirs." I continued, "I place an inordinate amount of emphasis on meeting efficiency and a huge component of that is starting on time and ending on time." Also, "I am a hardened advocate of managing calendars down to the minute. If I show up even two or three minutes late I am invalidating my position on timeliness. Therefore I am not living within integrity, so why should my people knock themselves out to live up to my standards if I won't? The point, as the leader of a team, is that it is more important for you to live within integrity than any other player on the team."

Of course, my teenager rolled his eyes and sauntered away, mumbling something indistinguishable. Someday he will understand. It is more powerful to lead by example minute by minute than it is to say 10,000 words trying to convince your people of their need for integrity.

In her book *Braving the Wilderness,* Brené Brown states, "Integrity—You choose courage over comfort. You choose what is right over what is fun, fast, or easy. And you choose to practice your values rather than simply professing them."[1] You can't be an effective manager of people without integrity. Get with it—otherwise, you're wasting people's time.

Let's cut to the chase though. Being on time and doing what you say you're going to do are both elementary. If you aren't doing those things as a manager, I trust you will be relieved of your position of responsibility quickly. So, let's go beyond the basics of integrity.

Hold Yourself to the Highest Standards

Think of the amazing managers in your past. Think about the teachers you respected the most. These folks were demanding and hell-bent on getting a strong performance from you. They held you to a high standard, but—more importantly I believe—they held themselves to equally high standards and thus you held them in high regard. Conversely, I remember a few people in my history who were demanding but at the same time didn't hold themselves to the same standard, and I simply considered them losers and jerks. The thread that makes a manager/teacher great is that they live with integrity or a strong adherence to an ethical or moral code.

This reminds me of stories about one of the great leaders in the history of my favorite sport, ice hockey: Steve Yzerman. "The Captain," as he was known, never said much, but he was always there on time and mentally ready to perform. He worked extremely hard, and he expected the same from his teammates. He was one of the most high-profile players in the game, and if he was willing to show up early, focus intensely, and stay late working out, then obviously everyone else should too. He didn't need many words as his actions spoke volumes, and it was the integrity with which he lived that was his superpower.

Golden nugget alert! Getting people to perform has less to do with them and their capability and commitment, and everything to do with your integrity and the respect you have earned. When we as managers understand this nuance, we unlock a powerful force, the magical force of trust. You must earn the right to manage people by living up to and preferably exceeding your own standards before you can expect people to allow you to hold them to account. You have to live with integrity so that others will grant you permission to lead.

Earning Respect Through Integrity

I've met too many managers who want to blame their employees for poor performance. It sounds like this: "People today have no work ethic"; or "Give them an inch and they will take a mile"; or "Most days I feel like I should just do the work myself"; or "If I had a nickel for every minute an employee wasted." What I am here to tell you is your employees don't suck. People want to be successful, but they are met by management that lets them down.

We need to earn our employees' respect first by demonstrating our respect for them. Then we set clear expectations for what we want and give people the resources to do their jobs. Prepare to be amazed at how your people will perform.

If you are outside of integrity, you aren't worthy of respect. Without respect you can't manage. If you aren't willing to show up and conduct yourself with the highest level of integrity, don't show up at all because being outside of integrity deteriorates the collective consciousness of the group. At a minimum, if you aren't present at least the group maintains their integrity and you haven't diminished them.

Fear Corrodes Integrity

Fear begins to fester when a team lacks integrity, which originates with the manager being outside of integrity. It's a domino effect: When you don't have trust, you don't have integrity, and without integrity you don't have safety. Without safety, fear becomes the predominant force on your team.

Everything starts with you. Your team takes your lead. If they trust you, the team can relax and think freely. Will you keep the environment safe, keep them safe, or do they need to be on guard for the unexpected because of your lack of integrity?

Richard Sheridan, in his book *Joy Inc.*, backs this theory: "If you are a leader, your team watches you. Do you actually mean what you say? The team will continuously look for clues and inconsistencies in your message and your actions. If they find those inconsistencies, you'll soon witness a rise in fear. It doesn't take much fear to wipe out that feel-safe culture, and suddenly you're commanding a being-safe culture."[2]

What is a being-safe culture? In a being-safe culture, people spend their time in a place of fear. They are spending time protecting themselves. Nobody wants to say the wrong thing for fear the boss or another team member will disagree and they will be on the outside looking in. Fear is cancerous on any team or in any organization.

As I talked about in the emotional stability chapter, creating an environment where people are more concerned about figuring out what you want to hear vs. telling you what you need to hear is poison. Spending time worrying what the boss is thinking or wants or trying to please the group is wasted time and gets in the way of real productivity. The more fear in the environment, the more time and energy is spent flavoring your opinions to get them just right for consumption by the leader. The brain spends too much time processing by contemplating one's own position and ideas but also trying to synthesize with the boss's position, all the while finding the right addition of spices and flavor to make sure points are landing in an agreeable way for everybody.

With enough fear one simply stops trying. It can be paralyzing. In fact, in many environments people spend their time keeping their head down, staying out of sight, and just trying to make it through the day. They surely aren't bringing their best thinking, passion, and resolve to the table to help with whatever problems need resolution. Leaders don't want to admit this is happening, and frankly most aren't aware they are the source of such behavior. On many teams it simply feels normal.

The solution? People feel safe if they know the rules of the game and they believe the rules will be enforced evenly. What are some of these rules? As a manager you will

- provide space for everyone to voice their opinion;

- acknowledge and strive to understand an opinion when it is brought to you;
- do the work to facilitate a healthy conversation when there is conflict;
- provide safety when someone is consuming too much air-time or attention by enforcing boundaries so the rest of the team can thrive;
- acknowledge everyone's talent and respect them for what they are bringing to the team and make sure their contribution is valued; and
- make sure everyone has the opportunity to bring themselves as a full human being, not just as a role within an organizational chart.

Trust is the baseline for every team and you must be the one who holds that trust. The team must match the trust each individual has placed in the group.

Stop Blowing Unicorns and Rainbows

For the past decade I have been swimming upstream against a management trend that has been gaining strength. I think it is completely outside of integrity and is doing significant harm. It is what I call the five-to-one ratio. It is very simple: for every critique you need to find five things to compliment. I also refer to this as a culture of praise, or blowing unicorns and rainbows.

I'm not alone in my thinking. "In other words, the notion of a 'right' ratio between praise and criticism is dangerous, because it can lead you to say things that are unnatural, insincere, or just plain ridiculous," says Kim Scott in her great book, *Radical Candor*, which I'll be referencing several other times in this book.[3] She says that if we don't feel the compliment inside, if it isn't sincere, then we should not give it. I think we should tell people when they are amazing, and I think we should also tell people when they need improvement. When they do an adequate job, I think we can point that out as well. If you do it any other way you are manipulating your employee, and that is outside of integrity. Being outside of integrity either in the negative or positive direction is corrosive to the relationship.

As I discussed in GRIND, the two worst traits combined in one person, be that a manager or an employee, are arrogance and ignorance. It is baffling how both can reside in one person, but I am amazed how often they do. This stems from a blowing-unicorns-and-rainbows culture. If all you have heard since you were little is that you are amazing and special, and everyone wins, you are not only going to be full of yourself, but you also won't have received the critical feedback you need to improve. When you believe you are special, you become arrogant; when you don't get or won't listen to feedback on how to improve, you become ignorant.

It is easy to understand how people fall into this trap. It isn't anyone's fault; tough love and constructive criticism are out of place and time now, and so it is our job as managers to create an environment where teaching and giving feedback is common, to believe and demonstrate that people can learn and grow. We are all equal parts of the team, here to make whatever contribution is necessary to propel the group to success. We can't do that unless everyone is growing and developing. People can't grow and develop without consistent, regular feedback flowing.

Here's an example from my personal life: My daughter, whom I adore, is a volleyball player. She enjoys the game, has a competitive spirit, and genuinely has the talent to be a good volleyball player. Our family went with the flow when she started playing for a private club team. The club was structured into travel and house. There were two travel teams per age group, one with some insane moniker like "National Team," and the other had a more regional feel. I don't know for sure, but my assumption was the travel teams generated real revenue for the club, and so they were aggressive in promoting kids to try out for one of the select national teams.

My daughter was hell-bent on playing for one of the select teams, and we let her try out without making commitments. You know where this is going. She made the regional select team. I was pleasantly surprised because she was a good but not outstanding player on her house team. We were talking through it at dinner one night, and the subject of cost came up. While it was a bit of a hard swallow, that wasn't going to be the reason we wouldn't provide her the opportunity. My wife shared her concerns about the schedule. I about fainted. Our daughter would be expected to travel more than half of the weekends over the coming three months. It was a hard no for me at that point.

Here was my response, and I quote, "You aren't that good, and you don't seem to care deeply about volleyball. It seems like too much for this family to make that level of sacrifice to provide you this opportunity." If she really wanted it, if she was practicing constantly, if there was truly passion for the game, maybe. But none of that was true. She was mad. My wife was mad—not for my position but for how harshly I presented it. I never relented. My daughter needed to hear the truth, and anything but the truth would have put me outside of integrity.

Today my daughter is still a volleyball player. She is committed and passionate. She is playing for her high school team and about to start on a travel team. I am proud of her. She took my challenge and is working hard.

Additionally, there was the bubble-bursting moment as we drove home from watching the University of Michigan volleyball team, and my daughter mentioned her goal to play for the university. I commended her spirit and genuinely loved the enthusiasm. A few days later I asked her if I could have an adult conversation with her about her goal of playing volleyball for the university. She reluctantly accepted, as my kids know when I land the "adult conversation" card it is most likely not going to be a comfortable conversation. I started by talking about how much I loved her goal of playing for the university but felt compelled to talk that through and get real about what it would take.

I simply stated, "For you to play at the university, you would have to not only be the best player currently at your club, but you would also have to be one of the best players ever to play there. I support you and I am willing to do what I can to make it happen, but you are going to have to bring your very best to the game of volleyball every day. Right now, I don't see it. I don't feel like your commitment level is anywhere near where it needs to be in order to make it happen." She understood. We shall see where it goes.

Was I too harsh? I don't think so. She believes I would support her in a quest to play Division I volleyball. I wasn't telling her I didn't think she could do it or telling her no. What was important for me, our family, and most importantly her was that we weren't going to live a fantasy. If we were going to make the massive sacrifice required to make it happen, we needed to understand the commitment it would take to justify such a huge undertaking. It is important for me to give my version of the truth, and I wanted her to live within integrity around her ambition and goals, too. Ultimately, I wanted her to be truthful with herself.

How does a unicorns-and-rainbows culture manifest in the workplace? In my world, when somebody gets done with a presentation, 9.5 out of 10 times they "killed it," or it was "amazing," or they "hit it out of the park." The fact of the matter is, we aren't always amazing, we don't kill it every time, and when we do hit it out of the park, it doesn't feel any different than our last seven presentations. We are left wondering if the platitudes are real. Did the person giving the praise really appreciate our work, or is this just our cultural habit of always telling everyone they are wonderful? For so many organizations it would be a refreshing dose of reality for people to hear the truth. Why? They know it internally, and when they get feedback that doesn't line up with that understanding, there is an erosion of integrity.

Here's another work example. In the early days, we were growing rapidly and staffed to handle growth. Growth started to level out and we were beginning to face some hard realities around budget. I kept emphasizing the need to grow and continue our pace. There was a moment in one budget meeting when a tenured leader brought the tough question about my obsession with growth. My reply went something like, "If our growth rate slows to 6–8 percent, and we become comfortable with our size and start plodding forward, then we won't need about half of the people in this organization because we are staffed for high growth. I don't want that day to come. I want to continue to employ everyone and provide opportunity for people to grow. We can only do that with growth."

The leader then expressed the importance of sending this message company-wide, and at the next opportunity I did. It was a hard message to send, but many people came to me and thanked me for my honest assessment. Authenticity and integrity are often very hard spaces to live within, but it is imperative that everyone knows where they stand so they can make the best decisions for themselves. This is really simple stuff. Treat people like mature adults. Treat others how you would want to be treated. Live within integrity.

A Cheater's Gonna Cheat

Many moons ago, the owner of a BIGGBY vendor—I'll call him Boss Hogg (how long has it been since you've heard a *Dukes of Hazzard* reference?)—took me to a Red Wings game along with two of his key managers. We met someplace convenient and drove to the game. After the game, Boss Hogg wanted to have a few more drinks and proposed we stop at a strip club on the way out of town. Not wanting to be a Debbie Downer but wishing I had driven my own car at that point, I went with the program. No big deal, go in have a drink or two and get on the road. Little did I know what I was in for.

Long story short, there was colorful activity. The driver and I sat out front by the bar sipping a drink while Boss Hogg and the nondriver manager (I'll call him Sheriff Rosco P. Coltrane) were neck-deep in inappropriate. Let me be clear, I am not judging what anybody does in their personal time. But first, this felt really awkward for a work event, and second, both Boss Hogg and Rosco were married. Maybe they had an understanding with their wives, and if so, my bad, but I think that's doubtful.

My relationship with this vendor was tarnished, and over time we moved our business. I didn't make a big deal about it, but I have an unspoken rule: if you can cheat on your spouse, you sure as anything will cheat on me in business. So that vendor lost my account, which at the time probably didn't seem like a big deal—but today, a few hundred stores later, phew, I am sure they would love the business. More dramatic was the impact on the two employees. Boss Hogg lost all credibility and integrity, and, for that matter, so did Rosco P. Coltrane with our driver.

For many folks, this bending of the rules or pretending there aren't rules is simply the way it is done; they are forced to roll their eyes and move forward, accepting status quo. I beg to differ. I think that is the way things are done within dysfunctional teams that are helmed by leaders who lack integrity. We as leaders have to keep and hold the trust of those within our care as if it is delicate and precious. People talk about trust as the essential ingredient to building a high-performing team. I agree, but the only way trust can be established is if there is integrity.

Moving Forward with Integrity

To maintain positive relationships with your team as you work with them to grow and develop as a unit, you must be fully engaged and work hard to build trust, but first you must recognize, mitigate, and root out fear. It starts by acting with integrity—by following your own personal values and the stated values of the company. When you properly hold everyone to those standards, people will trust, relax, and perform at the highest level, rather than worry about protecting themselves and running for cover.

Due Diligence on Your Integrity

Are you ready to live within integrity, every minute of every day, every day within every week, every week within every month, every month within every year? Ask yourself this:

- How often do you show up late to a meeting? If the answer is anything more than 1 percent of the time, you must take stock and evaluate your integrity.
- Do you have team members who might consider you outside of integrity? If you think so, go have a conversation, learn from them, get square, and move forward.
- Are any of your people scared of you? If so, who? Go have a conversation, learn, build trust and therefore safety, and move forward.
- When was the last time you told someone they were doing a great job when they were not? How often does this happen? Why does it happen?
- How many people on your team do you believe live within full integrity? If your answer is anything but 100 percent, you need to dive in, because there is work to do.
- Are you having the adult conversation–telling the truth, good and bad–with each and every one of your people? Every time?

PART 1 CONCLUSION

Taking Stock of Yourself

PART 1 ADDRESSED THE PRIMARY TRAITS critical to growing into an effective and strong leader—the kind of leader that can guide a company from bootstrapping enterprise to one that is sustainable. This is not a comprehensive list but meant to highlight the traits that you should prioritize. They are for you but also for your team. To recap:

- First, you must be fluid and adaptable.
- Second, you must be emotionally stable.
- Third, it is critical you are optimistic and inject your team with positive energy.
- Fourth and final, you must be of integrity.

Take stock of yourself. How well do you embody these principles?

As you grow as a leader and increase awareness of your impact on the team and the organization as a whole, use these principles as a foundation for your behavior. Then you will certainly be far along in the process of developing your team into a highly functioning group—a group that can build your company into an organization everyone is proud of. As you go, you must get square with the fact that the dynamic of the team and the health of your organization starts with you. The concept here is that you as a leader need to meet your company where it needs to be met. You must be the leader your team needs right now as it grows and transitions and becomes a strong, well-run organization that has kicked you from the nest and is sustainable and even thriving without you.

PART 2

BEYOND BEAN BAG CHAIRS AND KEGERATORS—BUILDING A BETTER WORKPLACE

Keith McFarland, in *The Breakthrough Company*, states that maybe the best way to "get the right people on the bus is to create a bus worth riding on in the first place."[1]

How does a bus worth riding on look and feel? My bus is green with gray racing stripes and long shag carpet; maybe yours is deep blue with black mag wheels and a star-scape on the ceiling inside; and maybe your finance manager likes all white with five rows of seats. I think a bus worth riding on is nurturing and supportive for everyone riding inside. When people climb aboard, they have to feel like they are being folded into a high-performing team—a team that will take care of them, that has their best interests at heart. Creating this kind of workplace is another major premise of GROW!

My dream is for every workplace everywhere to become an environment where people go home at night more invigorated than when they showed up in the morning. Where people face challenging problems and difficult situations and are supported by their team in doing good work, they will feel like they made a significant contribution at the end of the day. Everyone wants to feel like their work is worthy and that it is contributing to something powerful. If they do, people will walk on red hot coals and through walls simultaneously for you and the organization.

Allow me the liberty of an ice hockey analogy. The Stanley Cup, the trophy given to the NHL team that wins the championship at the end of the season, is considered by many to be the most grueling trophy in all of team sports. By the final seven-game series of the year, with only two teams left, there is always a moment when the camera sweeps the bench and shows every player banged up with cuts and bruises. They look like they have been in the fight of their life. The very definition of giving blood, sweat, and tears. They are laying it all down, giving every ounce of energy from their soul trying to reach the pinnacle of professional achievement as a hockey player. They feel great about what they are doing. They come to the rink for games or practices, grind hard, and go home feeling great about their progress. They are part of a unit, a unit that takes care of each other, nurtures each other, and supports each other day in and day out. They are part of a team; they make a strong contribution; they are willing to bleed to make it happen. Everyone on the winning team is willing to pay a dear price, but it is worth everything. It is fulfilling, and they love every minute of it.

It is one of your primary jobs as a manager to create a work environment that is like that of a championship team—an environment that encourages people to thrive, where they are nurtured and supported, and where they receive genuine feedback. It should be a place where people give everything they have to challenging work so that they go home at night a little bruised and battered but feeling great about contributing and being part of the team. If you are doing your job right, people come to work to grow, learn, and develop into a better person. If done properly, work should be an oasis of self-development.

This kind of workplace requires more than kegerators, ping-pong tables, and bean bag chairs. The days of those perks being meaningful are waning. People don't want fun at work. They want to be a part of something meaningful, bigger than themselves, something special. They want to be proud of their work, of what they do. They want to be challenged, held to account, and rewarded for what they do to achieve the company's purpose—its North Star.

Think of your workplace as a capsule (or bus, to stay on theme). People climb into it as a laboratory of personal development. We should be committing ourselves as leaders to the process of supporting each member of our capsule in becoming exactly the person they desire to be. We have all had classes we loved or teams we played on that were inspiring. We looked forward to showing up. We worked super hard and wanted to contribute. We felt great about the people and the process. This environment was created by the leader of the group.

Here's another sports analogy: Professional sports players enjoy posh environments where any and all needs are met. They have healthy food options available. They have a spa with amenities to take care of the player physically. There are areas for collaboration and meetings to facilitate learning. It is all about supporting the players at being their best. Shouldn't we do that with our work environments? Make them places that are built and organized around the premise of supporting your team? If a sports franchise invests in making sure their players are well cared for so that they can win games, this extends to our people as well, as we are all working to get our teams to perform/win at whatever game we are playing. Let's make sure our employees are entering an environment that is worthy of the effort and energy they are putting forth to further our quest, our cause, our purpose. Just like the high-profile sports franchises many of us love and support.

This part of the book describes the building blocks you need to create a high-performing environment for your team:

- Chapter 5: What's Love Got to Do with It? talks about how to make sure that your actions as a leader are coming from a place of love and respect.
- Chapter 6: Unbridled Truth explains how you can balance honest feedback with compassionate and caring coaching.

- Chapter 7: Gangs?—Proving You've Got Their Back addresses the emotional space within your workplace and how to make sure it is supportive and nurturing.
- Chapter 8: Architect a Collaborative, Supportive Environment gives examples of how the physical workplace and what happens within that space can enhance or detract from people's ability to work together effectively.
- Chapter 9: Time Management—Check More Boxes or Be a Better Human? explores the many ways in which you can make sure your most valuable asset—people—are using their most valuable asset—time—most effectively.

When you do the work to create this kind of a workplace, it will be the most rewarding work of your career, because your people will love it and love you for doing it.

CHAPTER 5

What's Love Got to Do with It?

PLEASE ALLOW ME TO INTRODUCE YOU to my concept of love—the HR-appropriate kind. I define it as the amount of energy and effort you put into supporting someone in building a life they love. The best example of this is the love of a parent for a child; it also happens between spouses and good friends. It is exemplified by the amount of time you spend with somebody as they go through crisis, or thoughtful acts you perform, or maybe favors you do for someone when life squeezes. In my experience, these moments are the exception, not the rule.

Typically, as Americans, we do a horrendous job of demonstrating love for one another. We are there for one another in a tragic moment, but day to day we rarely engage in loving expression. This is especially true in the workplace. Yet great managers are and always have been masterful at building loving environments. They are actively engaged in the lives of those within their care. Great managers are supporting their people in life, in their personal development journey. This is love.

Case in point: You will make any sacrifice for your child. Their well-being is more important than your own. You empathize with every struggle, and you are committed to making sure they are in a healthy environment, a place they can grow and thrive. One of my strongest management proclamations is the premise of treating everyone like you would want your child to be treated. As managers, we should show the kind of love and support that we would dream of for our own children in their work environment.

People have a strong desire to be loved and adored, and when you support them in this way, there is no limit to the trust and loyalty you create. How? If we are loving, supportive, and nurturing like parents, we will stay focused on the positive. Think of how a five-year-old is encouraged to read, or a one-year-old baby is supported in their efforts to walk. These are some of the steepest and most dramatic learning curves in life. As parents, do we scold our children for mixing up a few letters in the alphabet? Do we chide our one-year-old for falling down? No, in these moments, as parents, we are loving and supportive of our children. I'm not saying you should "blow rainbows" and pretend everything is happy or great all the time. But if our child is struggling, we encourage them and tell them they are amazing because what they're learning is breathtaking in scope. Often our people are also on a learning curve, and they need the same nurturing, love, and support as children do while they are learning to read and walk.

When our people are learning, when they are up to amazing things, we need to be fully engaged in making sure they feel supported, nurtured, and cared for with enthusiasm. They will continue to throw themselves at the impossible, tackling the hardest problems and striving to perform at their best. They will never give up! This is the power of a loving, supportive, nurturing environment.

Over the years in the retail coffee business, I have dealt with my fair share of scorned parents. They call me on behalf of their child to protest a termination or reprimand. Dismissively I think, "This is the kid's issue. What the heck are you doing getting involved?" That being said, I can relate. As parents, they want to protect their child from every indignity, every barb, and for sure any abuse. The truth of the matter is, once we are adults, we don't have anyone looking out for us anymore. A parent isn't going to intervene on our behalf. But wouldn't it be wonderful if they did? I posit, what if we as organizations, as managers, stepped in and became the nurturing, protective, caring force like a parent for a child? What if everyone on our team felt safe, protected, and loved? In this chapter, I'll explore what that looks like.

Coming from a Place of Love

I remember one of my employees showed up late a few times in a matter of weeks. This was unusual behavior, so I inquired. He was apologetic and sheepish, and he mentioned how recent snowstorms had gotten in his way. This was curious, because I knew he lived within two miles of the office. As I tilted my head sideways and raised an eyebrow it, all came gushing out. He had met somebody and had fallen madly in love. They had been together a few months and she was amazing, everything he hoped for. The problem was he had to commute almost two hours to see her. Many days his lover had to be at the hospital by 5:00 a.m. for rounds, and when she didn't, she had her kids and/or a commitment to play basketball. Long story short, to see each other they had to work around her very hectic schedule. He was making the drive two to three times a week, and it was killing him.

First and foremost, I congratulated him on finding a powerful lover, as he is a wonderful man and deserves to have somebody special in his life. We talked through what would work for him. We put together a different schedule and things leveled out. He showed up later the days he was traveling, and he committed to working every other weekend morning when his lover was going to be with her children. On the days he rolled in a little later, I would give him a wink, and he would blush and smile and get to work. As his leader I knew this moment would be fleeting. The puppy love stage doesn't last forever, and it didn't. In this case he was back to a more normal cadence within a year. His lover became his wife! She moved to a hospital within 45 minutes of the BIGGBY offices, and today they have a beautiful house and a dynamic blended family.

Looking back, I could have taken the traditional stance and forced him to stay within our schedule, our box. But it wasn't working for him, and he was miserable. When his situation became apparent, I approached him from a place of love and respect, and we easily came to a new agreement. He was a strong employee and a good person, and he deserved special attention as he navigated his circumstances. I could have easily gotten emotional and made his life difficult, but instead I chose to use this experience to build trust and to create one of the greatest and longest-lasting relationships I have enjoyed in my career. Getting over my frustration in the moment, I instead focused on listening and trusting, turning a potential breach of office norms into something powerful for us both.

This story illustrates how love and trust should operate in the workplace. The employee first trusted me by bringing me into the real circumstances of what was occurring, hoping I would accept them at face value. Then, I had to trust that he was being authentic. Love entered the equation, and we worked through it together. I reiterate: If this were my child, how would I want him to be treated in this situation?

For the Children

Here's a tip: If you truly want to connect with somebody, don't do them a favor–do something for one of their children. If they don't have kids, select another family member or a pet. There is nothing more heartwarming than somebody taking an interest in our children and others who are important to us. Try it!

Confirmation Bias: People Are Good

Why don't we automatically set up loving, supportive, nurturing relationships for everyone who joins our organization? Why don't we inherently trust people and believe they want to give their best from the outset? Traditionally, many managers live within the ethos that people are lazy, people are deceitful, and people will try to get away with the bare minimum. Here is the rub aptly stated by Danny Meyer in *Setting the Table*: "When you assume that people's stumbles are honest mistakes that come from a good place, you get farther with them during their victories. When you assume the worst of people, you get the worst from people."[1]

I support Mr. Meyer's position enthusiastically. When you focus on the positive, when you focus on their unique, beautiful nature, people blossom. It starts with the human connection—the connection between employee and manager. Again, from *Setting the Table*: "As managers, our primary job is to help make other people on our team successful. I urge them [managers] to use their position to maximize the positive impact they have on and for our team."[2] Who is Danny Meyer? Only one of the most successful restaurateurs in history. Look him up, buy his book—he is amazing!

Meyer's position is supported by the power of confirmation bias: People pay more attention to information that confirms or supports their beliefs or values than they do to contradictory information. If you start out with a positive attitude toward people, you will seek out facts and circumstances to support that position. Conversely, when you assume the negative, you'll be looking out for instances where people fail you. What you notice you will get more of, for better or worse. So why not make it for the better?

Stated differently, we as managers of human beings must remember that each and every employee is a distinct person on their own journey through life. If we can get beyond using the traditional lens of manager as all-knowing and the employee as guilty until proven otherwise, and if we can move into a space where all people are good, honest, loving, and caring and want to be a part of a high-performing team, then the dynamic within our organizations can go to the next level. It is our job to unlock that capability, and we have a much better chance of doing so from the perspective of a loving parent than we do a warden.

Lumens: The Most Important Metric in Business

In life we have units of measure for just about everything. I know my relative index in terms of my health with BMI, pounds, and inches. I know my monetary value in terms of what I earn and what I spend. I understand my kids' performance at school based on grades. I know my life expectancy from actuary tables. In business there are key performance indicators (KPIs) for every nuance, crook, and cranny of the operation.

How about we determine an index for the love we feel within a certain environment or relationship? From your big-box electronics store on Friday evening or the TSA checkpoint during your last travel experience, you're probably not feeling much love, so the metric would be low contrasted with your favorite uncle's house, where I assume the score would be relatively high.

What if we had a unit of measure for love? We could assign values to all of our relationships, both personal and professional, where you make deposits into your account through giving and receiving acts of love. We need an accounting mechanism. We can track credits/debits and have a running balance we monitor regularly. It would soon become clear to us with whom we should be investing and spending time.

To make that happen, we need a unit of measure for love so we can track our performance. I am going to propose we name it Lumens. What if we put the unit of measure of love on a scale between 1–10?

It is standard for many to feel good about their account status in certain areas of life, mainly personal relationships. We love our kids, we love our spouses, and we have some good friends. We have the holidays with our extended family, and we go to church on Sundays. Lots of Lumens in these areas. But outside of these primary relationships and events, most of us are going through the motions and are not worrying much about our Lumen account status. Why don't we extend the circle to include our relationships at work?

More specifically, how would you rate your manager or coworker on a scale of 1–10 in terms of how they are supporting you in building a life that you love? As importantly, on the same scale, how active are you in supporting another person in building a life they love? Each relationship therefore has a maximum of 20 Lumens available: the highest support coming from both sides.

There are two ways to increase the total Lumen value of your account: Either you work to develop higher scores with your primary relationships, or you add more people as primary relationships, which allows you to accumulate Lumens. When your account balance rises you will become aware that you have more deep, meaningful relationships.

In the end, I am proposing a new KPI within business. All managers should be graded on their average Lumens-per-employee rating. This should be a new unit of measure tracked, graphed, and reported out on in management meetings worldwide. I'd be much more confident in my organization if the ratings averaged 16 or higher; and if they were much lower, I'd know there was a lot more work to do to create the kind of workplace we need to achieve sustainability.

Wouldn't it be amazing to have Lumens monitored as closely as profit and dollars spent per customer acquired? The only way to make it a reality is to start. How would we measure, you ask? By asking each employee the question, "How well, on a scale of 1–10, is your manager/the organization supporting you in building a life you love?" Track the number. Report out and chart performance. We track 500 other metrics in our organizations, many of them less meaningful. Why not do it with love?

The Magic Sauce of Management

So, you picked up a book about creating a highly-profitable, sustainable business and end up reading about love. Crazy, eh? Maybe from the traditional, old-school perspective. Tomorrow's manager and the manager I am coaching you to be is concerned with actively loving everyone in your scope.

Love is and always has been the magic sauce of good management. It has almost never been talked about overtly in the context of working relationships. I grant you, love is a charged word and may make some uncomfortable. That's partly why I suggested establishing a new vernacular, and instead of calling the positive feeling "love," consider it a unit of measure called Lumens. We should all be aware of the number of Lumens we are creating or diminishing in our relationships, in the world. How we create Lumens is through having loving, caring, nurturing, supportive relationships.

If an employee is willing to give you personally as their manager and the company high marks on Lumen production, you have a powerful relationship, and powerful relationships create incredibly healthy and productive people. Loyalty will skyrocket. The team and each member will begin to soar. And that's the foundation you need to build a business that will last through both good times and hard times and persevere through to sustainability.

CHAPTER 6

Unbridled Truth

BACK TO THE PARENT ANALOGY. Being a parent isn't always about coddling and being sweet. Sometimes, especially as kids get older, they need to be confronted with hard truth. This is the job of a parent. But it is critical that the feedback happen from a place of love and support.

As managers, this concept rings true. Everyone needs strong input and direction to learn and grow. Giving people direct, honest feedback is a supreme act of love. Most—I would argue almost all—people maintain their relationships with pleasantries, rarely engaging in a genuine, authentic way. But being authentic with someone and pointing out deficiencies and areas for growth is a powerful act of love.

As managers we must be a coach; we need to be constantly pointing to areas for improvement with our people. Our people need to know what to be working on. Otherwise, how are people supposed to know where to put their focus in order to grow? Additionally, if there is no focus, how are we supposed to know where they need support? On the other hand, if an area of improvement has been identified and they have committed to improving, we now have a joint project. Super cool.

It is a curious phenomenon that in traditional management we expect people to show up to our organization with a full toolbox of skills, yet we all know everyone has weaknesses. Let's work hard to coach people in the areas where they need help and fill up their toolbox with useful tools. They need to know the tools they need to create, and they get that information from you, their manager, through unbridled truth about their performance.

Become a Magnet for Informal Feedback

It is important to understand that your squad—the people who report to you—is fully engaged in the success of your/their team, and you are a mission-critical component to the success of the group. Therefore, you need as much feedback as possible, and they know it. There are two types of feedback: formal and informal. The formal has some value, but generally it is often too broad in scope, coming from people who are removed from the minute-to-minute or from your team, and the comments are hedged to prevent you negative repercussions. So, there is only one way to get the real stuff—the stuff that can help you on your journey—and that is real-time feedback on real-time behavior, most often done informally: getting the feedback when events are raw and right in front of you, and often when the emotional gauge is redlining. This makes it a tricky puzzle with the highest stakes imaginable. It is where the magic happens.

The offering of in-the-moment, informal feedback must come from a spirit of care and compassion focused on helping the person improve and be more effective. It has to come from a place of love and support. For example, we have a woman who is and has been a powerful force in our organization for many years (she wrote the intro to this book). She is without doubt the closest embodiment of a Disney princess I have experienced outside of a Disney movie. She is loving and caring. She is effervescent and joyful. She is a performer. She has ridden these strengths very skillfully in her life. The problem we identified was that these strengths were beginning to get in her way. At times she presented as young and inexperienced. We had concern that people weren't taking her seriously. She was so sweet and pleasant that hard messages would fall short or flat.

Bob and I began to bring her this feedback. It was not the easiest message to land at first. It took a few months of being very specific with her about certain words, gestures, and body language that felt too much in line with the princess persona. (For informal feedback, it is critical to catch this stuff in the moment and then be specific enough that the person gets it square. If you wait, you will lose the moment.)

We started to point it out in front of the group. She was incredibly gracious, which most people are when they know the feedback is coming from a loving place. The rest of the team caught on and started to support her in her work of deactivating the princess in certain circumstances. With everyone engaging to support her, the pace of change increased rapidly. Today, she is more powerful but hasn't lost her ability to be a pleasant, charming, and delightful person.

As a manager, you need to provide feedback and coach the skills, then support the employee and give them positive feedback when you see improvements—calling it out in front of the group and making sure everyone acknowledges the gains being made, like putting gas on a fire. You will watch the behavior excel. As an example, if you had an employee who was never able to arrive to or end meetings on time, you could coach them on tactics such as the following:

- Hard-wiring ten minutes before every meeting into their calendar so they can come properly prepared
- Using timers throughout the day, in meetings and during work periods
- Building in 30 minutes each morning to review calendar appointments and get organized for the meetings (and also plan two to three days out)

When they eventually come to a meeting on time and prepared, recognize the improved effort in front of the group. Support the new behavior and celebrate the victories, as opposed to diminishing mistakes and missteps. When you diminish you confirm negative behavior; when you celebrate small victories you confirm positive behavior. Whatever behavior we support with confirmation will feed future behavior. Confirmation bias is hard at work, and we feed it as the boss.

Not Just a Work Issue

Be aware that what you identified as getting in your employee's way at work is likely getting in their way elsewhere. For a colleague who has a propensity to arrive tardy and show up as a shit show, we may assume they are doing the same for their children, an elderly parent, and even for their spouse. As you begin to see improvements, rest assured there is carryover in the rest of their life. Many times over the years I have had a spouse comment about the improvement they see at home from the work we are doing together on the job. Extremely gratifying.

Keep in mind, in the moment feedback may be a hard pill to swallow, but in the end, with acceptance and hard work, we can all move in a healthier direction. The only way we know what to work on is if those closest to us bring us the examples. A high-profile example of this that supports the importance of bringing the unbridled truth and authenticity as an act of love comes again from Kim Scott in her brilliant book, *Radical Candor*, which I mentioned before. On page 21, she talks about some advice Sheryl Sandberg gave her early in her tenure while working at Google. Ms. Sandberg was being fully supportive of Ms. Scott when she told her, "You are one of the smartest people I know but saying 'um' so much makes you sound stupid."[1] This was concrete, direct, and to the point while also coming from a caring, loving place. If Kim Scott wanted to advance her career, she was going to have to stop saying "um." Many would respond with anger and defensiveness, but when it is brought by someone who you know has your best interest at heart, the feedback can land well and be met with a thank you.

Another way to get to unbridled truth is by interrogating reality: searching for the truth behind appearances. This is a concept that Susan Scott (it certainly seems like the last name Scott is prerequisite to being an expert in candid conversations) brings out in her wonderful book, *Fierce Conversations*: "We believe that, in order to execute initiatives and deliver goals, leaders must have conversations that interrogate reality, provoke learning, tackle tough challenges and enrich relationships." But more than that, she goes on to say, "A fierce conversation is not about holding forth on your point of view, but about provoking learning by sitting with someone side by side and jointly interrogating reality."[2]

This is an image: Sitting side-by-side, interrogating reality embodies my concept of love. When we are alone in our own heads, we can create fanciful tales, both good and bad, that wander far astray from truth. Having a coach, mentor, boss, or friend help us interpret our reality, finding our unbridled truth, is a loving act and should be cherished. This has to become our reality as managers/leaders.

When people see truth, feel truth, and do the work to learn and grow, you will create a strong bond and relationship lasting a lifetime. You are now their mentor; you are guiding them along their path, and they will be forever grateful. Love your people enough to tell them the truth.

Pump Feedback in Both Directions

The most important responsibility as a manager is to have a healthy adult relationship with each member of your team based upon mutual respect. That leads to one very simple but very important fact about managing adults: They have valid and important feedback for you too. The feedback from those you manage is the most valuable information you receive in your professional life. Your people know the skinny, they know the tea, they know what is up, they know the truth, and you must listen.

The key component to making it happen is having the feedback loop be a two-way street. You must bring your people into your fold and highlight the stuff you are working on personally so they can be on the lookout, they can be supportive. By making people aware of the things you are trying to improve, and granting permission and asking for help, you give people agency and authority to engage. It makes people feel safe to bring you supportive, caring, nurturing feedback. Managers often feel like they need to be perfect, have no flaws, and arrive to work each day like a guardian angel from above. Everyone knows the truth; they see through you like a freshly cleaned window. Trying to be perfect is unauthentic and laughable.

Your people understand you are on a journey of improvement, growth, and awareness too. You can only grow and become more aware by being open to feedback. The real stuff, the stuff that hurts a little (or a lot).

Do this by the following actions:

1. Overtly state what you are working on to develop personally.
2. Invite your people to bring you feedback.
3. Accept feedback gracefully and always be thankful when somebody brings it.
4. Circle back and report out on your progress.
5. Always be looking for ways to loop your people into your development journey.

Honest, Loving, Supportive Feedback at All Costs

Strong, supportive, nurturing relationships happen through authentic conversations focused on direct and honest feedback brought from a place of love and support. The feedback is used to support everyone in building a life that they love. If we do this day in and day out, our professional teams will become powerful superorganisms that grow, adapt, and take on increasingly difficult challenges that will boggle the mind in scope.

CHAPTER 7

Gangs?–Proving You've Got Their Back

WHY DO YOUNG PEOPLE JOIN GANGS? They do it to survive. They are often adrift and need a mooring, a lifeline. When there is nobody to lean on, they join a gang to be part of something safe. These folks have shattered family units and are searching for protection. These aren't bad people but simply folks in tenuous situations looking for safety.

TRU Colors Brewing is a company run and managed by rival gang members in Wilmington, NC. On the company's YouTube channel (TRU Colors TV), you can find a video labeled "Path to Prosperity - Craig [Episode 2]," where an employee/gang member is explaining how and why he ended up in a gang. I think it supports my point. Craig says, "But a thing that changed me was like my pops died when I was seven, and my pops was like my go-to, like when I was growing up. So when after he died it was like all I had was my sister. When I first joined a gang, it taught me a lot about loyalty. I was about ten, eleven years old, and like all my friends—it was my brothers taught me like you gotta be there for the person that's beside you and a person that's also in a gang because if you're not it's like you have no loyalty, so that's just how it became. It's like natural."[1] After Craig's father passed away, it was just him and his sister. The gang became his family. Isn't this what we are all searching for? Something to provide safety.

Players on high-performing sports teams often talk about the chemistry on championship teams—the "magic in the room." This is the bond between players, the feeling of trust, loyalty, and safety within the group. Each team member has a role to play, and the rest of the group supports them in that role. Teammates have a vested interest in everyone's success; they want to see each player get better in their position. When you are on a team you are there to be supported and to support your teammates. Anecdotally, I would argue it is rare for a sports team to win without having this chemistry. With this chemistry the team performs well, meets its objectives, and wins games.

Highly functioning departments in corporate America create this same level of safety. When a safe culture is present, employees throw themselves at the cause. In return they are loved, trusted, and supported and are pushed to grow and develop. They are accepted for who they are. In short, they are protected, and they thrive!

Harrowing Stories from a Fearful Workplace

Indulge me in a couple of stories about an environment with a lack of safety. An environment where nobody had your back. In my early twenties I was working for a large corporation that I affectionately refer to as the Death Star. In my first week, I was coached to leave the lights on at the end of the day so our manager wouldn't know, by driving by, whether or not we were present. If the lights were off, we would walk into questions the next day about whether we were keeping banker's hours even if he drove by after dinner at 8:00 p.m.

Moreover, I will never forget Friday, May 10, 1996, working at the same company. I was at my desk and my phone rang. It was my boss's boss, Bob, at headquarters. Bob, with great enthusiasm, presented a request that turned into a dilemma for me. There was a tradeshow in Minneapolis where they were short staffed, and they needed me to get on a flight that afternoon to work the booth. I told Bob I couldn't go. There was a long silence and he told me he would get back with me. Five minutes later my boss walked into my cube and encouraged me to reconsider. I told him I had tickets to the opera that night and was taking my parents, as it was my mom's birthday. He proceeded to inform me that Bob encouraged me to reconsider and "man up," or it would be a black spot on my record. I held my ground and in related/unrelated activity was forced to resign a few weeks later. It was a toxic culture.

Working at this highly profitable Death Star, I felt the exact opposite of a member of a gang or a posse. The exact opposite of safe and supported. I felt disposable and only as good as my last bit of performance. They told us regularly that there were thousands of people who were lined up for our positions. I was told I was cream of the crop, but I needed to work hard to stay there. We weren't a team prepared to get through thick and thin; we were mercenaries for hire to be disposed of when no longer adding value. We all hated the place. It was a job. It paid moderately well, and for many it was where they stayed because moving to a new and likely equally toxic environment wasn't going to make it any better. For them, the Death Star environment seemed normal, the way it was supposed to be.

Fear doesn't foster thriving. It fosters survival. It fosters an environment of covering your tracks. It fosters an environment of ill will and deceit of your fellow employee, manager, and subordinate alike.

Safety is what allows us to trust. It is what allows us to be honest and bring our true selves to the table. It is what allows us to be accountable and hold others to account. Safety is what provides the notion that we are in it together, allowing us to bring our true ideas, thoughts, and opinions from a loving, caring, nurturing place so that we can all improve. Safety is the magic elixir for any underperforming team.

America Is a Lonely Place

Not to get onto a social pathology bent, as this is a book on business management, but America is a lonely place. What has made this country great is also what makes it hard to live in today. We are loners. We live in our little castles, even if they are 1,750-square-foot houses in the suburbs. I went three and a half years at my current house before I ever met my next-door neighbor. We are all ranchers who have staked our claim and are willing to protect it with our lives if necessary. OK, well whether you agree with my dramatic assessment or not, I hope you can agree with the fact that it is hard to connect with people in America today.

People struggle to find support in their day-to-day. It exists in small pockets, and those that find it are lucky. Most people are left wanting. We would all be more grounded and powerful if we could find more loving, supportive environments. We all need people we trust, people to lean on, to learn from so life isn't as daunting and we feel safe. When crisis arises, when the boogieman jumps out from behind that tree, and you feel alone and desperate, where do you go for support?

Here is one of the boldest premises of this book: You, the manager, need to provide extraordinary safety and security to your people. You need to be the place your people turn when they are under duress. You must make work a safe place, a judgment-free zone where people are members of your gang, your posse. A place where we are all improving and supporting one another to do the same. You need to be the gang leader of a gang that is focused on the individual development of each member and where the members are committed to taking care of each other and providing safety.

In fact, job responsibility #1 for any manager should be the emotional safety of your gang, posse, team. Foster an environment where people know they are valued, know they are being encouraged to grow and develop. This will be commonplace in the coming years, and if you don't prioritize building a nurturing and supportive environment, you are going to become irrelevant as a manager. This is going to be the baseline.

The Salve on the Wounds of Loneliness

I have often dreamed of being an alcoholic. Not because I want my life to be devastated by addiction, but because I want the support that goes with being in recovery. In college I wrote an extensive paper on

AA (more on this later in the book). I attended many meetings over a period of months in different geographies. I met with alcoholics in recovery, and my assertion at the end of the paper was that everyone needs a group like AA.

Why? Because in addiction or not, we are all struggling with something, and having a nurturing, supportive, loving group available to mentor and guide us is an amazing opportunity. When you have a safe place to immerse yourself and share your experiences and learn from everyone else's experience, you are living within a powerful ecosystem of support. A place where you are accepted for who you are and your specific place in the puzzle of life. Wouldn't this be magical?

How does this idea translate to the business world?

For many years, I have belonged to YPO (Young Presidents Organization), which is an assembly of CEOs who are managing a business of a certain scope. Members are typically under 40 years old when they join and age out at 50. There are a ton of educational opportunities available through YPO. There are amazing guest speakers brought in to offer learning opportunities. There are social events where members get to know each other and network, for lack of a better word.

But really the most powerful aspect of YPO is forum. Ask any YPO member, and I guarantee they will confirm my assertion. When you join YPO, you apply and are accepted into a forum. It is a group of members, typically six to eight members, who meet regularly. The cadence is usually monthly with some kind of annual retreat. Simply put, the forums are a support group for CEOs.

Each forum has its own governance documents and is self-managed. While fully autonomous, most forums follow best practices set forth by the broader YPO organization. The point of the forum is to provide members a place to go and share their stuff in both business and life. The assumption when you join, rightly so by many, is that the focus will be on business problems, but in reality, members bring any and all issues to the table. The groups focus on dealing with business issues, but it is also common to deal with personal issues and generally it is the tough stuff: aging parents, substance abuse, marital problems, the puzzle that is children, etc., that rules the day.

I found the YPO forum I attended to be an amazing place to take my dilemmas and have the support of smart, healthy people. It was a place of safety, a place of love and support. It might seem weird to have a group of CEOs sitting around talking about disciplining a seven-year-old who got into a scrape at school, but often these are the difficult issues we all face. One of the strongest practices that forums follow (like AA) is a strict adherence to confidentiality. We as members have a place to go to share our struggles, our frustrations, and our victories. Forum mates get to know each other intimately, and the camaraderie is difficult to duplicate. Why does this work? Because the members feel safe.

Business Heresy Creates Superheroes

Why are so many workplaces such dreadful environments? If AA can create a safe place for alcoholics, YPO for CEOs, gangs for ill-supported youth, and winning sports teams for their players, why can't corporate America do it for their employees? Somehow in businesses, managers often feel harsh environments are appropriate, where anxiety wins the day and people go home and immediately reach for a THC gummy or pour themselves a drink to unwind. We must change. To be high performing, we must figure out how to bring the same mentality as AA, YPO, gangs, and winning sports franchises to our workplaces.

How? There is no single answer, but it starts with love and then you figure out the details. At BIGGBY COFFEE, our purpose is to support you in building a life that you love. That is our starting point every single day. We believe all people should be supported in the process of exploring their passions and considering their perfect reality—and then be encouraged to make it happen. Our efforts are not about making each person a better employee with the sole goal of making the company more profit. It is truly about supporting our employees and helping them live the best life they can imagine. Yes, in that exploration they might even decide to leave the company and pursue another dream. We embrace this opportunity, give them a high five, and get behind them in their new endeavor.

Heresy, right? Most managers are thinking, "I spend my whole life trying to find good people, and now you are celebrating somebody leaving?" Yes, for sure, because we know those that go through a process of self-determination and decide that working at BIGGBY COFFEE fits well into their perfect life, the life they have always dreamed, these people will be superheroes. In the end, our team will be made up of people living their best lives by being involved in this massive project called BIGGBY COFFEE, and we will be filled with people who are fully supported in being themselves. If and when people leave, they will leave with love in their hearts and admiration for what we are doing. If we can create thousands of people who remember their time with us fondly, we win!

Managers today talk incessantly about the difficulty of finding and keeping good people. If this represents your mindset, I would posit that you need to evolve as a manager. The needle won't be found in the haystack; pining for some rock star employee is a fool's errand.

Create a safe environment for people to thrive, give them the tools and resources they need, and end the madness of constantly banging your head against the wall hoping for the right employees to appear. People want to be successful in their work; they want to work in a place that supports and nurtures them. People will love working with you and will rarely leave, and when they do it will be for healthy, amazing reasons.

So how do we make this happen? What are some of the ways we are doing this within BIGGBY? I've devoted most of chapter 19 to this issue of supporting professional and personal development, but here are some highlights:

- First, we provide individual coaching to each employee. This is independent of the organizational structure of their department, meaning this has nothing to do with their boss. Coaches are full-time employees of the company who are solely focused on supporting them in building a life that they love. Coaching happens monthly and the idea is to provide each person the support to first explore and secondly pursue their dreams and passions.
- Second, we offer a curriculum (the "Life You Love" courses from our LifeLab, internal within our company) designed to ensure that everyone has the foundational elements to pursue a life they love. These are six- to eight-week courses that meet weekly. They are focused on four fundamental areas: having a sense of belonging, exceeding your basic needs, discovering your personal vitality, and knowing who you want to be. There are group explorations of each topic. We believe work in these four areas is imperative to building a life you love. (For more information you can visit the website, www.biggby.com/lifelab.)

- Third, we are building out support-group-like forums for everyone in our company. Everyone in BIGGBY Nation deserves to have access to the magic of the forum experience. We know it is hard to take on anything challenging without support. Most great work comes from a loving and nurturing environment where others are vested in your work and ultimately your success. Our forums meet monthly—on the clock—and once you have committed to being in a forum, attendance is mandatory. Get and give support, build camaraderie, develop your posse, and you will love coming to work more each and every day, and so will your people.

Individualized coaching, the LifeLab curriculum, and forums have become instrumental in reinforcing our purpose in supporting all employees in building a life that they love. Simply put, if you look deeply into the intention of each one of these initiatives, they provide true safety—and safety is the magic elixir to toxicity.

Create a Safe Vessel for People to Travel In

To continue the long, arduous journey to sustainability, one key is to make your workplace a positive, upbeat, high-energy environment where people feel safe. A place where people bring themselves to the task at hand. A place where people are comfortable speaking their truth. It is a nurturing space bringing the very best out of each person. It is a laboratory of personal improvement where each person is getting the feedback they need to learn and grow. But also, you need to create a physical environment or a vessel of physical space for your people to travel within so the team dynamic can then take full effect. So, on to chapter 8.

CHAPTER 8

Architect a Collaborative, Supportive Environment

ARCHITECT AND DESIGN PROFESSOR LOUIS KAHN referred to his profession as the "thoughtful making of space."[1] That description seems pertinent in a chapter talking about how physical space can make it easier or harder for people to live their best lives at work.

When people show up to work, they are struck by a sensation. Is it dread and fear, or is it excitement and enthusiasm? Do your people look forward to work, or is "Sunday night stomach" a thing, where people approach the end of the weekend dreading the start of work on Monday? Either energy force is a direct reflection of you and the environment you create. Engage your physical environment with intention and be deliberate, as it is a critical component to building a healthy team.

Pulling off a healthy, supportive, nurturing environment is a supreme challenge. Perhaps because there is no one right answer, or at least no answer that works best in all situations across time. So be prepared to have to rethink how your physical space is designed and redesigned again and again and again . . .

Lessons from Trial and Error

Here are some examples of what we have tried at BIGGBY and my assessment of their effectiveness. Our first few iterations of corporate offices were generic affairs: a waiting room, offices, a larger meeting area, and a conference room or two. The first grand addition came in 2005 when we built a full-blown café in our third-floor office suite. People were amazed, and in fact, more than one person referenced its resemblance to Willy Wonka's chocolate factory. We left the café open to staff 24-7 so employees could bring in family and friends and make drinks. We never charged anyone. It is an amazing perk. We wanted people to be proud of our offices and show them off while sharing a latte or a caramel marvel with their loved ones. People enjoy this benefit, and not one time in 17 years has somebody abused anything about this benefit. It has been powerful.

At one point I became obsessed with turning our environment into a game room. I liked the idea of fun, and "work hard–play hard" was our mantra. We went for it. We ordered a foosball table and video games, and we filled an entire room with bean bag chairs. We enforced mandatory fun time (gall dang it) at every staff meeting. Activities ranged from team scavenger hunts to kick ball to euchre tournaments to office chair drag racing and coffee slamming contests. Our meetings were always a hoot. Sometimes things went a little too far (maybe over coffee sometime, I will tell you the story of getting duct-taped to an office chair, put on the elevator, and sent to the main lobby . . . sigh). For the most part I think people enjoyed these moments.

However, there was a problem, a disconnect. The fun physical environment we were trying to create didn't match the emotional environment of the space. We had a brutal culture, what I now recognize as an unhealthy environment; anxiety pumped through the veins of our organization. Bob Fish and I were maniacal, and our people were in a constant state of fear. We regularly dealt with midnight move-outs or people just ghosting their job. We had people who worked for us for over a decade who showed up every morning wondering if today was the day they would get axed. Tears were common. Our entire culture was built on covering your behind and trying to stay out of Bob's or my crosshairs.

But once a month we would get together and play kickball, have meetings on bean bag chairs, and show off the foosball table people never used. The disconnect was palpable. It was all very silly. It was like living in a beautiful home with an abuser. On its public face, it looked amazing, but internally it was a mess. The abuser analogy was real, and the beautiful home, our office space, was meaningless. I will never forget a longstanding vendor telling me his wife's assessment of our company: "Honey, it sounds like you are the spouse in an abusive relationship."

Needless to say, Bob and I have come a long way over our 25 years together. We started deep reflection and slowly began to realize we were a too-dominant force within our company and an unhealthy component to our culture. This realization prompted the next phase of change to our physical space. We moved into an era of walling ourselves off. We figured if we didn't have access to people and if people didn't have access to us, we could do less damage. Plus, if we could be separated from the day-to-day, the minute-to-minute, we could focus on our work.

So Bob and I built ourselves an apartment. It was walled off but had access to the boardroom, so we could enter from our private quarters. We had a full kitchen, a bar, and a living room, along with two private offices. The existing office space stayed the same, but we removed the foosball table, Nintendo player, and bean bag lounge.

This walled-off phase was relatively short-lived. For one thing, both Bob and I had moved from Lansing and were in town only two to three days per week. When we were there, most of our time was tied up in meetings. To have a thousand square feet dedicated to two people who only used it a few short hours every week was fiscally foolish. We opened up the space and it was repurposed.

The next big transition was focused on the future: to 2040 and beyond. It was mid-2018 and we had been talking for more than two years about opening up our space and having a communal environment. The concept was progressive. We wanted to make our space flexible with no dedicated environments. We wanted people shifting their seating and sitting next to new and different people every day. We offered a few different options for storage of private items. We had wagons, file cabinets that doubled as seats, and carts that worked like rolling credenzas. We were requiring people to pack up their things every night and clear the tables for tomorrow's move.

Here was our thinking: We wanted cross-pollination of people from marketing sitting with IT folks, and operations/training people sitting with the accounting team. We wanted our newest employee next to a veteran director and the next day sitting with my partner or me. We were preparing for the future. The future was paperless. The future was remote. No need for file cabinets and big desks with storage. If you could change up your workspace every day, then why not go to your local BIGGBY store or work from home? We designed it and pulled the trigger. There were quiet areas, rambunctious areas, and areas for people's pets to hang out. We had amazing communal seating areas with inspired designs. It was beyond progressive, and we thought it was great. Imagine, not everyone agreed!

We stayed firm for six months, but midway through 2019 we started to make some adjustments. There were teams who believed in sitting together for efficiency. There were people who struggled with making phone calls in public. There were people who wanted to set up as a team and be raucous. We were adjusting and compromising to make it more comfortable for everyone. Then COVID-19 landed, and instantaneously we went fully remote. People are finding equilibrium as the pandemic passes, but it will forever have changed our relationship to the physical space we work within. We were better prepared for the forced changes than most because of the transition we had been making, but what a pivot! We all got whiplash!

Creating a dynamic, healthy space for people to work in is a huge part of your job. I go into our story in some detail because I think it is important to understand that it is dynamic and not a static process. Dealing with the headache that is change is daunting, but you have to do it. You must constantly be looking for ways to improve the environment by thinking about the future, your growth, and the needs of your team. What are people asking for? What can you do to make the physical environment healthier and more productive?

Bring Artistry and Creativity to Your Space

Indulge me in another story. I was in my twenties, working in the hugely profitable but toxic Death Star. (Recall the lights-on story from p. 89.) My department's suite was on the top floor in the eastern half of the building and was built out as one big room with a sea of cubicles. From my seat, I could have had a nice view; well, not necessarily looking out at the Rockies, but still a vast Michigan landscape with flora and fauna. I considered it a gross injustice that my view was blocked by Herman Miller cubicle walls. One afternoon I decided to handle the situation and hunted down a building maintenance guy who I understood to have the key to unlock the cubicle maze. He was a hockey player and we had bonded over a Red Wings hat, so even though it was against the rules, he became complicit in my scheme. Within an hour I had removed both of the walls blocking my view and I had created one of the nicest spaces in our office. Everyone in our office thought it was great. Everyone but my manager. The next day when I came in, my walls were back in place, and I was expected to rat out the maintenance guy. I wouldn't and made up a little white tale about a friend at a bank having pilfered a key to the Herman Miller jungle.

Sure, I was a cocky twenty-something who was on track to have one of the shortest stints in corporate America history, but there are gold nuggets here if we dig a little deeper. My manager was responsible for overseeing the business for metro-Detroit, but he was a robot who didn't have the autonomy to allow us to reconfigure the cubicle farm. More egregiously, the cubicles were assigned based on availability when you arrived. I was the newest guy in the group and got lucky to be put at the end of a row, with my cube placed in a corner. With a few strokes of the Herman Miller magic key, I turned it into a dynamic corner office. There were really smart folks with over a decade of tenure buried deep in the maze of cubicles who had to walk for two minutes to find natural light. Who comes up with that silly system? It seems like those valued folks should have been on the glass and allowed to configure their Herman Miller walls however they wanted. Imagine the amazing configurations teams could design if they were allowed to treat cubicle walls like Erector Sets. But they weren't—what blasphemy. The system was the system, and we were going to follow it regardless. Thinking about this differently, it could have been a growth opportunity for me and my manager. Instead of changing it back and interrogating me like a criminal, we could have bonded and found a way to connect over this experience. We didn't, and I was gone a few months later.

This manager from back in the day at the Death Star is a good guy. I have followed him and his career for 25 years through a mutual friend. He is doing some pretty interesting things. I don't know what the culture is like where he works today, but I assume he has moved on and found a place where he can create a healthier culture. Here is the rub: He wasn't allowed to manage the physical environment, and I think this is one of the flaws of many organizations. The physical environment and setting it up in a healthy way are critical to the success of the team. If you take that away from the manager, you are taking away one of the primary tools they have in their belt. There isn't a one-size-fits-all approach to building environments in which people can thrive. In addition, the needs of teams shift over time; managers need to shift the physical environment too.

Break Down the Gates of the Fortress

Convention in most organizational space demonstrates how generic environments have become. Go into one conference room, and you have been in them all. The most you can hope for is some original art and a comfortable chair. Lobbies are horrendous—they all look the same, many of which feel like the entrances to fortresses with security at the door.

Take the time as a manager to make your environment comfortable, healthy, and interesting. Your people spend nearly half of their waking hours in the space. Let's make it an environment they feel great about. Cubicle farms, like jails, are not inspiring. What about interesting? Do we ever wonder what a space should look like in order to be inspiring, or how our space could make work more interesting? People are well accustomed to making their own personal spaces a reflection of themselves, so why not make the space a reflection of the team?

I used to love going into my professors' offices in college. They were all unique and interesting because most of my teachers were eccentric characters. One I remember resided in the same office for going on 40 years. He traveled extensively, and there were 5,000 books strewn throughout his tiny office. He had a work surface with a computer and a couple of chairs for guests, but generally you had to shovel them off to sit down. There were half-alive plants fighting for survival next to artifacts he brought back from his travels. It was crazy and I loved it.

I had a boss once who was a Lego enthusiast. He had the back shelf under his window covered in different Lego creations. There must have been 30 different vehicles and settings.

My godfather was an engineer for General Motors. He had the same desk-top blotter (huge notepad) for 40 years. There wasn't a mark on it . . . not a mark in 40 years!

My boss at an internship during college kept her space meticulous. She was incredibly fastidious and had a compulsion with the aesthetic. The art was perfect and fitting, and my guess is I will never be in a more beautifully adorned office again.

There was also my colleague at the aforementioned Death Star who was a huge college football fan. When you walked into her office, you felt like you were entering a pep rally.

My personal favorite office story is about a vegan lawyer here in Ann Arbor. His wife and kids were vegan. His family was pretty extreme; they wouldn't even wear clothes made from animal products. Sadly, he passed, and when his daughters were cleaning out his office, they found a leather coat behind the door and a drawer full of beef jerky and meat sticks. I find many of these stories comical, amazing, and heartwarming. We all like to make our spaces our own. As leaders I think we should take it one step further and make our workspaces a reflection of our teams. Bring people together and make them feel like they are part of something bigger than themselves.

Every Pillar, Every Wall Is a Blank Canvas for Your Team

Our quest should be to create environments that are comfortable enough for people to thrive within. It might be one thing today, and something else in six months. The important part is allowing the team to create their environment. Just by spending time together being creative and thinking of how they would like to set up their environment can be a fun and engaging team-building exercise.

Menlo Innovations here in Ann Arbor allows their people to reset the environment at their discretion. Richard Sheridan, the CEO, wrote a book about his culture called *Joy, Inc.*, in which he addresses allowing his people to have control of their physical space. He says, "The second reason for rearranging is change for the sake of change. If projects have been in the same part of the factory for too many weeks, the team grabs a twelve pack of beer on a Friday evening and spends a few hours rearranging tables and computers just to shake things up. The team sees every pillar and wall in our space as a blank canvas, to be adorned for practicality or whimsy."[2] It also lets people say, "This space is ours; we feel ownership and commitment to making it what we want it to be."

At BIGGBY, we built many different communal seating areas in our latest configuration. We had two different living rooms and a dining room table setup. We had a series of standing desks that could be configured, however. Based on mood and group size, we could choose our own arrangement.

A friend of mine within his company has built giant birdhouses and tree forts throughout his environment so people can climb up and remove themselves from the day-to-day, looking down on the world. He has some whimsical story about how good it felt as a kid to go and hide away in your tree fort. It is endearing.

It isn't just about arranging the physical features though. What about capturing your purpose, capturing your values in the space so everyone is reminded of what the company stands for? Your purpose should be dripping from the light fixtures. Who are you, and what do you represent? If your space doesn't scream it, then you are missing an opportunity to inspire your people.

What is the answer for you and your team? Complete flexibility where nobody has their own space, or big walls with cubicle farms, or dedicated offices? The debate will rage on and on. One week you read an article defending open spaces and another criticizing them. In the end, organizations are going to be amorphous, with some people being extremely fluid and others being more stationary. Technology has changed how we convene, and we are infants when it comes to this transition. Keep an open mind and do what is best for your team in the moment.

Physical Space Is a Message

In *Conscious Capitalism*, Whole Foods founder John Mackey and Professor Raj Sisodia state, "To put it bluntly, the most important task for any manager today is to create a work environment that inspires exceptional contribution and that merits an outpouring of passion, imagination and initiative."[3]

Culture, purpose, vision, and values don't have to be represented by silly posters of rock climbers scaling mountains or magical backlit trees espousing integrity. Make the messaging in your space powerful, and make it your own. Design interesting effects that will get people talking, get people engaged. The space should be designed for bringing the team together. Think of a sports locker room. You don't have players making the space about themselves, the space is about community and team. Your space is a big part of how your team identifies. It is up to you to make sure your environment is having the intended impact.

78

In the mid-90s, there was a movement to privatize government agencies and social services like welfare and food subsidies. Lockheed Martin formed a company to develop

continued

these projects. The leader of the company was Gerald Miller. He was in *Time* magazine's top 100 most influential people in the U.S. and was meeting with and advising the president. His company was poised to grow and grow aggressively. He had his entire company boiled down to one metric. They needed to hit this metric. The metric was 78. Whatever it meant doesn't matter, but that was the number. Over one weekend he went in and installed "78" everywhere in his offices. He had been collecting 78s. He had balloons with 78 on them. Dice with only sevens and eights. Coffee mugs with sevens and eights all over them. He hid the number 78 everywhere. For weeks people were discovering the number 78 throughout the office and thinking and talking about 78–this was the exact effect he wanted. He was purposefully engaging his environment in a way he felt was powerful, and I agree, as I remember it nearly 30 years later.

You can also use your physical space to celebrate major victories. Build a trophy wall with framed certificates of external awards. Create your own awards, post them, and make them a big deal. BIGGBY gives awards every year for who exemplifies our core values, along with some fun mock elections, and our exclamation point is the year's MVP. We take a photo each year with the winners and make a nice placard to hold the photo and list each award winner. Over time this board has told and continues to tell a fascinating story of the dynamic people who have made up the history of our company.

Or build a timeline from the company's inception and highlight significant historical milestones. Mark where you intend to be in ten, twenty, even thirty years. Paint a literal picture of where you are going and what you are up to. Don't make the timeline only about business metrics. Make sure to add significant, emotionally relevant events. For example, maybe when an employee retires. The birth of babies within the company. The date a key product launched or a successful campaign was retired. Let people put their own marks on the wall with things they believe to be significant.

What about paying homage to an event that shook the company? We at BIGGBY had an employee lose a baby boy. It shook our company to the core. What about a place to honor him and let people know we are all human beings and that we are connected? When one member of the team is hurting, we are all hurting.

Another idea: frame positive quotes from customers and display them in a prominent location. In our office, there was a long hall that led to our training center, and we hung hundreds of quotes from our customers with date and name. It was invigorating and a strong reminder of the love we spread in the world.

Hang your logo and cool historical pictures everywhere. Honor the past, your foundation. People need to know they are part of something bigger than the current headache. In sports locker rooms, they have trophies from past championships and pictures of all the historical greats. I have heard professional athletes talk about getting chills because of the deep history of an organization. In the great high school sports programs, it is done as well. This is powerful and done intentionally by management. You are part of something important—you are a key part of our history. There is a powerful expectation.

Most of all, be intentional. Build your physical space powerfully. Let it say who you are, what you have done, and what amazing things you are going to create in the future.

CHAPTER 9

Time Management–Check More Boxes or Be a Better Human?

WHAT IS THE POINT OF MANAGING YOUR TIME? Is it so you can fill your calendar with more work? Get more accomplished in a day? Check more boxes? Most people go home dreaming of having another hour in the day so they can get more done. However, more meetings, more phone calls, and more emails is not the objective. Higher-quality work and greater effectiveness for those on your team is the point of managing time.

With the evolution of technology, we have all become infinitely more efficient. It was only a few years ago that people in leadership positions would have to snail mail documents for review and wait for weeks on end for the response. Imagine. Now we can review and sign documents within a few hours or even instantaneously online. We can have meetings with people around the globe with a few touches of our electronic device.

Time frames have gone from weeks and months to hours and minutes. So what are we doing with all of this saved time? Are we enjoying our lives more? Spending more time on self-care? Sharing more time with our loved ones? Spending time thinking and creating new and dynamic methods, products, messages, and relationships? For most, the answer is no.

What the heck is all this efficiency about then? Getting more done or doing better work? I argue that for most it is probably the first, but shouldn't it be the latter? This is one of the primary messages I want you to take from this chapter. Let's be efficient, let's improve, let's take advantage of our era of technology, take all of this bonus time, and figure out how to be better. Not just better cogs in the wheel but better coworkers, better managers, better parents, better friends. In this chapter, I want to explore time and demonstrate that how we manage it can impact our ability to be more effective on the job and lead happier, more fulfilling lives all around.

Workaholics Anonymous

Allow me the opportunity for a rant. This may land poorly with some, but it is something I have always lived by and believed in the marrow of my bones: Anyone who is a workaholic is a really poor manager. Unless you are Elon Musk, trying to inhabit Mars, upend the auto industry, and bring solar power to the masses (all at the same time), being a workaholic exposes significant deficiencies in your life. Maybe it is worth it, and maybe if you are Mr. Musk you are OK with the sacrifice. Twelve-hour workdays six days a week represents an extraordinary level of dysfunction or incompetence for you as a person and/or manager. You are running or hiding from something. Also, I don't believe a person can work hard and bring their best self for 12 straight hours in perpetuity.

World-class athletes practice and work out up to four hours per day. I was talking to an NFL wide receiver the other day and we were strategizing about how he could best use his immense amount of downtime. He was shocked at how little there is to do. When he was in college at Stanford, he had to both go to class/study and workout/practice football. Now, he just plays football. Believe me, if NFL teams thought having the players working out, reviewing video, and running practices 8 hours or 12 hours a day would give them a better chance of winning, they would do it. They don't.

Why, then, do some managers think they can bring their best stuff for 12 hours a day? They can't! They waste time in their day doing things that are not strategic, or important, or relevant. How many meetings do they run that should last 17 minutes but somehow get stretched out to 30, 40, or even 60 minutes? From my vantage point, most.

Don't be like these managers. Have a sense of urgency in every interaction. Get your work done in 6 to 8 hours a day and build a life you love with the rest of your time.

Also, I think if you are willing to work 72 hours a week, you need to take a good hard look at what is going on in your life that you are trying to avoid. People who are workaholics don't have joyful, fulfilling lives outside of work; if they did, they would be more focused at work to get what they need done and go home ASAP. Period.

Bob, my business partner, used to be this guy. When we went into business together, he worked seven days a week. The business was his life.

In contrast, I had a rule that I didn't work weekends. I was in my twenties, and I wanted to party with my friends. I was playing hockey four nights a week and was a one-handicap golfer. My life was more important to me than the business. My position is and has always been that if I have to work 60 to 70 hours a week to grow my business, then I don't want the business. My business is not my life; it is a blast and I enjoy my work immensely, but I have so many other passions and interests. A successful business is only one.

Bob has credited me with saving his life by setting this example. He was on a track to work himself into the grave. He has had an amazing transformation over the past 20 years. Today, he has a beautiful wife he adores, a son he is proud of, and a busy social calendar. He travels extensively and finds time to work out every day. He is now a wonderful example for me in multiple areas of how to live a balanced and full life. I know he is a better manager today because he is healthy.

I got myself into hot water at a talk a few years back by telling a room full of college students that working harder than everyone else—being the first one in the office and the last one to leave—was immature and silly. Many accomplished folks speaking to students will ask, "Are you willing to do the work? Are you willing to outwork everyone?" If yes, then you have a fighting chance to make something of yourself.

I totally disagree with this mentality. The "secret" to success is knowing when to dive headlong and do the doggie paddle as hard as you can and when to flip over and float gently around the pool, watching wispy clouds float past. The secret is to know when to apply yourself and bring it hard and when you need to throw it in neutral and coast. You can't bring it hard, every day, for months and years on end. I advocate being smarter than everyone else by knowing when to throttle up and when to throttle down.

Limiting your availability at work, committing yourself to eight-hour days with breaks to rejuvenate, forces you to focus. You will work on the important stuff and let the rest of it go. You will be deliberate and forceful with your time and encourage everyone around you to do the same. If somebody on your team is a mess and can't get their work done, you have a job to do as the manager: You need to coach them to figure out what isn't working.

Back to my talk at the college class. Yep, you guessed it, I got a call from an angry father. He was beside himself that I would send that message to a room full of young, impressionable students. I listened to him for ten minutes and politely interrupted, "Sir, I respect your opinion and your opinion is shared by many people. I think you know I disagree with you. I am asked to present in front of groups regularly, and they want me to share my 'secrets' and my opinions. I feel very strongly about this one, and there is no way in the world I can share anything but my truth. Maybe someday my business will slow down, and people will decide I am not somebody they want to hear from. Until that happens, and as long as people want me to present, I will bring my authentic self. You have your way of doing it, or at least thinking about it, and I commend you for your success." I politely tried to end the meeting. He was a lawyer and surely wasn't used to short, 11-minute conversations. He tried to continue. I wasn't going to give him any more time. I interrupted and ended the call. Eleven minutes was too much in the first place. He expected people to accept his pontification, but luckily, I am in a position to refuse his idiocy. To me it was a waste of time. I moved on with my day and engaged in meaningful work—and for the record, I keep getting invited back to classes to speak.

The lawyer/dad's message is the standard message, the one everyone spouts. Typically, it is not genuine. I know many successful people who want you to believe they are workaholics, but in truth, they aren't. Managers have a ton of tactics they deploy to make it seem like they are working 72 hours a week. It's a sickness, some puritanical work ethic that has a strangle hold on our culture. Needing to play games and manipulate people and convince them you are working harder than you are means your default position is people should be working harder. I am sorry for all the people in the world that have to live in this environment. This is a sickness that needs to be cured before we can have healthy, engaged, hyper-powerful work environments.

My business partner at times still has guilt when he feels like he isn't working hard enough. He is self-aware and understands what is going on for him, but the guilt is still present. This guilt is an unhealthy reflection on our culture. I would much prefer to be the person who built an amazing and well-respected business because of intelligence and efficiency than because I worked harder than everybody else. Why be a martyr? It is so unbecoming.

Rant over! Let's now look at specific ways in which you can get more done in less time in the workplace, allowing you to make room for rejuvenation, relaxation, and learning off the job.

Giving 100 Percent, Eight Hours at a Time

I was fortunate to be in the audience once when Matt Ishbia of United Wholesale Mortgage was speaking about company culture. He is a graduate of Michigan State University, a former basketball player who played under Tom Izzo, and a fellow YPO member in the Detroit Chapter. He molded his

continued

culture after his time playing under Coach Izzo. He asks his people to show up and give 100 percent when they work. Give everything they have that day, an eight-hour day, then put the electronics away, go home, and enjoy life. The contract is to show up and give him 100 percent, and the company won't expect you to work more than the prescribed eight hours. This is healthy. I imagine his people go home tired after giving a full effort, but they feel good about their work and their job. They are meeting the prescribed expectation and not spending their days, evenings, late nights, and weekends trying to figure out what their boss truly expects of them after reading an email that arrives Sunday morning at 6:15 a.m.

Tip 1: Prune the Rosebush

Let's say you have bought into my theory that time should be treated as our most valuable resource, that you as the manager should respect your employees' time more fiercely than you do your own. You should make sure your people are carving out time for thinking and rejuvenation and not just jamming in more tasks and responsibilities. Make your expectation clear in relation to time so your people aren't left in the nebulas. If you buy into my approach, let's explore some practical things you can do to free up time and create a healthy environment.

First, all of us must always be pruning our workload. We bosses are constantly adding new tasks and responsibilities to our people, which is natural for any thriving organization. But the only way that people have room to take on more is to get rid of tasks and responsibilities that are no longer important. Anyone who gardens knows plants have to be pruned to maintain their vigor. We should approach our own workload and that of our employees the same way.

I've done a lot of pruning of my own workload in recent years. For example, at one point I was fielding requests for information from prospective franchisees. Or sitting in store development meetings where we reviewed status of every store in great detail. Up until three years ago, I read our franchise agreement word-for-word every year. I used to handle my own email and scheduling. Not very long ago I approved any expenditure in the business over $15.00. Etc. Etc. I pruned all of these tasks so I could spend time on more complex strategy and cultural improvement. Not only does it free me up, but it also allows somebody else in the organization to take these responsibilities and grow. These kinds of changes are scary for people like me because if we manage ourselves out of a job, we'll begin to wonder, Are we necessary? If you fill the void with bigger and broader items, you will always be growing and valuable to the company. Always prune your workload.

Tip 2: Slow-Roll Your Response; They Will Figure It Out

Another tip is to take your time responding to calls, texts, or emails, which will free you up and send a healthy message to your team. Most managers are controlling and tend to micromanage. It wastes a ton of time but also doesn't allow others to grow. People desire your input. Your experience is valuable, and it provides cover for them. If you weigh in, they have your blessing, which is natural. However, if you give it 24 to 48 hours before responding, the issue has often been resolved. The delay forces the person to move forward, figure it out, and get to a resolution. If they don't, it is a coaching opportunity.

This leads to yet another tip for managing time effectively, which is to be careful about your inbox. Email can become your de facto to-do list, and a clean inbox, while gratifying, is such a waste of time. Just because somebody sent you an email does not make it important. As the manager you are copied on everything. If you are reading and responding to everything, you are providing them cover. Be aware of the unhealthy dynamic this creates on your team. People will never fully own their work if you are engaging, critiquing, and de facto approving everything. Moreover, because something is urgent and important in somebody else's world does not mean it is urgent and important in your world. If it is an actual emergency, then people should call, interrupt, and get what they need. Try this: Guarantee a ten-day turnaround time on email and then start living within that structure. People will stop sending you silly stuff for review because they know it won't be engaged. Ten days!

Make them call you. Calling sets a higher bar. Take the time and show enough respect to reach out to me if you need my attention. Don't be passive aggressive by hiding behind email. When I hear somebody say, "Well I sent you an email," my response is typically, "Did you get what you needed from me?" If not, then email was not an effective way to communicate. I have never committed to stay current with my email in any time increment. I have committed internally to returning a phone call by 10:00 a.m. the next day, and I do because a phone call expresses a degree of urgency. By making email urgent, you are actually setting up a dysfunctional culture within your organization.

One last tip about allocating time: Make sure you include blocks of time for doing important work. Often people are trapped in the urgent list and keep pushing off the important work because it can wait. Therefore, I recommend making a list of strategically important projects—the stuff that is not urgent but will move the company forward. Typically, I have four to six items on the list. I block out time in two-hour increments. Then I break it down and spend 30 minutes on the four most important items. I think giving yourself 30 minutes creates a focus and forces you to take action. If you give yourself two hours on a project, there is no urgency and you piddle time away watering Hank the plant, daydreaming about the lovely walk you took Sunday, and of course checking social media. As with anything, you have to be flexible (fluidability!), and there are times I am crushing it and I will ignore the time limit until the feeling of flow goes away. Setting aside two-hour blocks gives you this flexibility.

Tip 3: Celebrate Inchpebbles Instead of Milestones

There are a couple of things to cover before we dive into more how-tos of saving time. Saving aggregate time is important, but getting people to perform and utilize their time to its maximum is also critically important to managers. There are only two ways to have more time: either work longer or be more effective during the hours you work. Building momentum and being more effective is critical to managing time.

There is a beautiful quote in the book *Switch* by Chip and Dan Heath: "People find it more motivating to be partly finished with a longer journey than to be at the starting gate of a shorter one. One way to motivate action, then, is to make people feel as though they're already closer to the finish line than they might have thought."[1] The point here is to ensure people realize they are making progress on a regular basis with the end goal being closer than it appears. In *Switch,* the Heaths refer to a term their father created by quantifying work in "inchpebbles" rather than milestones. It is your job as the manager to organize a person's work in such a way that they are regularly accomplishing and celebrating. They will race to each and every finish line, and their work will be fulfilling. As a manager it is incredibly difficult to be involved in other people's work intimately enough to know how to establish these inchpebbles, but it is also some of the most important work you can do for your people.

Often there is a monumental task ahead of us, and everyone is bogged down. I know from my experience writing books that breaking the project into bite-sized inchpebbles and celebrating the wins works well for me. When I think about the enormity of publishing a book, it slows me down and I can easily lose motivation. When I know I need to write a small subsection with a chapter, I find all kinds of moments to sit down and bang on the keyboard, sometimes just 15 minutes. Then I could walk away feeling great because I had made progress. We need to sit, strategize, and contemplate how to break projects down into pebbles, as opposed to stones, rocks, or boulders.

Again, spending time breaking the boulder into smaller pieces that are more easily quantifiable and executable is the most important work we can do for our people. It is tedious work because, in the moment, taking an hour or two to form pebbles can feel unproductive. But when people start checking boxes and you watch them begin to blaze through work, you will realize the power of momentum. Your people will get more and more done each day and feel great about it.

Celebrating inchpebbles is a powerful tool for building positive momentum. Check the box on a bite-sized task, celebrate, move on to the next pebble, check the box, celebrate, and keep going. With this real momentum, the size of the pebbles will start to get bigger. In my life, when I have that momentum flowing, I am joyous. I wake up on fire, ready to take on my day. I also know the reverse of that, which is when I wake up and I am carrying the weight of a boulder; I quickly get bogged down because I don't know where to start and I don't know what to work on. Line your pebbles up and start flicking them off the table. If you want to learn more, pick up the Heaths' book called *Switch*. It's a great read.

Tip 4: Become Fanatical about Meeting Time

So we have covered pruning your work load and maximizing your productivity per minute by getting more done with focused work, as opposed to functioning in the state of overwhelm, leading to lethargy.

Next, be intentional about blocking time, particularly in relation to meetings. Produce laser-like focus. At the start of a meeting, if everyone is clear about the intention, then everyone is rowing in the same direction. Setting the intention gives the group focus. When someone goes down a rabbit hole or dives into the weeds, it becomes blatantly obvious. It keeps us on track and allows us to check in at the end of a meeting to see if the intention was met. The key is to get very clear at the outset of the meeting to cover the intention. Crystal clear.

Also, meeting end-times should be a variable. The scheduled end-time is the maximum allocation. By ending a meeting eight minutes early, you are providing people with a gift. It sets a different expectation around time. The expectation is to end a meeting when the intention is met, rather than when the clock dictates. This adds a level of urgency to every meeting. Has this minute contributed to our stated intention? If not, somebody needs to interrupt and get the group back on track.

This approach shifts mentality. Meetings should be run in increments of minutes, not five-, fifteen-, or thirty-minute blocks. Most meetings get scheduled in 30-minute increments, as it is convenient for our calendars. If we can get to resolution and meet our intention in 14 minutes, perfect. Most people spend a crazy amount of time in the weeds, and I have spent my career pulling us out. Staying focused. Pulling the rip cord when our intention is met is mission critical to effective meeting management.

Here is the rub. Typically, managers set the tone of too little focus, too much time, and too many people. Keep in mind, the manager's job is easier if everyone is involved, as it lifts the burden of responsibility to communicate crucial information to members of the team who aren't attending. But in doing so, the manager is wasting a lot of employee time by forcing attendance. Also, some managers enjoy pontificating to an audience so that their genius is confirmed (more on this in the next chapter on communication). The more people in the room, the better. Showing off as a manager, being the big dog, being the cherry on top of the whipped cream, is not only bad culturally, but it is also a huge waste of time.

These patterns can no longer be tolerated.

Understand, as the manager you set the expectation on meeting attendance. Having too many people on a call or in a meeting is endemic in corporate America and a colossal waste of time. At BIGGBY, there used to be an unsaid rule that people should attend every meeting even when they didn't see value or thought they should be focused elsewhere. They didn't have control over their calendar. Now, the rule at BIGGBY is that only the people absolutely necessary to achieve a meeting's purpose should attend. That means only people who have relevant knowledge or decision-making authority.

Today in my organization, I love it when I hear somebody opt out of a meeting. To me it is a sign of health and efficiency. I have full respect for anyone who is willing to say, "I have other things to work on. I will be available if you need me, and I look forward to getting briefed after the meeting." Generally, I hear this from more senior people in the organization, but I am always impressed and I think it is a sign of maturity when I hear a more junior person take this position.

As a manager, you must always address the issues of meeting attendance. Ask, "Who needs to be in this meeting?" of the group. Ask the question of each individual. Encourage people to ask themselves, "Do I need to attend this meeting?" You should be setting the example by pulling out of meetings if you have other things to do—while expressing confidence in the group and making sure you are available if needed. Ask for a five-minute briefing after a meeting. This is empowering to your people, as it sets a tone that you trust them and also demonstrates that your time, like theirs, is valuable.

Tip 5: Others' Freneticism Is Not Your Gong Show

Another huge time suck in all of our worlds is the chance encounter. Let me be clear, there is value in running into someone and catching up. It happens all day, every day in various ways. The trick is to keep these interruptions brief. Spend a few minutes at most, then move along.

What about the interrupting phone call? If you are making the call, get to the point, state your intention, tackle it, and move on. Typically, what is said in 40 words can be said in 12 and should be said in 6. Be quick, be hasty, and watch time blossom on your calendar.

I am critically aware of these time killers, and I fight against them at every turn. What do I do? I always start a conversation with the amount of time I have available. Before I answer my phone, I generally look at my watch and then tell the caller how much time I have. The "deadline" doesn't actually have to be an appointment on my calendar; maybe my commitment is to go for a walk around the block or to sit down and read an article, but there is always a commitment. Everyone is respectful when I establish a time parameter by saying, "I have a commitment at 11:45 a.m." Nine out of ten times, as we approach my time limit, the other person is still rambling, and I interrupt, "Sorry, but remember I have a commitment." Often, I think the person gets what they need. If not, it is on them, as the time parameter was established at the beginning of the call. Plus, we can always schedule more time later in the day or week.

As a boss, subordinate, colleague, or friend, always be respectful. If you are the person doing the interruption, ask if the other person has time for the interaction. If you set boundaries around your availability, others will respect them. Remember, no one knows what your calendar and commitments are. Get in the habit of looking at your watch and communicate that you have a commitment at the next logical intersection of time. It is a beautiful tool.

Another great tactic is to place outbound phone calls when you have a hard commitment on your calendar. My line is, "I have been wanting to reach out on 'X' topic. I have eight minutes before my next meeting." I am being deliberate about squeezing in this call in a way that forces you to get right to the point. If more time is needed, then we can schedule a ten-minute call later in the week. Try this stuff; it works like magic.

Manage the interruption of fatigue. Getting a good handle on your work preferences and styles and being deliberate about your calendar allow for peak performance. For example, I am significantly more creative in the morning. I tell people my last book was written before 8:00 a.m. It is true. I write best in the morning. Afternoons are not as productive, as I get less focused. If I try to write in the afternoon, it is frustrating, but casual conversations work well in the afternoon. I have a list of people I am interested in connecting with, and I call later in the day. It is more comfortable for me and for my psyche. When I try to force work into the wrong moment in time, I get tired and frustrated, and little "good" work gets done.

Everyone is different. It is your job as a manager to ensure people are aware of their preferences and maximize their workflow. We had a brilliant programmer working for us who did all of his best work in the evening. An 8:00 a.m. meeting was a disaster. I was frustrated with this quirk, as he would show up to a morning meeting unable to engage. His argument was, "I was up writing valuable code until 3:00 a.m. I can't do both." Being aware of this dynamic is critical, and maximizing efficiency takes awareness of each person on your part. Once I got over my issues and understood the programmer's dynamic, he became a much more valuable team member. When I stopped forcing 8:00 a.m. meetings, he became a much more responsive and healthier employee.

Another great precedent to set with your people is encouraging them to recharge throughout their day. If somebody is feeling unproductive and getting frustrated, they should stop immediately and recharge. Again, everyone is different. I like to nap. I wake up and am reset. I know people who like to meditate or go for a walk. Recharging in the middle of the day is critical to performance. Remember, 40 hours of targeted, well-planned work are better than 60–70 hours of ill-focused time. A 20-minute recharge in the early afternoon can make the final hours infinitely more productive.

Finally, the trite and yet important message we all know but is important enough to mention here again that I will take three lines to say it: Turn off your email, text, and social media alerts, as they are distracting. Turn them off and schedule specific time to do email, respond to texts, and muddle around on social media. Be deliberate about it, and then engage aggressively when it is time. Stay focused on the important work and avoid the videos of cute kittens and text messages from friends making fun of a coworker when trying to get work done.

Tip 6: Self-Care Is the Most Important Event on Your Calendar

Let's be deliberate about scheduling time to do things that will actually make us better and healthier, such as work out, read, or meditate. These are proven to make you smarter, healthier, and more productive—and, in the long run, make you a better manager.

Schedule time in your day to work out? We all know it helps us be better people, better managers. How many of us schedule the time to do so?

Schedule time in our day to read a book and learn? There are the standards on management and leadership (like what you are reading right now), or then again, maybe a book on nutrition. What? C'mon! Nutrition? Sure! When I learn about better nutrition, I get healthier. I come to work with healthier food, I maintain my glucose levels throughout the day, and I am much better at maintaining my energy levels. Or, maybe I am reading a book on cross-country skiing and when sitting with a customer, I learn their spouse is an avid cross-country skier, so we connect. Or, maybe I am reading a book about living with a child who has ADHD, and my coworker's daughter was diagnosed with ADHD, so I can share insights from my reading. I am regularly amazed at the connections I make with people based on what I am reading at a given moment in time.

Maybe we develop a meditation practice and become aware of our breathing and how important it is for our ability to focus. Then, when we are scrambling to finish an assignment and prep a presentation, we can take a few short minutes to concentrate on our breathing. We lower our anxiety and increase the potential for a strong outcome.

Being deliberate about our use of time is good for us as people and makes us better managers, but it also sets the example for our people so they feel comfortable scheduling healthy moments in their calendar. Healthier people on your team makes the team more powerful, and isn't that our job as managers? In the modern era we have been given the gift of time—the most valuable gift anyone could receive. Let's make good on that gift and use it in important ways.

The gift of time doesn't need to be exercised only with self-improvement. The gift can be used for rest and rejuvenation. Anxiety gets in the way of good, clear thinking. We all need to take time away from stress and anxiety. There have been countless times I have escaped the rat race to enjoy an epiphany. I will never forget the time I was playing with one of my babies, constructing a Lego house, and bang, a concept called BIGGBY in a Box was born. It was a prefab box built within a store. It never changed, and we could only lease spaces where it would fit. It cost 50 percent less to build. It turned into one of the larger strategic shifts in the history of our company. It hit me like a ton of bricks while constructing Legos with my six-year-old.

Said differently, I have never had a big idea when grinding away at email, or engaged in a meeting, or formatting a spreadsheet. Good ideas enter my brain when I least expect it, when my head is clear, when I am relaxed and invigorated. We need to schedule this time not only for ourselves but also to serve as a role model for our people. We need their epiphanies too. We, the collective we, don't unwind easily. We have to practice it and get better and better at disconnecting from our busywork.

Larry Meyer, the former chairman and CEO of the Michigan Retailers Association, mentored me on this topic. He required his people to take a minimum of two weeks' vacation at a time. His point was you spend three or four days unwinding to get to a relaxed state, and then you start ramping back up two or three days before you go back to work. To actually experience a week's worth of vacation, you need to take two weeks off. I have always remembered this recommendation. I haven't required that of the BIGGBY team because it seems too paternalistic; people should spend their vacation time how they want. But Larry's point is extremely valid. We all need downtime to rejuvenate and be at our best.

Typically, I advocate being deliberate with the calendar and blocking time for a walk, or meditation, or a nap in the middle of the day. We can't run at full speed for eight hours straight. We need our people to take charge and build rejuvenation into their days, but remember—it starts with you. If you set the example, others will follow your lead. Everyone in my organization knows I love to nap. Make it a practice, and they will too.

Finding the Right Balance

It is a proven fact that people's cognitive capability goes down when stress and anxiety tip over some unmanageable point. It is different for everyone and different depending on the task at hand or day of the week. From the HBR article, "Managing Yourself, Are You Too Stressed to Be Productive? Or Not Stressed Enough?" by Francesca Gino (April 14, 2016): "According to what is known as 'the Yerkes-Dodson law,' performance increases with physiological or mental arousal (stress) but only to a point. When the level of stress becomes too high, performance decreases."[2]

Gino's quote demonstrates how important it is to understand that your job as the manager is not to create a stress-free environment but to find the right balance. If there were no stress in the world, we would all be hanging in hammocks on a beach. What is critical is that you are aware of what stress is occurring. You and your people should take the test in the previously mentioned HBR article. Here's another quote from her article: "Given this relationship between stress and performance, it's probably beneficial to understand how much stress you are currently experiencing at work." She advises people to research available tests based on the Perceived Stress Scale[3] (created by Sheldon Cohen and others in the early 1980s) to find ways to do this evaluation.

Help people manage their stress level and you will have a much more powerful team. Create space and time for people to de-stress and rejuvenate.

Next Gen Thinking about PTO

If you could (and you can) wrap up time in a box with a nice bow and present it to your employees, it will be one of their favorite gifts of all time. It is called PTO (paid time off). One thing we have in our organization is a liberal PTO policy. Everyone gets 15 personal days a year over and above the nine standard holidays and their vacation. Our hope is that people get enough time to manage their lives so they can come to work as stress free and grounded as possible.

Anyone who advocates leaving your personal problems at the door is living in Fantasy Land. If your car needs new tires, or your kid has a dentist appointment, or you need to finally get that tree removed from the front yard, or you need to finish planting your vegetable garden, you should have the time to get this stuff done without turmoil. If you have a family member ill or in crisis and you are able to compartmentalize and be good at work instead of caring for them, you may have a personality disorder. People need to take care of themselves and their loved ones first so that they may come to work with as free and easy a mindset as possible.

The other day I was talking to an owner of another business about my belief that we as leaders need to provide people the ability to manage their day-to-day lives. She weighed in, saying that she regularly grants people time off to handle personal situations. She gave me the following example: An employee's daughter was struggling with her first semester of medical school. The employee went to visit her daughter on a Sunday and on Monday morning called my friend, asking if she could remain with her daughter for the week. Though frustrated based on the sudden notice, my friend consented, telling her employee to take good care of her daughter. My friend then joked with her employee, "Tell her she has to become a cardiologist because this kind of shit is gonna give me a heart attack." They had a good laugh, and the employee felt supported. My friend reflected that if she had demanded that her employee come home and get to work, or if the culture of the organization was such that the employee wouldn't have felt comfortable to ask for time off, the situation would have resulted in a miserable employee doing terrible work and resenting both the boss and the company. In addition, asking the team to rally and support their colleague builds camaraderie, as everyone understands to expect the same in their time of need. This is an example of solid management, and my friend's business is growing so fast she can hardly keep up. She attributes their success to her amazing team. Telling.

To reiterate a critical point, the concept of leave your life at the door when you show up to work is bunk. It is impossible. Companies are an assembly of human beings. Human beings have issues that need attention, and you as the manager will have a stronger, higher-performing team when people know you have their back.

It isn't simply about managing crises though. It is also about getting your oil changed, meeting the nursing staff at your mom's nursing home, taking the dog to the vet, and the myriad of maintenance of life activities we all endure. Your mindset as a manager might be, "Well, that is for the weekend." I disagree. I think the weekend is to be with friends and family, or to go for a long walk in the woods. The weekend is to rejuvenate so when we show up to work on Monday morning, we are ready to inspire and be inspired. If you are spending your weekends managing life, when do you get to level out the plane and get your noodle screwed on straight?

Time Is More Valuable than Dolla Bills Y'all

We all know people who seem to have all the time in the world. These are the people who are being deliberate about managing their world.

Making sure a conversation that should take 7 minutes doesn't take 30. Making sure you are focused and performing your best when working allows you to get significantly more work done in a shorter period of time. I hope you have pulled a nugget or two from this chapter that will help you make gains so you can free up time in your world and enjoy a more carefree life. What I'd like you to remember is the following:

- First, becoming better at managing time has more to do with being hypervigilant than eliminating things from your calendar.
- Second, you have to be deliberate in managing your calendar, building blocks of time in increments of minutes to protect time for either important work and/or rejuvenation.
- Third, you as the manager are the example. If you are healthy in relation to time, your people will adapt and learn how to be healthy too. This needs to be one of the great gifts you offer.

If you had to be successful in your role and work four hours a day, could you do it? Let me say it more powerfully. If I was willing to write you a check at the end of the year for $50K to be successful in your role, but you could only be in contact with work four hours a day for five days a week, could you do it? My guess is yes, but you would have to approach your world differently. Do it now. Use the extra four hours a day working on important work, strategic work, and make rejuvenation critically important so you are at your best all the time.

PART 2 CONCLUSION

The Path to Sustainability

IT IS IMPERATIVE AS MANAGERS TO UNDERSTAND that the most important component to getting our organizations from chaos to calm, or to sustainability, is the people working together to make the journey possible. They are where you need to put all of your time and energy. Assembling your team is the first step. The second is making sure the work environment they show up to puts them in a position that encourages them to thrive.

I talked in the opening to part 2 about treating your workplace as a capsule we climb into every day. We show up and we immerse ourselves in an environment, and we open the hatch and exit the environment to go home. How each person is treated in that capsule is critical to each person's experience but also critical to the overall performance of the company.

The environment within this capsule needs to be nurturing and supportive of each person so they go home at night and are more invigorated than when they leave the house in the morning. Imagine the impact on the world. If everyone arrived home and was in a better place mentally and emotionally, think of the different conversations that could occur around the dinner table. If people were not carrying the burdens of the workday home with them, think of what they could do instead of pouring a stiff drink or reaching for a THC gummy. They could kneel and greet their kids with a huge hug and start a genuine conversation about their day. Or they could hug their spouse and express how happy they were at work and how excited they were to spend the evening together. Or they might wrestle with the dog or pet the cat. They might be present and aware, as opposed to anxious and distracted. Imagine the powerful change in the world.

This could be normal life—and it starts with building work environments that support everyone emotionally and nurture them in their personal growth so they are invigorated and excited about life each day. We can limit substance abuse and help people build more authentic, loving relationships. If this isn't a noble cause, then I have never seen one. The rewards will be astronomical, and we as leaders can feel amazing about our contribution to the world.

How does this benefit the company? When you have well-adjusted, powerful, vibrant, loving people showing up to your organization each morning committed to furthering the purpose and supporting the growth, and therefore impact, of your company, you will have superheroes in your midst committed to being the absolute best they can be, plus loyal and devoted to the organization. Isn't this every manager's dream? Apply the principles of part 2 and you will realize the amazing benefits of creating an environment that encourages the individual growth and development of each member of the team, and then sit back and watch the team perform at the highest level.

PART 3

WELCOMING ALL VOICES

Companies are a conglomeration of people. Without the people and the work they do, there is no organization. Your people are not individual units performing tasks; they are an intertwined ball of relationships. Some good, some bad, and some indifferent. Relationships are the fuel of high-performing teams. Communication is the backbone of all relationships.

Communication can be healthy and productive—supporting a strong bond—or it can be corrosive and destructive. Healthy, vibrant, robust conversation is a primary responsibility of management. This chapter is about facilitating strong communication on your team. High-performing teams are extremely good at communicating.

Good communication doesn't happen by accident. Communication that facilitates a healthy team dynamic and a strong culture within the organization is about respect and making sure everyone has a voice. It is also about making sure that everyone on the team understands that people are different in terms of communication style and needs. It is your job as the leader to build an environment where all the nuances are honored and where each member of the team has the opportunity to engage. We need to put rules and processes in place that develop cultural norms so good communication is simply a standard.

The concepts in the following chapters will help you and your team communicate in a healthy way so you can have incredible relationships on thriving teams.

- Chapter 10: Truth, Transparency, and Authenticity—The Essential Foundation for Healthy Communication is about the foundation you need to build so healthy communication can occur.

- Chapter 11: Seven Critical Forms of Business Communication describes different communication scenarios—ranging from feedback to problem-solving—and provides tips on how to make sure they add value.
- Chapter 12: Communication Rules of Engagement presents a dozen rules that, when enforced as standards, lead to effective and productive communication while avoiding many of the pitfalls that can occur when human beings interact.
- Chapter 13: The Magic of Five—Tools to Enhance Communication describes three simple but highly effective methods that help you use time more effectively and make better decisions.

There are many things we need to focus on as leaders as we help our companies traverse the GROW phase and reach sustainability, but at the top of the list is engendering healthy, supportive, productive communication. You will get immense value from the following chapters, and I promise you will walk away with some new tools in your belt to help you facilitate better communication on your team.

CHAPTER 10

Trust, Transparency, and Authenticity–The Essential Foundation for Healthy Communication

LET'S SUPPOSE YOU'RE WRITING THE DEFINITIVE RESOURCE on Texas barbecue. You'd want to start the book by talking about the rancher or farmer who raises the cattle that eventually become the cut of meat you purchase from a butcher. There is no tasty brisket without the essential foundation of high-quality beef raised by a farmer in West Texas who cared for the land and raised the cow.

In the same way, there is no healthy communication without three ingredients: soul-cleansing trust and its prerequisites of absolute transparency and authenticity. When we communicate day to day, it is easy to forget the fundamentals of good communication, the roots which form a baseline of those three ingredients. Let's explore each of them in more depth.

Soul-Cleansing Trust

Trust is the foundation for all healthy communication. Why? Our intention when communicating is to convey a message and find understanding. The words are important, but equally important is the brain space of the person listening. The same words coming from two different people can have very different meanings and generate very different reactions. For example, the words "Sweetie, you look pretty tonight" from your grandfather are endearing. Those very same words on public transit from a man who has been ogling you for ten minutes are threatening. Based on your trust level with these two people, your reaction is dramatically different. With your grandfather it sounds like a loving statement and fills your heart with joy. From a man on the bus, you are in a state of panic, wondering what he might he do next.

This is obviously an extreme example, but these same dynamics occur in all interactions. When we have a baseline of trust, we naturally interpret words in a positive and constructive way. The a-hole manager from accounting who has a poor reputation, bad breath, and is known for expressing severe bias is stupid. He has always been stupid and therefore anything coming from his mouth is stupid. You don't trust him. Any communication is doomed.

Trust allows for healthy communication, as it encourages us to be open, understanding, and interested in engaging with and learning from the speaker. When we have trust with colleagues, we accept feedback as an act of love and understanding. They simply want to facilitate our growth and encourage success. When there is a lack of trust, the slightest misstep by a colleague bathes our brain in cortisol and we shut down (see sidebar). Once we shut down, there is no chance for healthy dialogue.

Preventing the Cortisol Effect

Personal attacks, sarcastic comments, and condescension are among many forms of engagement that send the brain sideways and release a stress hormone called cortisol that decimates one's cognitive ability. From "'Stress Hormone' Cortisol Linked to Early Toll on Thinking Ability (*Scientific American*, October 25, 2018), written by Karen Weintraub, "The study of more than 2,000 people, most of them in their 40s, found those with the highest levels of the stress hormone cortisol performed worse on a test of memory, organization, visual perception and attention." Additionally, from the same article, "The link between high cortisol levels and low performance was particularly strong for women."[1] Your job as a manager is to keep cortisol out of the group dynamic. It is an invasive weed in your garden of groupthink that needs to be pulled quickly, or the group will lose its power.

For example, "Your arrogance is getting in your way" is a harsh statement I once received in my career as poignant and valuable feedback. When coming from somebody I love and trust, it is constructive, and I want to learn more. Coming from a lawyer on the other side of a negotiating table might culminate in blood dripping from noses.

In many manager/employee relationships, there is a lack of trust. The employee doesn't feel the manager is committed to their personal growth, and criticism lands like a personal attack. Conversely, when the manager is offered feedback from an employee without trust, the manager gets defensive and interprets the words as an attack on their management capability. This seems to be the default dynamic in many workplace relationships today. If the employee is vested in the success of the team and genuinely thinks there is a better way for the group to engage, or if the boss is bringing feedback because they genuinely care about the employee's growth, trust will develop. However, without trust, meaningful communication is unlikely, as words without trust land on deaf ears.

Most managers seem to think there is a default trust setting: They should receive full trust from their employees simply because they are the manager. Nothing could be further from the truth; in fact, the inverse is true. When people work for you, my assertion is that they start out hopeful but skeptical that you will be a trustworthy person. You must earn trust.

Trust is tenuous and has to be considered, shaped, molded, and cared for in every interaction. It needs to be the priority, above and beyond anything topical. Every engagement contributes to or detracts from building trust. We develop or negate trust in every reaction—every nod, every eye roll, every sigh—every minute of every day.

Did your interactions build trust today? How could you have engaged differently to build trust to make your environment more caring, nurturing, and supportive?

How Do You Build Trust?

So how do you build trust? You must make the investment of time by starting from a place of giving: get to know your employee as a person; learn what their ambitions are and what inspires them; offer to sign them up for a class they want to take; invite them to join you for an interesting meeting; etc. Most importantly though is to listen intently and absorb what is occurring for them in the moment. In the end opportunities are endless. Make the effort to support them with what matters to them first, and trust will follow.

Transparency Built on Truth and Accuracy

Transparency is pivotal to trust. If you as a leader are opaque—hiding information and your thoughts from others—people feel you don't trust them, and hence they don't trust you. They sense you feel they can't handle—or their position is too menial, or they aren't important enough for the broad perspective—the full picture. You must first trust, share the full picture, and your people will in turn start to trust you. When you don't, you are damaging trust, therefore hindering the relationship and effective communication.

The fact is that people want to be involved, they want the full picture, they want to understand the complexity, and they want to help. Many mid-level managers live in a quiet hell because they feel trapped between senior management with extraordinary expectations and their team who is not empathetic, supportive, and understanding because they don't know the whole story.

Here is what I believe happens when there is a void of information: The healthy, well-rounded, rational, trusting employee typically doesn't fill the void. It is the people on tilt looking for answers and justification who colorfully fill in the gaps. When these people don't know the whole story, they fill in the gaps with drama. The stories are born at this mythical place called the watercooler. I imagine this watercooler as a place of chocolate rivers and gnomes chewing blueberry bubble gum while sipping drinks that have smoke billowing from within. This is the place where yarns are spun in mythical proportion. I am regularly dumbfounded by the stories I hear about me and my company that likely originated from the mythical watercooler.

These watercooler stories are ruinous to the culture of love and trust. The only way to pull your team out of this cesspool is through transparency. Where there is full transparency, there is no room for the blueberry gum–chewing gnomes to tell their fanciful tales.

That's why, if you freely share information about what's going on with you in your business and in your life, then people will be more engaged and certainly empathetic. They will more fully understand your difficult decisions and the complexity you are facing. Transparency is a manager's best friend. Bringing your group together around the tough topics builds trust. Without transparency, it is difficult to build a powerful team dynamic.

The Lightness of Transparency

I have never understood why some managers resist transparency. Do you remember lying as a child or withholding information from your parents? It felt horrible. You worried

continued

> that others would find out. You carried the weight of the world until you decided to come clean and then, poof, you were light as a feather. This is what being transparent feels like as a manager. You no longer carry the burden of everything.

A couple of stories. It took many years for Bob and me to open our financial records to employees. Early on, we didn't do that because we were embarrassed by our lack of performance. We felt employees didn't need to know that the company's situation was fiscally tenuous. However, the further we traversed the GROW phase of development, it became clear that our people wanted to know more. As we stabilized by becoming more profitable, we started wondering about opening up our books and letting people in on the financial machinations of the company.

It took us two years to make the decision to share financial information, and the first time we did it, we went with partial information. It was a mess and caused even more questions and mistrust. The next iteration was better, but still much of the detail was missing.

Eventually we learned to produce summary reports backed by all the detail. Nobody cared about the summary; they dove deep into the details. It created a whole bunch of really healthy conversations. Not easy, but healthy. It took a great deal of time to answer questions and clarify how our financial statements work. It was an educational process that was worth its weight in gold. Now we have a broad team of people that understand the details of how our business works, giving them a broader perspective and more power in their positions.

When we first decided to disclose the full financial statements, I had anxiety that people were going to be put off by the amount of money my partner and I were making via the profitability of the company. After a few quarters of presenting the information, nobody had said anything and so I decided to ask, thinking that maybe people were too intimidated to bring up the subject. I didn't present it to the whole group but went to one particular team member who I deeply trust, and I asked him, "Have you heard anything out there about the overall profitability of the company? Has there been any chatter? What is your opinion on our profit level?" His response sticks with me many years later. He said, "You guys have built one of the strongest brands and coolest companies in Michigan. It sure seems like you should be making a lot of money. Frankly, Mike, I am proud of you and happy for your success." It was a cathartic moment. We have always been fiscally responsible, and I am proud of growing a profitable company. It was nice to hear it confirmed by somebody who has worked in the organization for decades.

A young manager at a massive organization asked me to present to her group. In a short period of time, this manager has taken on a great deal of responsibility managing a team of hundreds. I was curious why a manager of a massive company would want me to speak inside of a behemoth corporation. She said after reading GRIND, she realized the attitude and perspective I convey in becoming a successful entrepreneur is all the same stuff that she believes it takes for people to be successful in their careers. Typically, when I plan to spend time with a group, I enjoy getting to know the leader. Spending time with this woman was amazing. She was dynamic and engaged, and she cared a great deal about her company but more importantly about the people on her team. She was clear about the fact that she discloses everything, absolutely everything, to her team. Her take was that it was condescending and disrespectful to hold back. Everyone deserved to know what was happening; anything that might impact the group was important.

Unfortunately, too many managers operate from the perspective of Jack Nicholson in *A Few Good Men*, believing that their people can't handle the truth. People, all people, have the ability to engage and comprehend complexity. Big company, small company, and if I really dive into the philosophy of it, life in general.

Secrets are like cancer on a team. They grow and morph and spread to other parts of the organization. The only way to cure this disease is to shine a bright light on the secret and then talk it through, getting people on the only page that matters, and that is the truth. If you are hiding something from your team, I advocate taking the time to explore why. There are times when things shouldn't be disclosed. These typically involve NDAs (nondisclosure agreements) or maybe information about people's private lives they don't want shared, but otherwise being an open book is the answer.

If people know the challenge and are given all the information, they will commit themselves to their work in powerful and meaningful ways. Generally, people will work themselves to exhaustion if they know the size of the problem and they are part of a team charged with its resolution. Watching your team resolve difficult, complex issues will be some of the most rewarding moments you have, I promise.

Let me end this section with a crazy idea: I have been chewing on an idea that BIGGBY actually flirted with a few years back around disclosing everyone's pay rate within the company, giving each person the opportunity to compare what they make with the whole team. In short, should we be fully transparent around how much people earn?

I know I'm in a minority here, but in thinking about full disclosure of compensation, I think the upsides outweigh the downsides. If an employee felt like they were underpaid in comparison—if someone else is making more money with the same level of seniority and responsibility—the inequity would be highlighted and get addressed through a healthy conversation between the employee and management. There may be things the employee needs to improve, it may be a simple oversight, it could be based on bias, or other factors. In the end, isn't it important that we uncover the discrepancy?

Let me restate the powerful message from this section. Transparency is the magic elixir for managers. Open up, bring people into the fold, trust them to be responsible, and be free of the burden of holding everything and trying to figure out appropriate disclosure. Transparency allows you to be free.

Authenticity

Healthy communication is authentic. Authenticity can be defined as bringing your heart and soul to the conversation through being honest, real, and genuine—telling your truth. Authenticity is the ingredient that brings incredible value to your relationships. If your dialogue with others is neutral/vanilla, little value is being created. As the manager we need to focus on value creation through authenticity in all communications. When people feel value and are getting meaningful things from you, they are likely engaged and growing.

Why is authenticity critical? Leaders and managers who are deemed inauthentic are dead in the water. But know this: Authenticity is hard. Many managers live outside of authenticity because of different reasons:

- The first is "ruinous empathy"[2] (I need to give credit to Kim Scott here), which is telling an employee that they are doing quality work even if they aren't because it is easy in the moment.

Also, culturally, positivity is now the norm. Finally, bringing the real feedback if less than positive can be awkward. (More on the need for "radical candor" later in this chapter.)

- The second is a place of frustration and anger. Speaking what we think is "truth" because we are angry or frustrated can feel authentic because we finally say what we feel—however, it is often inappropriate because our emotions are raging and outsized for the given situation. The inauthenticity stems from emotions dictating our behavior and affecting our communication.
- The third is simple laziness. Oftentimes the authentic conversation leads to a much bigger conversation, which leads to a bunch of work. It is much easier to give somebody a glib platitude and go about our day.

Ruinous empathy and anger often clutter the landscape. The problem is that neither of these reactions are authentic or healthy. Always be on the lookout for ruinous empathy or anger.

Another important aspect of authenticity is that it isn't only about you: it is about creating an environment where everyone on your team can be authentic. Let me bring a granular example. Within BIGGBY, compliance has always been a bugaboo. It is a big part of the role a franchisor plays. People want to know that other stores in their market will be held to a high standard. If your fellow franchise owner in town has dirty bathrooms, it reflects poorly on the business you own, as you both fly under the same flag. We have been working tirelessly to improve on the enforcement of the brand standards. It is an ongoing quest, and I think an ongoing quest for most franchise companies.

We were in a meeting when Nikki Walsh, the woman who is charged with building the systems to help us with compliance, landed one of the most authentic statements in my career. She said, "Mike, you are the problem. Every time we build a mechanism to hold a franchise owner accountable, you let them wiggle out. You always take the side of the owner as opposed to supporting our team. You have to stop doing that, or we are never going to make any progress." Boom! This certainly wasn't easy for her to say, or for me to hear, but it was absolutely her truth and very close to the real truth, and I think we advanced compliance in a giant leap forward in that one moment. Bringing you authentic opinion, cutting through all the nonsense, and landing authenticity is a critical component to powerful communication. Giving your people the agency to bring the stuff bubbling deep in their soul is critical to healthy communication and ultimately to a productive and healthy team.

Keep in mind, as is the case throughout this book, your reaction is critical. When somebody opens up and bares their soul, it is most important that you support them as the leader. The content is irrelevant; it will get sorted out—the person who trusted you and the team enough to be authentic needs to be supported and taken care of. This is your role as the leader. Get good at knowing when authenticity is present. Support it fully, and it will begin to appear more and more often.

Exchanging Information

Most often I think we consider communication to be a methodology to exchange information. It is infinitely more complex than that. To me, opportunities to communicate with others are opportunities to build the relationship. When we have strong relationships, built on trust, and we have transparent and authentic engagements that help us build strong bonds and communicate in ways that are healthier and more effective, it is a virtuous cycle. It takes trust, transparency, and authenticity to make it happen.

CHAPTER 11

Seven Critical Forms of Business Communication

COMMUNICATION HAPPENS IN INFINITE FORMS. Whatever the purpose or form, when we communicate, we need to bring value, every time. Some real-world applications may help give a flavor for the power of truth, transparency, and authenticity in healthy communication, so in this chapter, I'll cover seven forms of communication that are critical in a business setting:

1. Updating your team about a recent development
2. Giving feedback regarding an employee's performance
3. Getting feedback on your own behavior or performance
4. Solving a specific problem

5. Blending the professional and personal
6. Listening to an issue an employee is facing
7. Asking for help

1. Updating Your Team

Let's say you need to communicate something seemingly innocuous, like a change in policy around travel expenses. HR decided to make some changes, ran it around senior leadership, and now you need to present it to your team. The message you need to convey is factual and simply a statement of truth from your perspective: There has been a policy change and we all need to adapt.

But releasing the statement may not be as simple as you envision. First, "truth" is a matter of perspective. There very well could be significant feelings about the new policy regarding travel expenses. People on your team who travel often will be impacted more than others. There are always nuances you aren't considering. What matters is how you choose to frame the decision. You can bring it as a fact, dropping the bomb and expecting people to suck it up as the new reality. Or you could spend a few extra minutes talking about the new policy and asking people how they feel about the decision. Asking how people feel when communicating something new is critical, like syrup on a pancake or mustard on a hot dog. Without it, you still get the pancake, but it isn't anywhere near as tasty. Give people a chance to speak their piece. If there are no concerns, great, but if there are feelings, you must engage. Take notes on the feedback and repeat back what you heard to make sure you understand.

Depending on what you learn from the input, there are different courses of action. One, you could agree to take the feedback to senior leadership. You could agree to check back in a few months and see how everyone feels after the new policy has been road-tested. Or maybe you respond in the moment to the concerns by backing the process that senior leadership used and supporting the outcome. Or you might ask what your team wants you to do. The key is that your team has the opportunity to engage and speak their minds—by sharing their feelings.

In my career, countless times I have thought something I was bringing to the group was simple, no big deal and wham, two weeks later it has turned into a "thing." Just take a moment to check in after bringing what may seem like rudimentary stuff. Most often, just checking is enough, but on occasion it is not and that is when you have the opportunity to do good work. Always remember you are the conduit between your team and the organization. Facilitating the right dialogue within the team regarding company happenings/decisions is one of your primary functions. Do this like the health of your team depends on it, because it does.

2. Giving Performance Feedback to an Employee

Communication can pertain to the role and function of an employee and how to help them grow and develop. You should always know where each of your people are on their personal development continuum. Some of their goals will relate to their skills and abilities in their job; others may relate to their personal lives. Knowing where they are focused in their development journey is important to bringing the right performance feedback.

As a manager you should have a method for keeping track of each person's work. Don't make it a long laundry list; select two or three performance areas where they want to improve and brand them, "20XX is going to be the year of X." It helps everyone stay on track. It takes a ton of work getting everything boiled down, but once you have the performance gems for each person identified for the year and have them branded so they are easy to identify, then you can stay focused and get/give regular feedback.

You should be giving feedback and input regularly. When doing so, make sure you frame it properly. Before you bring difficult content to the conversation, it is always helpful to start with an affirmative statement, something like, "You know I have deep respect for you, and I am committed to supporting you in your growth. Thus, I have some feedback." This is a reminder that the feedback is coming from a place of love. When you open up in this way, you position yourself and your commentary such that it can land well and be absorbed.

Your people should never need to inquire about performance or their progress. You should be in a consistent cadence with ongoing conversation, regular check-ins, and updates. As you go about your daily routine, you should constantly watch for nuggets to bring to your next meeting. In my organization we have a formal review system that touches on this specifically, but meetings only happen a few times a year. It is way too hard to make any real progress when your interval for feedback is measured in months or quarters. The informal feedback brought regularly, daily/weekly, is where you find the gold. Keeping everyone's development goals and objectives top of mind by talking about them often is how real progress gets made.

Professional goals may seem more natural in the work setting. Maybe someone aspires to be better at public speaking or wants to set up two mentoring relationships by year-end. Or they may want to read 25 books or have an article published on an industry website or in a journal related to their profession. Maybe your goal as a leader is to have conversations once a week with everyone on your team about their goals for the year. This stuff seems natural and appropriate for the work setting.

As I hinted previously, I think it is appropriate to allow people to have personal goals, as well as professional goals. Personal goals we've seen at BIGGBY range from physical fitness (I want to lose 20 pounds) to arranging a weekly date night with their spouse or lowering their golf handicap by four strokes. By checking in regularly on their personal goals, you bring a level of accountability but also connect with them on a more intimate level. When you help them move forward in important ways personally, you are building strong connectivity. There is no judgment, only support.

With either kind of goal, engagement as manager doesn't need to be big dramatic strokes; you can do simple small things that have impact. For the woman who wanted a date night, we took care of a weekend getaway sans kids. For the gentleman who wanted to lower his golf handicap, I sent links to articles on golf instruction. These things are simple little perks, but the real power is in the regular communication asking about their progress. The magic happens with the small, consistent gestures, not the grandiose, big strokes.

Just make sure you are constantly, daily engaged in each person's development. It has to be a regular part of the conversation you are having with people in order for you and each member of your team to excel.

3. Receiving Feedback on Your Behavior and Performance

It is imperative as a manager that you work hard to make feedback a two-way street by not just expressing and commanding but requesting input and feedback. Asking for feedback and getting direct engagement on your performance from your people is essential.

If you are fortunate to have a formal review process in your company, that is a step forward. (For example, the popular 360-degree review process provides multiple sources of feedback on each employee's performance from many different sources— employees, peers, and supervisors/bosses—which is valuable information.) Keep in mind though, something mandated from the organization will be viewed skeptically. The quality of the feedback is suspect because you are forced to fill out standard forms and it feels like administrative busy work, and you cram it in because you have to, not because you want to. There is always some value, but the impact is marginal.

The real magic occurs by going to someone on your team directly and asking for their help in monitoring and assessing your performance in relation to specific, tangible objectives (e.g., "I am working on ______. Would you be willing to keep an eye out for this behavior and point it out to me when it occurs?"). I am regularly amazed at what comes of these conversations. It is nothing short of magical.

As the relationship progresses and deepens, you can begin to ask them for things you could be improving. Get nuggets from their perspective. At first people won't feel comfortable sharing their honest feedback. They aren't prepared. Additionally, few managers ask for feedback, so it comes as a bit of a shock. Be prepared for a lackluster response in the moment and let them off the hook gently, but leave them with, "Can you think about it and try to bring me something in the coming weeks?"

As time goes on, the conversation usually gets better and more meaningful. The feedback you get is the primary benefit, but nearly as important is the fact you are asking. It changes the dynamic of the relationship in a healthy way. You shed the know-it-all persona. You are attempting to be better, and you need their feedback to do so. Asking for authentic engagement and feedback from your people is meaningful and will propel your relationships forward.

Whenever somebody complies with your request for feedback or takes the initiative to bring you feedback on their own, take the time to reiterate what they said so you make sure you understand and they know you heard them. Also thank them for being willing to speak up. They cared enough to share their opinion.

I also recommend sharing the person's feedback with the rest of your team. Publicly talking about it is critical for any manager. You are the magic elixir who can eliminate fear. Public acknowledgment makes it safe for other people to bring you—and hopefully their coworkers as well—the real stuff. I have gone out of my way in large group settings to acknowledge somebody for bringing me useful feedback. It is always helpful to dive in and make sure you understand the specifics of any feedback by discussing the details with the group and getting additional perspectives, rather than confining your processing to the mucky gray area of your singular brain. More brains and more perspectives is always better.

4. Solving a Specific Problem

Communication in a business setting is often about problem-solving. You are facing a problem and think you could make a better decision if you discuss the issues and get input on ideas and potential solutions by engaging your team. Tapping into the collective brain of your team is something you need to do on a regular basis, both with the group and individuals alike.

Most managers know the importance of getting input— it can be make or break for new initiatives or problems that need to be solved. How we do it is critical. Typically, we throw out the question, "Is there any feedback or input from the group?" This is routinized behavior and the same cast of characters share a thought or two before the group rolls forward to the next agenda item.

As the manager/leader of the group, it is your responsibility to get everyone involved and bring out the collective as well as the individual genius. This is how groups function effectively. It starts with facilitating conversation and communication and encouraging/expecting everyone to contribute. Not everybody provides input the same way, thus, you need to encourage people to contribute from their authentic position. How? Here are two ideas:

First, call on people by name to share their ideas. "Sarah, what are your thoughts on this?" Everyone benefits from commentary and discussion in real time. The more perspectives running around in each brain the better. You need to provide safety and openings for everyone so you don't leave genius on the sidelines.

An example: Kevin, a manager in our IT department, is quiet and reserved and rarely spoke up in meetings. He joined us on a leadership retreat early in his management tenure. We all got to know him better. Upon returning from the retreat, as was normal, he rarely engaged. The group started pausing and asking him for his opinion. At first there were long, long awkward silences. He would hem and haw for what seemed like eternity. Frequently, we would have to self-govern and stop to correct members of the team who would nervously start talking and interrupt his thinking. The silence continued. Then, bingo, out would come some thought so profound that we would sit with it for a minute to let it sink in. His insights proved to be powerful. This routine happened regularly enough over the years to call it magic. Kevin was an amazingly strategic thinker. If we had never inquired and specifically asked him to share his ideas, we would have left his genius buried within.

Second, offer the opportunity to talk one on one. If a person is not comfortable weighing in with the entire group listening, try calling them aside directly after a meeting and saying, "Tom, I noticed when we were talking that you didn't share any ideas. I know you have thoughts, and I would love to hear them." You may get positive and supportive nonsense at first, but go deeper by summarizing what you think you heard, then asking for more depth: "Ok, you are generally supportive, but if this isn't going to work, why not?" Or maybe, "What are some blind spots we are not seeing on this? Where do you see this thing going sideways?" People need permission to go negative and it is your job to provide them the safety and opportunity to critique. From my experience it isn't natural to open up, especially if they think their ideas will feel contrarian or judgmental. You need to provide them safety to do so, and sometimes you have to do that by approaching them for feedback in private.

When solving problems, get as much feedback and different perspectives as possible. Make sure to get to everyone by whatever means necessary. It is critical to hear every voice.

5. Blending the Professional and Personal

Admittedly, diving into an employee's personal life can seem like a big hairy abyss, with snakes and spiders squirming and crawling all over. It's a place many managers avoid like the plague. The thinking goes, if you open Pandora's box by broaching personal issues, it will overwhelm you. You may end up in an inappropriate conversation and learn things you never wanted to hear. It goes with the territory.

The fact of the matter is people live lives without brick walls between work and home. The two are meshed in inextricable ways. Traditionalists would like you to believe it is possible to leave personal issues at the door—but that is as impossible as leaving the office in the car when you pull into the driveway at home. Case in point: How many people go straight to the bottle or grab a THC gummy when they walk across the threshold at home? Just like you need to vent sometimes about work at home, sometimes you need to vent at work about what is happening in your personal life. Life is life, no matter the setting.

Ironically, avoiding people's personal stuff has always been a mantra for me. I like to buckle down and get to business. As you may have picked up, I am a huge proponent of efficiency. Therefore, I like to skip right over the fuzzy stuff. On the flipside, Bob, my business partner, is magically powerful when it comes to engaging people about their lives. He does it because he genuinely cares about what is happening for them and wants to be supportive. He remembers details of people's lives, he follows up on an important personal event, he loves stories about pets and children, he loves to hear about personal victories but also engages in the heartfelt moments of struggle. He is a strong leader because of it.

Going back through all of time, you will find the best managers, the managers with the highest-performing teams, were engaged in supporting each member of their team on a personal level. This is simply what good managers do. They know what is going on with people authentically. They care, and it starts with taking the time to ask.

For example, you have a healthy relationship with a man you have worked with for many years. He is seemingly off one day, and you ask, from a position of love and support, "Frank, are things all right? It looks like you saw a ghost this morning in the parking garage." Traditional response follows: "It's nothing, just some family stuff." Here is the tipping point, the point with which you can engage or pull flaps. You choose to ask. It can be as simple as, "Like what?" In my experience it takes very little for people to open up.

Frank gets emotional and tears up a bit. "My wife's brother's oldest, my nephew, is going through a really tough time. He is transitioning gender. He has been going through it for a few years openly, but frankly it has been a struggle most of his life. We are supporting him as much as possible, but he has been threatening suicide. It is killing my wife and me."

Heavy #@*%!

Long silence.

Your response: "Are you talking about Tommy? The kid you talk about all the time? Oh, my goodness. I am so sorry. What can I do?"

Frank, as is typical, declines any help but is thankful to you for taking a minute. Over the coming weeks you check in occasionally on his nephew.

A few weeks later you are at a school function and have a conversation with a friend on a similar subject. The friend mentions a family retreat they attended in Boston centered on teens transitioning. It was amazing and frankly she thought it might have saved her daughter's life. Boom! You get the information and simply pass it along to your employee. Nothing more. What did it take? Maybe five minutes. The results are powerful for everyone. You do it out of love and support. You do it because you care. Let people bring their whole self to the conversation at work. You will be amazed at the results.

We have been working on folding personal and professional together for many years now in our organization. In a traditional environment managers check in with the obligatory, "How are you? How are things?" and 99 out of 100 times you get, "Good. Things are going well." The manager moves on and gets down to business. Today in our company we make a deliberate effort to check in "for real." We open our engagements with, "How are you? How are things?" We still often get the obligatory response. The manager is expected to slow their roll and ask, "No really, what is going on for you right now? What is working? What are you struggling with?" There is always a much deeper and more heartfelt answer, and now you are in a meaningful conversation. It is amazing how simple it is; just make a little room, extend the invitation, and bingo, you are in a healthy, authentic dialogue. Most people are starved for authenticity and love to be open.

Also, in formal meetings, we start by going around the table with everyone taking two minutes to give their personal and professional highs and lows. It is a powerful touchpoint and keeps everybody looped in. For example, we have a woman who is a leader in our organization. Her mom fell quite ill and was hospitalized. We were all worried. Everyone checking in with her independently was cumbersome and awkward. Because of the weekly check-in, we were all kept in the loop. Intermittently, we were able to engage with support and care. For a few months at every departmental meeting, I eagerly waited for her update regarding her mother. It was a great way to efficiently stay connected to each other that was also comfortable for her and everybody else.

The following story from Kim Scott's book, *Radical Candor*, offers an exchange that summarizes the transition managers must make in their thinking in order to be effective:

> "I'd gotten only a few steps into the office when a colleague suddenly ran up. He needed to talk right away. He had just learned that he might need a kidney transplant and was completely freaked out. After an hour and two cups of tea, he seemed calmer.
>
> "Next, I walked toward my desk, past an engineer whose child was in the ICU. 'How'd your son do last night?' I asked. He hadn't improved. As he told me how the night had gone we both had tears in our eyes. I convinced him to leave the office and go take care of himself for an hour before returning to the hospital.
>
> "I left his desk drained, passing by our quality assurance manager. His child had better news: she'd just received the highest score in the entire state on a standardized math test. He wanted to talk about it. I felt emotional whiplash as I jumped from sympathy to celebration.
>
> "By the time I got back to my desk, I had no time or emotional reserves to think about pricing. I cared about each of these people, but I also felt worn out and frustrated that I couldn't get any 'real' work done. Later that day, I called my CEO coach, Leslie Koch, to complain. Is my job to build a great company, I asked, or am I really just some sort of emotional babysitter? Leslie, a fiercely opinionated ex-Microsoft

executive, could barely contain herself. 'This is not babysitting,' she said. 'It's called management, and it is your job!'"[1]

Taking care of people on your team is more than assisting them in becoming better employees who take on more responsibility, get a promotion, make more money, and produce greater profits for the company. If this is your mindset, you are going to be left behind as a manager; you are a dinosaur. As leaders we have an obligation to engage people from the heart and to contribute to their growth and development as people. It all starts with a willingness to support. It all starts with communication. It starts with a question: How are you? No, really, how are you doing?

6. Listening

There are countless statistics supporting the notion that most people are poor listeners. They spend their time considering their response rather than trying to understand the speaker. Why don't people listen? There are a number of variables impacting a person's ability to listen. For example, if the CEO is in the room, people may be running a filter front and center, attempting to get her attention. Maybe somebody is present with whom we are in conflict, so they are taking the lion's share of our mind space. Maybe there are outside events limiting our ability to be fully present. If you are posturing based on who is in the room, modifying your behavior to get an advantageous outcome, or checking out mentally because your dog was diagnosed with cancer, you are not bringing your full self to the table. You as the leader are susceptible to distraction the same as anyone else. You have to be cognizant and aware of your listening but also the quality of listening for the whole group.

Often the issue at the surface is tangential to the bigger issue. I liken this process to mining for gold. You must invest the time and energy to uncover the gold nuggets through listening. Nuggets are the moments you uncover the meaningful, heartfelt issue behind the issue at hand. You dig and you dig, and occasionally you find gold. We listen and we listen, and occasionally you gain insight into what is occurring for people. The harder you dig and the harder you listen, the more nuggets you uncover.

When you sense strife, anxiety, anger, remorse, etc., when the light blinks yellow, you must ask the individual directly what is happening for them and allow the person time to open up. There, you will often find a treasure trove of insight. When you get nuggets, you have to treat them with the highest degree of integrity. When people get vulnerable and share, you have considerable responsibility to be thoughtful and cautious. If you breach trust, you will crush the relationship and the possibility of any future insights. To bring value to the group you have to know the skinny, the real stuff, the true picture. The only source of that information is the team itself, and you only get it through listening deeply.

When I uncover nuggets, I rarely take the content head on. We must use what we learn in nuanced ways. This nuance is complicated. If I want to use a nugget I learned to coach the team or an individual, I ask for permission. If I don't have permission, I generally don't use it, or I keep it so broad as to avoid a breach of trust. When somebody on my team shares their truth, it allows me to bring that reality to the whole team. The only way you get these insights is to listen for what is underlying in the issues people bring, and not necessarily attempt to solve the problem at hand.

We all know that even in the most trusting relationships, the words we choose are critical and should be considered/debated before they are launched. Most people run a filter to make certain they are not doing damage to their relationships (Communicating 101 or Communicating for Dummies). Equally or maybe even more important than your choice of words is how you listen. Listening appropriately is a key component to building trust, and being purposeful when listening is a superpower. We are all magically drawn in by good listeners because when we feel like our opinion matters and is valued, we feel acknowledged and heard. When we feel heard, we connect. When we have the opportunity to connect, we build trust. Listening is 50 percent of healthy communication. If you aren't listening, you can't effectively communicate.

7. Asking for Help

Traditional management culture signifies the need for bosses to be powerful by inculcating a feeling of indebtedness from their team. The boss is always giving. This is the framework for servant leadership. That's why most people believe we build relationships by doing favors and helping others. Servant leadership is a great construct. I appreciate the premise very much, and it has done great things for the world of management and leadership.

However, it only tells part of the story. There is another powerful way to build a relationship by communicating and asking someone to support you. In my experience, people want to be involved and help but aren't provided opportunities. By engaging a peer or a member of your team in a personal favor, you open yourself up; you become human and vulnerable, and the relationship transitions to symbiosis or helping one another. The symbiotic, two-way bond is stronger and healthier than one-way bonds. That's why I am advocating evolving beyond servant leadership, because those relationships are one sided;

instead, we need to become half of a symbiotic partnership with each member of our team.

When somebody feels like they are contributing and are appreciated for their efforts, they feel valued. It is even more powerful if the indebtedness originates with the boss. They become vested and connected, and it feels great. This principle could be its own chapter in a book on management, but I think it can start with the willingness to ask for help—to be vulnerable and share your struggles. Most managers shy away from asking for help. Get over yourself and let people know you need help too. They want to support you and will be honored to be engaged.

An example: Suppose you have a daughter who is interested in playing lacrosse and a woman who works for you has a son playing college lacrosse. You'd like your daughter and her son to connect, so you ask the mom for help in arranging a phone call between the two kids. She then invites you to attend one of her son's games. You'd probably sit together. What a nice opportunity. Imagine the connectivity you will create with the lacrosse mom. You will know each other better.

Ongoing, you and your daughter track her son's career. At some point, the help cycle comes full circle when he reaches out directly and asks for a networking connection or a letter of reference. You are happy to do it, and you feel great about it. You are now connected to his mom at another level, and you both carry that forward. All you did was ask for a phone call between your children. Don't be shy. Ask for help.

Add Value or Bust

We have covered different scenarios where effective communication is critical, from simple updates to requesting feedback, sorting out group dynamics, asking for help, engaging people's personal lives, focusing on the power of listening. The gamut is wide ranging, but the key takeaway is that the strength of your relationships starts with quality of communication. Are you adding value to the relationship each time you have the opportunity to engage? How do you know? You ask your people, "Are you getting value out of our engagements?" If the answer isn't a strong affirmative, then you need to start asking for feedback on how you can better communicate and therefore connect.

CHAPTER 12

Communication Rules of Engagement

RULES OF ENGAGEMENT ALLOW YOU TO SET THE STANDARD and hold everyone accountable to the same standard. This is as true for communication as with any other form of human interaction. There are simple rules to follow and processes to engage that help keep people in sync and acting with integrity. This simple stuff is hard to abide by in the heat of the moment but critical to the health of the group. It is the stuff you learned in kindergarten, and it still works today. Here are 11 rules that I've found essential to effective communication.

Rule 1: Understanding, Verified

Most listeners, therefore most people, think they understand what someone says to them. You and your arrogance believe you get what the person is trying to tell you. The problem is you are listening through the filters your bias has created, and every word coming out of the speaker is landing in relation to your own experience and bias.

Just last week I was talking to my therapist about a major premise of my next book, which is going to be on "redefining capitalism." And because I am a CEO of a company, she assumed many things about me, namely that I am a fiscal conservative and that I vote Republican. I found this amusing because neither of those assumptions is true. I was trying to make a point to her about one of the primary premises of my book, and she scoffed and told me, "Impossible." I was taken aback and just reiterated my point to her, only to be met with another scoff and eye roll. I stopped her and said, "I don't think you are hearing me because what I am trying to say is actually supporting your position on this." Her reply was, "It can never happen." Let me remind you, this is a trained therapist who is paid to listen, and her bias was squarely in the way of her hearing what I was saying. How often does this happen in the world? More often than not, I am afraid.

Clarify, verify, clarify. And repeat as often as necessary. The following phrase is magical: "Let me make sure I understand what you are saying. Do you mind if I repeat it back to you?" Boom! Instantly the person feels heard. You are telling them their opinion is important because you want to make sure you understand. You are listening. After you have repeated their position, they then have the ability to weigh in and clarify whether you have it or not. Feeling heard puts everyone in a great space for a healthy conversation.

Another option that helps with a nuanced misunderstanding is to say something like, "Before I weigh in with my opinion, I want to make sure I understand your position properly." You are attempting to understand, and they are made aware you might have a different opinion. This is important because stating your understanding can be interpreted as agreement. It has happened to me numerous times. Clarifying your understanding is not agreement. I oftentimes will go as far as to say, "We are in agreement that we understand each other, but not necessarily in agreement on the topic at hand." If a speaker interprets your statement as agreement, that can be ruinous down the road when the person overhears you state something counter to their position. They can react justifiably harshly, as if you are going back on your word.

My business partner and I engage in this checking-for-understanding practice regularly. It is daunting how often we get it wrong; the number of times we repeat back to each other what we thought we heard only to have the other say we are way off is staggering. It is really on the listener to cue up verification. As the listener, you sense when maybe something is a little off, and at that exact moment you must interject with, "Hang on, let me repeat back what I am hearing just to make sure we are aligned." You will find 90 percent of the time that you are missing something or the speaker has a point to clarify.

Rule 2: Don't Control by the Way You Listen

Active listening can also present in the form of responding with positive cues. You make the speaker feel engaged by acknowledging points with "ahhhhh," or demonstrating understanding with "uh-huh." There is also the quick "sure" or "right" when in agreement. You are attempting to make the speaker feel comfortable and at home. Who could argue that?

Another part of listening is leaving space before responding. People have a lot to say, and you want to make sure you are providing ample opportunity for them to get everything on the table. Try to avoid the quick response, as it typically shuts down conversation. Practice waiting five to seven seconds after you think somebody else is done speaking before you chime in. It doesn't sound like much, but in the moment five seconds feels like forever. You will be surprised how often somebody has more to say—they just need permission to say it, and silence offers that permission.

There is a downside to active listening, and this is the nuance. If the active listening is overt—the sounds or words of encouragement too intrusive—the speaker cues their focus on the active listener as if he or she is the only person in the room. A leader who is an aggressive listener draws all of the intention to themselves. This relegates the group to the sideshow and not primary to the presentation, discussion, or dialogue. The leader unconsciously wants to be in charge, and with aggressive active listening it is clear to everyone that he or she is. Imagine if a junior member of the team was aggressively listening and engaging a speaker. It would feel odd. Or imagine if everyone in the room was aggressively listening; it would be chaos. As the leader, get clear about your engagement when listening.

A leader actively listening generally has no bad intentions, but like nonverbal communication, one must understand the impact the leader's active engagement has on the group. This is a subtle form of communication and not recognized by many but can have a powerful impact on the dynamic in a room. When you are actively engaging or actively listening, you are drawing all the attention. Try sitting back and saying nothing. I enjoy trying to mask my leadership role when outsiders are present. I enjoy watching them interact with the team. If you are inappropriately actively engaged as the leader, it impacts this dynamic by making you the center of attention. If you are the center of attention, then you are absorbing 80 percent of the energy in the room, sucking away resources and not allowing others to flourish. Try sitting in the back seat and watching others flourish, and you will learn truckloads.

Rule 3: Don't Interrupt

Interrupting, especially from a position of authority, plagues most groups, more specifically interrupting women. (Frankly the issue is men interrupting women; women don't interrupt so much.) If you don't believe me, and most people don't, start paying attention. It is an amazing phenomenon. I have been blown away by this behavior. This is something I am paying close attention to, as I have been held to account for interrupting. Recently, after having been made acutely aware of this issue, I was flagged again for violating this rule, even after paying attention for many years. Interrupting is a show of dominance and can feel as dramatic as a punch in the face.

If you want fluid communication and productive idea exchange, nobody can feel dominated. Make interrupting anathema. Also, appoint someone to look out for whether you interrupt or not. If you are a white male in your forties or fifties, I think you might be surprised by how often you interrupt. Stop it by putting somebody in charge of interrupting you when you interrupt.

Rule 4: Don't Disguise Statements as Questions

This rule is a spin-off of rule 3: When someone else is speaking, do not interrupt with questions unless you are absolutely certain your intent is simple clarification.

People often consider questions to be a great tactic in listening, but it is important to understand that questions often manipulate and guide conversation. The act of asking questions can be an insidious way of controlling the conversation directionally. Questions are often statements dressed up with a mask. Simply because your brain leaps to a certain place given what a speaker is saying, that doesn't mean your certain place is the appropriate place to leap, and potentially it isn't what the speaker needs and or wants from you. When you quickly leap to a certain line of questioning, you are leaping to a conclusion, and so often your conclusion is inappropriate.

So limit yourself to questions of clarification—"When you said the customer was unhappy, what did you mean?" or "I don't understand what the complaint was. Can you give us more details?"—whenever someone else is speaking.

Maybe an example of a statement disguised as a question would be helpful. A coworker is talking about a relationship with a customer that is proving frustrating. If you jump in and ask, "What tech platform are they running?" you have just moved the conversation in the direction of technology, and the conversation will focus on how the tech platform is the problem. Within the speaker's response, you uncover an issue and ask a few more questions about the technology deployment. They answer your questions. Your colleague is riding with you on the line of questioning because it is almost impossible to divert you from your questions without appearing rude or dismissive. They even may begin to think that technology is the real issue and exit the conversation. You feel good about yourself—you brought value.

The fact of the matter is your colleague was struggling interpersonally with the VP of marketing at the customer; the frustration had nothing to do with technology, and he really needed to dive in on the customer. He needed a sounding board because he felt like he was losing the account due to his interpersonal struggles. He thought of you as somebody who might be able to talk him through his approach. By immediately asking a question about technology, you took him down the technology path because it was on top of your mind. You controlled that conversation and left feeling great. He walked away not getting what he needed.

People will pause their thinking to accommodate your questions in order to understand your intention in order to line up with your direction. As the boss you have sway and you have to be careful with your line of questioning. By staying stuck on the technology questions you are saying you think that is the issue. There were hundreds of questions you could have asked; you made a statement with the one you chose.

Venting Alert: Avoid the Socratic Method of Questioning

For many, the Socratic method is considered a more advanced form of communication whereby you ask a series of questions that steer people to your conclusion but leave them feeling as if they have arrived of their own accord. The flawed assumption starts with you thinking you know the answer and then manipulating your team to agree through a series of questions that act like statements.

If done with discipline and training, the Socratic method can, at times, be effective, but in management it needs to

continued

be monitored, making sure it isn't used to manipulate, steer, or cajole. Questions from a place of authority are often statements: "Where have we seen this before, and was it effective?" The underlying statement is that we have seen this before, and it wasn't effective. The manager knows the answer to the question and is steering the group to that conclusion. Or, "Have you considered other methods to resolve this situation?" (implying that the speaker has not yet found the right answer and should keep working). What if in their line of thinking either your answer or a better answer was just around the corner before you interrupted?

Don't interrupt with questions, especially if you are going to use them to try to restrict the path the group will take in its discussion.

Rule 5: Value Candor and Sincere Expression

The concept of candor is another of my favorite ideas that I got from Kim Scott's great book *Radical Candor*.[1] Ms. Scott presents the idea of "ruinous empathy" as the opposite of candor. Empathy becomes a problem in relationships when you are more interested in being kind and understanding than in being honest and authentic. Managers leave authenticity out of the conversation because they invest so heavily in false praise. The manager is afraid of bringing their truth and tells someone they did quality work when they didn't. It is more harmful than not saying anything at all. It is much easier and feels better to tell somebody they were awesome than to suggest areas for improvement. Flip your mindset. Bringing the truth, the real stuff to a relationship, is a loving act. You are supporting that person in growing and bringing them valuable information so they can improve and develop. Also, when you bring the critique, it makes the compliment more meaningful. If everything is always sushi and puppy parties, then the compliments lose value in the end. Without the counterweight of the critique, compliments are not authentic.

There is a modern movement to keep your compliment-to-critique ratio appropriate. Something crazy, like four compliments to one critique. As I discussed earlier (p. 55), if you are working hard to find compliments, there is a problem. You shouldn't work hard to find four positives every time you want to land a critique. If you have to search for something positive to say, those compliments will lack authenticity. People need to know when they do good work and when their work needs to improve, period. When they know the feedback is genuine, it is infinitely more powerful. Celebrate the positives and bring the negatives from the perspective of love and empathy, and in the end people will trust you and believe in you as a manager.

Rule 6: Criticize and Compliment, for Real

Criticism must be used sparingly and done in a way in which you are not questioning the individual but rather their opinion or decision. Steve Jobs said it best (which I quote from the introduction of Kim Scott's book *Radical Candor*):

"'You need to do that [criticize] in a way that does not call into question your confidence in their abilities but also does not leave too much room for interpretation and that's a hard thing to do.' He went on to say, 'I don't mind being wrong. And I'll admit that I'm wrong a lot. It doesn't really matter to me too much. What matters to me is that we do the right thing.' Amen: Who could argue with that?"[2]

Keep the cortisol levels at bay and facilitate a powerful outcome by criticizing the content and the opinion, not the person.

Rule 7: Clearly State Your Intention

We build powerful teams by aligning around the purpose and intention of a specific conversation and ultimately presenting our truth for everyone's consideration. Anything short of that is wasted time. The key to understanding truth is that everyone's truth is different, and reality lies somewhere in the mess. In order to get to a mutual reality, we need every morsel of truth the team has on a given topic. Where there are differences in truth is where the gems are hiding.

That's why another rule to establish in your organization is that people should state their intentions prior to communicating. If everyone is aware of the intention behind a forthcoming statement, it is much easier for them to listen and respond appropriately.

For example, if my intention is to highlight a risk and I am generally supportive of the idea, it is important for people to know I am bringing my concern from a place of support, not dissent. Stating my intention might sound something like, "Generally I am quite supportive of this idea and I am concerned that we need to be considering . . ." This has a completely different vibe than, "I am concerned that we need to be considering . . ."

Also, if you disagree with something, it is imperative the group knows you are willing to accept the wisdom of the group, even if you disagree. You might state, "I hope all of you trust I will line up with the group in the end and support the direction we decide to go, but I would be doing the group a disservice if I didn't express my concern based on . . ."

When delivering an opinion that might trigger extreme or unpleasant reactions for certain members of the group, make sure to set up the conversation in a way that allows for openness but also provides a release for people who might get triggered. This can sound something like, "There is a chance that what I am about to present could land wrong for some people. Please know I am bringing this up because I think it is something we need to think about. If you want to reach out to me directly after this meeting and talk it over, please call." People feel like you are open to feedback by setting up the conversation for a healthy outcome.

One of my favorite moments in any meeting is when someone makes a statement or pitches a solution and somebody pipes up with, "First, allow me to clarify your position, and if I understand it correctly, I have to politely disagree." At that moment I know we are headed somewhere productive—not necessarily somewhere comfortable, but productive. All teams face difficult challenges and strong teams bring differing opinions. As I have said before and will say again, resolution is where the magic happens. It doesn't happen without people bringing their truth, and one of the primary ways we bring our truth is by being discerning with the words that leave our mouths and making sure they land gently in our listeners' ears. Bring it clearly, land it gently, and work hard to find resolution.

Rule 8: Pay Attention to Nonverbal Communication

Nonverbal communication is as powerful as any spoken word. You must be acutely aware of how you are communicating nonverbally. Most of us are pretty good at blowing smoke, pontificating, and sounding smart, especially those in leadership positions. We have become adept at saying the "right" things in the appropriate moment. On the flipside, most of us are blundering idiots when it comes to understanding the impact our body language and actions have on the group. Even though I have been made aware of and am sensitive to the impact my body language and distracted tendencies have on others, I still get it wrong all the time!

As the leader you must be critically aware of how you are presenting. People are watching your every move, intently. They look at your facial expression. If you tip your hand quickly with a smile, or a nod, or a sigh, or slight eye roll, you are influencing groupthink. Sitting back in your chair, arms folded, means struggle. Leaning into the table with chin in palm is showing interest and support. Everyone is motivated to line up with you as the leader, and strong nonverbal engagement signals your position. People get in line.

Keep a poker face with a positive air and people won't feed off you but instead develop their own opinion. In case you haven't guessed, diverse opinions are the gems we are all searching for as managers/leaders. When you are steering the group through positive or negative body language, you are submerging all the gems about to be mined. How does this work? Let's say that during a presentation online, your body language signals your disinterest or disagreement. However, a junior associate happens to have data supporting the presenter's position. When you signal negativity, maybe the junior associate decides not to mention their data for fear of your opinion. You just lost potentially powerful information that could have altered the course of the decision because your body language signaled negativity.

Freeing up space and not influencing the group with nonverbal communication has been my nemesis. For many years I walked into every room knowing the answer in advance (or so I thought!). I would inadvertently impact the trajectory of thinking and discussion by how I was sitting or expressing quirky behavior everyone grew familiar with.

There is arrogance in thinking you have the answers. It took me a long time to realize the genius behind collaborative creativity, and my nonverbal cues were limiting our ability to reap its rewards. Even when I became aware of the power of group exploration, I still struggled with nonverbal cues that changed the group dynamic. An example: When struggling to understand an idea, I put my glasses on the top of my head and rub my eyes. Those gestures became widely known and people would point out, "It's clear Mike isn't on board. He is rubbing his eyes." I didn't even know I was doing it. People knew where I stood, and as an owner and co-CEO, this small gesture impacted a group's direction.

Another example: I would lean my head back and close my eyes whenever I lacked enthusiasm or was frustrated. Upon seeing those gestures from me, the presenter would get nervous, which impacted their performance. Everyone would sense my lack of enthusiasm. I was sucking the energy out of the room. The group disengaged: If Mike isn't on board, this thing isn't getting off the ground anyway, so why try? My behavior manifested even when I was acutely aware of the dynamic. These behaviors are hard to control.

Another insidious nonverbal behavior is being distracted. How often do you look at your phone? How often do you respond to a text or an email in a meeting? When you do that, you are screaming "What you're doing isn't important to me!" to everyone else in the room. During an update from your CFO regarding a crisis with the future of your company in the balance, I imagine you aren't on your phone. It would be considered negligent. When a junior associate is presenting a topic of little relevance to your day-to-day, you will be more prone to distraction. Looking down at your phone is catastrophic to the junior associate, creating a dynamic the cost of which is immeasurable. Your attention is a highly sought commodity. Be engaged or exit.

It is hard to understand your own body language or how your engagement is impacting the group. It is almost impossible to gauge this stuff yourself, especially in the heat of the moment. In order to be a strong leader, you must get feedback from others.

Just the other day, a woman colleague who I respect pointed out a behavior of mine that was sending the wrong message. We have a weekly Zoom call with the collective body of our franchise owners called "town hall." We cover different topics and bring different people from the organization to provide status updates on current topics. It has proven to be a powerful communication tool. In a meeting shortly after one town hall, my colleague commented, "You seemed really bored and distracted during that town hall again." This wasn't the first time she noted my behavior; she'd made me aware of it on prior occasions and commented on the negative impact. She pointed out that everyone reads my body language, and it hits people squarely. Both presenter and audience are cueing off me. The fact of the matter is I wasn't bored or disinterested, I was tired. I have been growing increasingly aware of my Zoom fatigue. Obviously, it wasn't getting better and in fact was actually getting worse. I had been having a "day." I was on the periphery of the issues discussed in the town hall, but my impact was negative. It would have been better if I wasn't there.

Asking somebody on your team or the whole team to provide you feedback on your nonverbal behavior is imperative. When emotions get bumping, it is difficult to check your voice and even harder to control your body language, but these are the exact times you need to be in complete control. Ask somebody you trust to watch your behaviors and gestures. Spread the workload a bit. I have gone as far as having different people on my team look out for different things.

Fortunately, my business partner is always on the lookout for my glasses getting flipped up on my forehead and my fingers massaging my eyeballs. I have asked a female member of my team to pay close attention to when I interrupt. (Yes, interrupting is a form of nonverbal communication; when you interrupt you are communicating that they are lesser or what they are saying is not important.) I have asked the whole team to be on the lookout for moments I represent disinterest. Your people know you better than you do—take advantage of it!

When supporting a team, what you don't say can be more impactful on the group than what you do say. Leaving space for others is critical for the group's development and performance. Also, what you communicate with your body language and facial expressions is the secret code of leadership. Great leaders are aware of how they impact the group with their nonverbal communication. This can go as far as what clothes you wear to the kind of car you rent on a business trip. Pay attention to the details of what you are communicating with things other than words.

Rule 9: The Manager Should Speak Last (Limiting the Impact of Outsized Voices)

Your role is to keep the group focused and on task, but you must also manage the outsized voice—comments from those with the most authority by virtue of their job title or seniority. That person with the outsized voice is often you! When you say something, it changes the course of any conversation.

The rule I like to use is that you, as the manager or leader, communicate last, if at all. You are more experienced than most. You have been put in your position for a reason. You are confident in your capability. Let me give you a fundamental truth: You are not smarter than the collective wisdom of the group. But when you speak, you pull the group in your direction where cognition dissipates and dissention evaporates. The group is keenly aware of your power: You are the arbiter of resources and hold the keys to their future, so they subconsciously line up with your thinking. Maybe your idea is a good idea, but any real thinking in your group can stop when you speak up. Shut up and let the group unfold an idea and wander down paths you haven't considered. Then you can weigh in. There is alchemy in the conversation.

One quick example from my career: For many years, and even today at times, I fall into a mode dubbed by my colleagues as "command and control." My behavior becomes extremely controlling, bordering on maniacal. When I am in this space, I am not listening to anybody. I feel like I have the answer, and everyone else be damned. I am acting as if it is my God-given right to tell everyone what to do. Needless to say, this is most unhealthy.

On a leadership retreat, we dove deep on this one and really got into what is happening in those moments. We uncovered that I react this way when I am scared. Fear has taken me to a place where I feel like I need to control everything.

In subsequent years, when this behavior started to emerge, it was extremely helpful when somebody interjected, "Mike, it appears from your behavior that you are operating from a place of fear. What are you scared of right now? Why are you approaching this with so much anxiety?" For some members of our group, interrupting me could be difficult, especially when I am in command-and-control mode. My reaction in the moment is critical to the overall health of the team. My visceral reaction at that point is to increase intensity and blow the doors off the room. I now know it is the unhealthiest thing I can do and at that point I need to sit back and close my lips.

The healthy response is to think, thank, and consider. So if I'm hearing feedback from someone I trust, I sit back, take a breath, and assess. When it works well, the group can dive into the question about my fear, and we often have a healthy conversation that exposes a quite reasonable concern. It is the behavior that the concern created that is worrisome, not the concern itself. After the exchange, I try to thank the person who brought it to my attention so that everyone else in the room can be more comfortable in the future challenging me when command and control is present. This moment can build significant trust within the group, which should be the aspiration.

Here's a positive example of how I've learned to create a safe space for people to voice opinions, even if they think I might disagree: I had built a tool early on in our company for projecting revenue, and it had been reliable. The process, though, was arduous, and it took a great deal of time for me to churn out results each period because there were tons of different data points and manual calculations. One year, Kevin, our IT manager, whom you met in chapter 11, raised his hand and said, "I have been sitting on something for too long. I think you are spending a lot of time on something a computer was designed to do. Would you like me to create an algorithm that would automate this calculation? We could run it multiple times a year; in fact, we could run it every day if we wanted."

There was a long pause in the room. Kevin was suggesting that my tool could be improved. A tool that was sacrosanct in my little world! His suggestion was bold. He was being honest and sincere. How would I react? I let him speak and explain his ideas, and I thanked him for his input. Ultimately, the team asked Kevin to write the new algorithm and we would run it beside my tool for the time being. It took two full years to get the algorithm fully polished and tested, but finally we proved that Kevin's tool was more accurate than my manual calculations and took almost zero work. We transitioned.

This is an IT guy. What the heck did he know about financial modeling? An IQ of six billion lends itself to bringing value in many different areas of the organization. Had I not shut up and opened the door for Kevin to speak—making our meeting a safe place for all opinions—I would still be grinding on a spreadsheet for countless hours every year. But because we did, Kevin felt comfortable sharing all of his ideas—being his authentic self—and the company (and me personally) have benefited greatly.

Leaving space for others to engage is critical. Also, as my example portrays, knowing and understanding when and why you don't leave space is important. If you aren't willing to leave space for others to fill the void, you are directing the course of conversation and having undue influence. Leave space; talk at the end—if at all.

Rule 10: Limit Sarcasm and Ill-Timed Humor

One of the silliest and most irresponsible ways to communicate as a manager is through sarcasm (critical or caustic remarks disguised as humor) or words marked by hostility and bitterness with the power to cut or sting. Sarcastic implies the intentional inflicting of pain usually by making someone feel foolish.

It is said that there is truth in all sarcastic statements. So when people hear a sarcastic statement, they naturally wonder if the speaker is hiding a truth by making joke. How much truth is there in the statement? Was she kidding? Maybe I am supposed to engage the topic? How serious was that comment? Nobody really knows. I am especially amused when, down the road, a manager comes back to a sarcastic comment and says, "We talked about this. I thought I was pretty clear." Well, no. You weren't clear. You let sarcasm confound the moment, so nobody really knew. Leave sarcasm out of the equation when you are communicating at work.

It's not just sarcasm though; humor can also be used badly. Managers may deal with tense moments by cracking a joke. Everybody laughs, the tension is broken, and everyone is relieved. However, it is in those awkward moments that growth can occur, if you let it. As the manager, don't fill the void or let others fill it with humor. Don't let the moment get off the hook. Let somebody else step in; see what others have to say. Where there is pain and awkwardness, there is golden opportunity for learning.

I have taken it upon myself to interrupt a group when sarcasm or an ill-timed joke lands by saying, "What exactly did you mean by that comment? Because I am unclear." Or I will interrupt after a joke has landed and everyone giggles with relief and pull the group back to the moment: "Let's go back and look at that and try to discover what was going on before we were all interrupted by the joke." The essence of our job as managers is to provide our teams with the opportunity to learn. Don't mask real communication with humor and sarcasm;

let awkward happen and watch the powerful stuff bubble up before you shut it down with a silly comment or joke. Don't take this the wrong way. Humor can be healthy. People connect and build trust over laughing together. It can be a very powerful tool for people to bond. Simply make certain it is well timed and not a release valve in a high-pressure, high-value moment.

Rule 11: Use Silence to Mine for Gold

The final rule I want to land regarding the rules of communication is the power of silence. Recently I was interviewed for a segment on advice from one CEO to another. My closing comment was supposed to be one word (I hyphenated) of advice to every CEO: "Shut-up!"

Silence is a powerful tool yet used too rarely, particularly with an immature manager. I don't understand why there is anxiety in moments without spoken words, but people are uncomfortable with silence. Observe what happens in your group when moments of silence occur. People, usually the same people, interrupt the silence by cracking a joke or making a sarcastic comment. You need to be aware of this dynamic and coach those prone to breaking silence, as it is impacting the functioning of the group. Most groups have outspoken members who consume 80 percent of the airspace, and 20 percent is left over for everyone else. Be careful not to let this dynamic occur in your group. You need to make space for everyone, and oftentimes this is simply demanding silence.

During heated discussion, people need to collect their thoughts. With no silence, discussion ends up as a rubber bouncy ball slamming around a room, impeding new and different considerations. Deeper insights occur only upon reflection. Force moments of reflection by posing a question and providing a few minutes for people to prepare a response, and then indulge everyone's thoughts. At this point you must open the room for opinions or ideas from everyone.

Simply presenting the issue/problem at hand and letting the group chew, swallow, and digest is healthy. The largest contributor to facilitating strong dialogue and discussion is forcing silence and applying a governor on those who are prone to dominate. Remember, if you want to go beyond surface level and get deeper into issues, silence is your friend. Allow space, and let the magic bubble up. If silence is allowed to happen and you slow the roll of the dominant folks, you will begin to see others step forward. Here is a golden rule: Because somebody is not outspoken and loud does not mean they don't have an opinion. Quite the contrary. Those who are not spending their time engaging are the people who might just be thinking and who will land a different perspective. At first, it may present awkwardly. These people are not used to engaging, so their voice might crack a little and the "ums" will dominate. They might stumble around for a minute. Let it happen. You will find the group being catapulted in a new and different direction. It is powerful to witness.

The Rules Are about Respect

The cumulative effect of all these rules of engagement can be summarized in one word: respect. Each individual must feel respected; disagreement must be focused on a notion, opinion, or idea, not on an individual personally. If attacks get personal, people quickly shut down because of our cortisol responses (see p. 140). We must respect each member of the group and make space for the quiet introverts to weigh in. We must respect the group enough not to use jokes and sarcasm to deflect from the harder topics that need to be addressed. We need to make sure we are aware of our nonverbal communication and the impact it is having on the group. It is also extremely helpful to state our intention in every engagement so people can help us get there. Always verify your understanding before believing it, don't interrupt, don't control with your listening, and finally, value candor above all else.

In applying the rules, you make sure that everyone on your team feels respected and that they show respect when others are speaking. That's how you can ensure that all communication brings value to each member of your team and then therefore your organization as a whole.

CHAPTER 13

The Magic of Five–Tools to Enhance Communication

AT BIGGBY, MY COLLEAGUES AND I are constantly looking for new ways to improve our communication. On that journey, we've discovered three communication tools that share a theme: They all involve the number five. In this chapter I'll describe these five-themed communication tools you can deploy to expedite discussions, help with decision-making, and get to the root of an issue quickly and effectively.

Fist to Five: The Fast Directional Check

Hundreds of hours are wasted in meetings when most everyone is lined up in agreement, but we don't stop talking to check in. People add their two cents with little value, and time is wasted because we don't have a tool to move forward. How often do people sit through meetings because they have no mutually acceptable way to interrupt the madness and help move the group forward?

The Fist to Five method helps you avoid this wasted time. It is a widely used nonverbal method of having people express their opinions about an idea by holding up a hand with anywhere from one to five fingers showing (one variant method includes a "closed fist" as a sixth option). This is brilliant in its simplicity, and anyone in the room can announce their desire to throw a Fist to Five as a way to either resolve the issue at hand or identify that more work is needed.

The process is simple:

- Someone summarizes the issue and requests a Fist to Five.
- People think about how they want to vote.
- At a given signal, everyone exposes their vote by holding out a certain number of fingers.

We have been using Fist to Five for many years. Our voting scale goes like this:

- One finger (we don't used closed fists): You are strongly opposed to the proposal, and it will be difficult to persuade you to change your opinion. In our company, ones are rare.
- Two fingers: You have some questions or concerns, and you would like the opportunity to get more clarity around the proposal before you agree to get on board.
- Three fingers: You don't have a strong opinion either way so can either get on board with the proposal moving forward or lean toward opposing it, depending on the data and perspectives that you hear from the group.
- Four fingers: You are in favor of the proposal.

- Five fingers: You support the proposal to the extent you are willing to take on a leadership position to make sure the proposed solution gets implemented.

Here's an example of Fist to Five: "I want to take the temperature of the group, so I would like to propose a Fist to Five. I suggest we stock the break room with strawberry jam, as well as grape jelly. As has been discussed, only stocking grape jelly means that a significant percentage of people are not interested in making PB and J sandwiches because they don't like grape jelly. After much discussion, it feels to me like we should bring in strawberry jam. Let's get ready to throw our vote."

Everyone in the meeting places their voting hand on the table, covering it with their other hand. We refer to this as cradling. Typically the person proposing the Fist to Five will say, "Is everyone cradled?" Invariably there will be somebody who isn't cradled, typically due to indecision. Once everyone in the group is cradled, the proposing member of the group counts off "One, two, three . . . Shoot!" Everyone lands their voting hand (with one to five fingers showing) on the table so that everyone else in the group can see their vote.

After everyone has voted, the proposer asks to hear from the people who held up just one or two fingers because we need them to share their concerns or questions. Nobody interrupts or responds until all of the ones and twos have been heard. What would a typical two sound like? In the strawberry jam scenario, here are four concerns typical of someone who is voting a two:

- "I am worried about cost. We are now going to be inventorying two different jams. My guess is people are going to be eating more PB and J sandwiches with the addition of strawberry. It doesn't sound like much at first glance, but over the years it is going to add up."

- "Not all strawberry jams are equal. If we are going to do this, how are we going to choose the strawberry jam? Is there going to be a process for choosing which product? Much needs to be considered when choosing a jam."
- "I have heard some rumblings that this is a ploy to replace grape jelly. Keep in mind there are a ton of people who love grape jelly in this company. I don't want to deal with the blowback from the grape jelly lovers."
- "First let me say I am in love with this idea, but we all remember the many feathers we ruffled when adding blow dryers in the bathroom. Let's keep in mind the lessons we learned from that so we can make this transition successful."

Hearing the reasoning behind each one- or two-finger vote before having a discussion is a critical part of the process and difficult to maintain, especially if you as the leader are the one proposing the Fist to Five. Typically, ones and twos are dissenting, and it is natural to want to rebut. You can't! You need to get all of the opinions on the table before discussion because you don't want to interrupt and influence others by defending your position before others have had a chance to talk.

This is especially true if you are a senior manager and you come out strong against the first person who presented a one or a two. What if there are three other people who held out two fingers who are thinking along the same line, and you bring the hammer on the first two-finger vote? You are going to potentially change the opinion of the other two before they have their opportunity to share their idea. You lose the impact of knowing three people were thinking the same way.

The presentation and discussion of the dissenting opinions (people who threw ones or twos) is the perfect opportunity for the group to learn about and vet the details for what is happening for the team. Keep calm and keep quiet during this phase so everyone has the opportunity to say their piece without influence from the group. We work hard to prevent that. When we have a meeting, it is common to hear people say, "Wait, wait, wait, we have to hear from all the ones and twos before we discuss." This is incredibly healthy.

I like this method because it's a very quick way to take the temperature of the room, to check and see where everybody is on a given topic without having a major interruption. It is also a quick way to move the group forward. Often there will be no ones or twos, and your idea passes quickly. Awesome! By proposing a Fist to Five, you've gotten beyond meaningless discussion and made progress in the direction of the stated intention. When groups get charged up on a topic and everyone is landing support, it is great when somebody interjects, "I want to check the group. I think we might all be violently agreeing. Let's see, and if so, we can move on." This is such a beautiful moment.

If you check the room and you uncover concerns, you can tackle them and attempt resolution. It keeps the conversation relevant and allows for dissent in a healthy, methodic way. Fist to Five can feel childish at first. Try it, practice with it as we have. You'll find it remarkably efficient.

Being Flexible with Five Levels of Decision-Making

There was a time in corporate America when decisions were made by a boss. They would then share the decision with employees, who were expected to implement. Decisions were made quickly and only the boss felt the burden of responsibility for the decision, but often there was little buy-in.

More recently, the pendulum swung in the opposite direction and overcorrected to the side of consensus, where all the parties involved have to agree on the decision. But consensus takes more time than a boss-made decision. And sometimes people settled for compromise—each side giving up something they want—rather than true consensus.

The fact is that both of these decision-making modes—plus others—have value if they are used at the right time for the right purpose. The key is "deciding how to decide," then informing your team of where and how a decision is going to be made.

It is important for everyone to understand who is making the decision and how they are expected to contribute. All you'll get is confusion and resentment if people have different understandings of how decisions are made or whether they are going to be offered the opportunity to weigh in. Clarity around who is making the decision as well as how or whether people should give input is critical to efficient and effective decision-making.

At BIGGBY, we employ the five levels of decision-making:

1. Leadership is going to make the decision and inform everyone of the outcome.
2. Leadership is going to make the decision but would like to get input from the group.
3. The decision is going to be made by consensus.
4. The group is going to make the decision with input from the leader.
5. The group is going to make the decision without input from the leader (that is, the leader hands over responsibility for the decision to a different person or group).

Identifying which of the five levels is appropriate for different decisions adds clarity to the process. People are generally good with whatever level the decision is going to be, and they enjoy knowing in advance. If somebody objects to the level suggested, they can voice their opinion and interject with a Fist to Five.

This is what it might sound like when announcing a level five decision. The leader will say, "We have a decision to be made about our upcoming annual meeting. I am comfortable with the group making this decision. I don't have much in the way of input and I look forward to hearing what you decide."

Or maybe there is a decision that is going to be controversial and you as the leader think it is important to give your people cover, so you announce that the decision is going to be a level one. As a reminder, level one decisions are decisions the leader is going to make, with no input needed from the team. People will frequently object to a level one decision, hoping to give input. If the idea is to provide cover for a difficult and awkward decision, then zero engagement by the team is important. Of course, as the leader, you can change your mind at any time and agree to accept input, making it a level two decision.

There are also times when level three, consensus, is the best course. These are usually decisions when having everybody on board with the final outcome is critical to its success, such as when announcing a major new initiative that will need full buy-in and support from those responsible for implementation.

In the real world, the majority of decisions are going to be level two, three, or four—meaning both the leader and team are involved, but it varies who has input and who has the decision-making authority. Input is generally a good thing and consensus is what we would like to try to get to in most decisions, but sometimes consensus is simply too arduous. A good outcome when a decision is taking too long can be that the leader interrupts and suggests that the decision move from a level three (consensus) to a level two (the leader will make the decision based on all the discussions they've heard). It might sound like this: "I think I have a good understanding of everyone's position. I appreciate the healthy dialogue and debate. I think our best course at this point would be for me to take this thing offline and make the call. I will make sure to report back to the group with my final decision."

Consciously deciding what level a decision is going to be is meant to make communication and decision-making efficient and streamlined. How many times have you been in a meeting where you want to fall backward over your chair because you feel like the discussion will never end? If you had the power to suggest a change in the level of decision-making or if you could just throw a quick Fist to Five to try to move things along, you would rejoice and thank the heavens and stars for the ability to get the group out of the quagmire of endless discussion.

Ask *Why* Five Times

The "5 Whys?" method is a tried-and-true approach for digging out the root causes of a problem. The principle is simple: ask why something is happening, get an answer, then ask why that thing is happening, and continue until you've asked why five times.

This method can be applied to any discussion. If a discussion feels light or if you are left wanting a better understanding of an argument, start asking, Why? Ask why five times—waiting for answers in between!—before engaging with input or discussion. You will be amazed at the mysteries that will surface. I have observed that from the start of asking why to the completion of the fifth why, there are often profound discoveries in the process. It is a great practice to always be asking why.

Let me give a quick example. A manager in our group was frustrated by the relationship with a franchisee. He wanted to get the owner on board with a new menu item without the mental gymnastics of 40 questions and 17 suggestions for improvement.

So another team member asks the manager, Why? (#1.) The manager replied, "It is just so frustrating that I have to burn time and energy. Why can't they just once get on board with an initiative?"

"Why?" (#2.) Answer: "Well, it takes an enormous amount of time, time I don't have."

Why? (#3.) Answer: "Well, they don't understand the rationale and they want me to clarify every detail before they can be on board."

Why? (#4.) Answer: (Long silence.) "Well, they do have their life savings on the line and their store is underperforming, so they are scared. I guess they are looking to me to help provide the answers that lead to an in-depth understanding of the new product because they want to do a good job of implementation."

Why? (#5.) Answer: (Even longer silence . . . followed by a sheepish reply.) "Well, they see me as the leader who can provide them with the direction they need."

Yes, yes, yes! Exactly! This is the job of a leader. This series of why questions led to a healthy conversation around preparation regarding the rollout process for the new initiatives. We talked about having the manager do a role-play with their team and think through every question this franchise owner would surface, then prepare a pre-brief document answering all those questions. The manager agreed that he and his team could do a better job of preparing their rollout documents. We would be more thorough as we got ready to launch.

Yes, yes, yes! This is exactly how this is supposed to go. Asking the one-word question—Why?—is one of the most powerful communication tools in a manager's tool belt.

Your team will start to recognize this tool and will get comfortable with its use. A mature group will start to do it automatically, which forces them to think deeply on what is happening, a critical part of communication.

The magic is that they are developing their own answer, not simply listening to your answer and/or recommendation. Previously, I presented my criticism of the Socratic method where a leader asks questions that steer the group, but by asking why, you force people to go deeper. Asking why doesn't steer the individual, it simply forces them into the roots of their brain to find out what is really happening.

As a manager, or frankly as any member of a group, it is beautiful to make people in the room think deeply. Make them go beyond the quick and easy answer. You will find people take real time to ponder their answers. In our world today, taking time and being forced to ponder is often in short supply.

Deceptively Simple Tools

At first glance these tools—Fist to Five, five levels of decision-making, and the "5 Whys?"—may seem elementary, but don't let their simplicity fool you. Though very easy to use, they are powerful when it comes to improving team communication and effectiveness. Use them, and you'll find your team will waste less time in meetings, leverage decision-making more effectively, and uncover the root causes of issues that are leading to frustration. If we are accomplishing these three objectives, I am certain our communication will be much more powerful and effective.

PART 3 CONCLUSION

Everything Is Relationships

LISA OAK, WHO WROTE THE FOREWORD TO MY FIRST BOOK, GRIND, once managed a company called Franchise Brands, a company Fred DeLuca, founder of Subway sandwich shops, established to make investments in companies in the franchise space. BIGGBY worked with Lisa and her team for ten years trying to put a deal together, as Fred and Lisa wanted to invest in our company. We did eventually structure a deal, only to have it undone by the untimely death of Fred DeLuca. One of the golden nuggets I learned about Lisa's team at Franchise Brands was an expectation they had to add value every time they interacted with a company. I remember the days of interacting with Lisa and Franchise Brands fondly. I looked forward to our interactions and I felt great every time I walked away. Lisa and I were able to maintain a healthy relationship through some difficult conversations. What I learned from those interactions was the effort she brought to the table with each and every conversation in order to leave behind value is what made the relationship powerful. In fact, those conversations were what built the relationship.

I challenge you to think about your relationships. Do people look forward to a meeting with you? Do they expect to walk away feeling better, as if they got value? When you approach every conversation to create value, you will end up with authentic relationships.

You hear from old-school cronies, "All you have is your word." I would suggest that you only have the relationships that your word builds.

There is a ton of content in this section. You won't remember it all. I hope there are a few tools you can internalize and begin to implement for better communication within your group. What I hope people take away is that communication is the foundation of our relationships. We must approach all communication from a place of respect and make sure that everyone can engage and bring their individual perspective to the group.

If all we do as leaders is act as facilitators of healthy communication within the tangled web of all the dynamics and often complicated relationships on our team, we will have had an incredible impact on the performance of our group. Conversations occurring in our lives are meant to improve our relationships. Our conversations are the relationships. I am a firm believer in trying to bring value to everyone with whom I interact on a daily basis. Be authentic, be genuine, and watch the power of your key relationships propel you to wherever you want to go.

PART 4

THE POWER OF LEARNING AND NEW PERSPECTIVES

It is critical as a leader to constantly be learning and considering new ways of doing things. We must be open to gutting the old and starting fresh with new perspectives. In the following chapters I advance some ways to get new perspectives and advocate two new things you can try to start fresh and approach the business differently. I believe if you can embrace these concepts, you will find yourself in a new and different paradigm in short order, perhaps two to three years.

- Chapter 14: Supercharging Your Environment with the Entrepreneurial Operating System is about a powerful platform for you or any leader to execute the day-to-day operations of your business.[1]
- Chapter 15: Outside Vantage Points Deliver an Advantage discusses the importance of systematizing voyeurism in your company. (If that isn't intriguing to you, we need to get a defibrillator.)
- Chapter 16: Learning from the Greatest Leaders of All Time explores the many things to be gained by reading. There are few things as important to leadership than to be continuously learning.
- Chapter 17: Lessening Our Addiction to Financials will come as a shock because I advocate that the leader ignore the financials for the most part. I suspect this will make many uncomfortable, but I want to act as a counterbalance to the incredible focus on financials as a tool to manage and lead. We will see what you think.

Much of what is in these chapters may seem routine and simple, but sometimes genius is found in simple changes. The last point in this chapter—disregarding financials as a primary tool in managing the business—is anything but routine and simple and will be inflammatory to many. I hope I have gained enough of your trust at this point to at least have you hear me out.

CHAPTER 14

Supercharging Your Environment with the Entrepreneurial Operating System

THERE ARE THINGS THAT COME ALONG IN LIFE when you just have to sit back and say, "Thank you." Healthy children, the democratic process, national parks, the iPhone . . . and now I add EOS to that list, standing for Entrepreneurial Operating System, which is a set of concepts and tools that helps entrepreneurs coordinate and align all the working parts of their organization.

In this chapter, I'll explain how I stumbled across EOS and recognized it as something that BIGGBY needed, and why I'm now a strong proponent that other entrepreneurs adopt it as well. If you already know what EOS is, consider this chapter an endorsement of that approach; if you are unfamiliar with EOS, I hope to explain how it can strengthen your business in ways you didn't think possible.

Why I Needed EOS

I had been working for years in my organization trying to come up with a way to communicate as well as facilitate a method of aligning the day-to-day operations in our company with our strategic initiatives, and more importantly, our purpose. I kept fumbling. My exploration was the quintessential example of a monkey copulating with a football. I knew we were struggling. I knew we needed focus. I knew we needed a cadence. I knew our meetings were a cluster bang. I knew we weren't presenting our future properly. I knew the roles in our company weren't clearly defined. And on and on and on.

One of my early attempts at a solution was a tool I called "levers and pulleys" that I developed to show how all the parts of our company were interconnected. I had drawn a diagram of what I was trying to accomplish with ropes hanging from pulleys and detailed depictions of handles drawn on levers. I had developed a cadence for the development of and reporting out on each lever and pulley. My leadership team was interested in the concept and helped me in my quest. It was good thinking, but I knew it wasn't enough; the end result was a sorry piece of work. I felt like a newly born fawn trying to stand up for the first time with a pack of coyotes howling in the distance. My tool was going to take three to five years to develop, and in the end, who knew if it was even going to be effective.

The important part of this moment was that I knew we needed something to improve communication and alignment. I just didn't know what would allow us to do that. It felt like I was driving a car down a curvy country road at night with no headlights.

Then I stumbled on EOS (Entrepreneurial Operating System). We were in the middle of recruiting John Gilkey, who was a friend of mine for more than 20 years. John had owned a technology company and was a primary vendor of BIGGBY. He had gone through the process of selling his company, and his new role within the company he merged with wasn't a perfect fit. After two years of discussion, we were in the final stages of the conversation, and we were close to putting a deal together for him to join our company.

In one of our final meetings, I took 15 minutes to lay out my concept of levers and pulleys. I was diving deep into the problem I was trying to solve. At one point I stopped talking to take a breath and John said, "You are describing EOS." Then he went on to outline how EOS works and the power behind the tool. I sat in awe and listened as he unfolded the different processes and methodologies. He was quite experienced. He had done an EOS implementation at the company he owned and was about two years into the implementation of EOS at the company he had sold to. All he had was positive things to say.

What had sold him on EOS? The underlying premise is that all organizations need a business operating system that guides how all the pieces of the enterprise work together to produce the best results most efficiently. EOS could be called a people operating system—meaning it helps you get your people aligned and pulling in the same direction. Which, since leading and managing people is the core theme of this book, is why I instantly felt compelled to include and heavily endorse EOS.

The "system" of EOS comprises concepts and tools that help you define and align six major components relevant to all businesses:

1. Vision—developing a company-wide, shared understanding of the destination you want to reach
2. People—having the right people in the right jobs
3. Data—identifying the most important metrics that give you reliable insights for managing your company
4. Issues—becoming proficient at quickly identifying and resolving the specific challenges that arise in your business
5. Process—developing standardized systems (as much as possible) for conducting business
6. Traction®—achieving disciplined execution of what is most important to your business

EOS has tools for tackling each of these components in a coordinated fashion (available at EOSworldwide.com). The following paragraphs describe some examples of how EOS works within our world and some of the more powerful components from my perspective.

First is the quarterly company-wide meeting. This is a cadence for review of our purpose and vision and connecting and restating the three-year picture and one-year plan. This meeting is done in the same way with the same rhythm each quarter, and the group starts to get quite comfortable with the rhythm. We are touching base each quarter to realign on the critical components of our progress as an organization.

Second, there is a simple process we implement each quarter to determine the most important initiatives for us to complete within the quarter in order to meet our one-year plan. These initiatives are called rocks. As a team we agree on the two or three things the team needs to focus on and also the two or three things each team member needs to be doing. This provides focus. The list isn't seven or ten things; it is two or three. Go do them, report back, and everyone stays focused on the work that will help us reach our quarterly and one-year plan.

Third is the L10 (Level 10) meetings, which occur weekly. Each member of the meeting checks in on our progress for rock completion, and then we "IDS"—identify issues, discuss them, and solve them. It is the moment to bring issues to your team for support and engagement. These meetings follow a tight process and are effective in keeping everything straight.

All-in-all, EOS is a great tool to simply keep everyone moving in the same direction and for tracking whether the group is on target. There are many other components to EOS, but I have highlighted the things I think have made the most impact on our company as we learn and grow.

Implementing EOS at BIGGBY

At the very end of our "negotiation," I asked John if he would be willing to head up the charge for BIGGBY COFFEE to become an EOS company. He initially accepted the job as VP of Technology but in short order became the president of our company and accepted the challenge of deploying EOS. I will remember forever the moment we came to this conclusion—we hugged and I knew we were going to move forward. He was fired up to bring EOS into our world, and I was eternally thankful to have somebody of his talent level willing to come support us and our company. It is one of the proudest moments of my career. He then asked my partner and I to read a couple of books before he got started. This was one of the top five most pivotal moments in the history of our company.

The books couldn't arrive quickly enough (yes, I still read ink on paper). I engaged and was immediately spellbound. You know the moment when you are reading and you can't sit still, you want to scream from heaven to earth, the world makes sense now, you have arrived? This was what I was feeling as I read the book *Traction: Get a Grip on Your Business*, by Gino Wickman.[1]

Needless to say, we went all in. We hired an implementer who walked us through the process of deployment. We differentiated our roles. John became what is known as our integrator; my partner and I accepted the role as visionaries. Both "integrator" and "visionary" are specific roles defined in the EOS model, with clearly defined responsibilities and boundaries for each. We have found the definition of roles essential, as it prevents Bob and me from straying into areas that don't reflect the best use of our energy or talents. Additionally, it protects the business from our natural propensity to engage willy-nilly and muck about in things where our involvement proves counterproductive.

We had the requisite meetings, and now, over three years later, we are fully walking in line with the EOS model. It has been a game changer. It took us 18 months before we settled into the new rhythm with all the components, but we are now gaining many efficiencies and feeling the positive impact within our organization from the deployment of EOS. The speed at which we are completing projects is increasing. We continue to see more value as time goes on and we are getting better and better at EOSing. For example, my partner and I understand our role as visionaries more completely. Daily I find myself catching old habits or poking my nose into things that are not part of the visionary function. Today, I stop myself and I autocorrect the behavior. I have a better understanding of where I am supposed to engage and what to avoid so as to not impede the progress and learning of others.

A Game Changer Analogy

The best analogy I can make that illustrates the value of EOS is to the deployment of a new software suite. You buy it, you install it, you learn it, and bam, you now have new efficiencies that you couldn't have imagined before.

That was the experience I had with Waze, the satellite navigation app.[2] Before installing the app on my phone, I always fumbled with GPS and didn't gain much value from using it. Waze won application of the year at CES, which prompted me to read an article, and I was hooked. I learned how to use it and I have been a devoted user since. It has added a ton of utility to my life and I can't imagine the world before I adopted it. I will never forget the time I was driving home from Chicago and got directed to exit the freeway, after which I spent 45 minutes on winding country roads. I reentered the freeway, and the whole episode cost me a 15-minute delay getting home. Later that week I learned there was a tanker truck overturned on the freeway ahead of me, and a friend was stuck in traffic for over three hours. Hallelujah!!!

My introduction, adoption, and pure devotion to Waze feels very similar to EOS. We are finding new efficiencies and magic as we get deeper and deeper into our deployment.

The other day I had the honor of talking to Gino Wickman, the founder of EOS and the author of *Traction*. I asked him, "Why is the sweet spot of EOS small to mid-sized companies?" His response was beautifully entrepreneurial, and I could relate. He said, "Big companies get bureaucratic. They hire a bunch of MBAs who are smarter than the rest of us, and those MBAs ensure job security by making their organizations so complex that the only people who can understand the mechanisms are the MBAs hired to manage it. They are not entrepreneurial. We do have huge companies using EOS beautifully. It does work with all organizations big and small, and it works best if you stay true to the principles and execute."[3]

I couldn't agree more. People think they are smarter than the system; they aren't. No one individual is smarter than hundreds of people collectively deploying and improving one system. EOS has become that for us; it is a system we can execute, like a franchise that has hundreds of people engaged and improving the system every day. The benefits have been immense.

Take the EOS Plunge

If you are in a role within a company to take on broad-reaching initiatives and if you are the founder (I assume you are), I highly recommend exploring the EOS management tool. It will take you down important paths and lay out a framework for you to execute. If you take on the quest of EOS, take it pure. We operate a franchise company, so we understand the importance of systems and we always tell people to follow the system, because it has been proven time and time again. It works. We are committed to this same thinking with our engagement of EOS. We want to implement EOS purely and extract as many benefits as possible. Maybe someday you will want to tweak EOS and make it your own, but from our experience at BIGGBY, that doesn't seem necessary.

Give yourself a gift and do a deep dive into EOS by starting with the book *Traction*. You won't regret it.

CHAPTER 15

Outside Vantage Points Deliver an Advantage

FOR MANY YEARS I LIVED WITHIN THE FALLACY that I could figure everything out on my own. I didn't believe in working with third parties. I just believed in my partner and myself and our ability to work our way through circumstances, develop solutions and systems to mitigate problems, and take advantage of opportunities. There were two reasons why I thought this way: First, typically I was disappointed in the performance of third parties, and second, I didn't like the price tag. When we were getting BIGGBY started, every nickel was precious. My expectations were outlandish. I would expect people to bring exceptional value for little remuneration. It wasn't fair, and I have guilt over how I treated people at times. As I talked about in chapter 8, the wife of one of our vendors told him that doing work with BIGGBY sounded like being in an abusive relationship.

What I learned over the years is the value of turning to outsiders—and even acting like an outsider yourself at times—so you can draw on the expertise of others and get insights into your business. In this chapter, I'll share some of my experiences at BIGGBY to illustrate why I'm now pro-outsider.

The Best Experts Are Worth It

What opened my mind to working more with outsiders was an experience our leadership team had when exploring the idea of taking a leadership retreat—not because we thought we needed it, of course, but because we were going to be facilitating a retreat for a group of our owners and we wanted to make sure we understood the experience and how it would bring significant value.

Thus, we looked into retreat options to launch these groups and decided to try Crux Move Consulting, a company I had worked with many years prior when I was in college. Key point: I had history with this vendor and therefore some inherent trust. Crux quoted us a number I considered absurd. Mike and Jim at Crux Move were salty dogs, and they didn't move off their number. They knew what a two-day retreat was worth, and they stuck to their guns. I consented, which was not normal behavior at the time.

Our leadership team went on the two-day retreat and had a mind-blowing experience. Mike and Jim worked in the woods at an amazing facility with killer activities—things like a setup called the "wobbly woozy" and the high ropes course. The experience wasn't made hanging from ropes 30 feet in the air; the value came from the leadership and guidance of Mike and Jim. They took us on many journeys deep into the soul of our team. They knew when to push a little harder and when to back off. They knew when to check in with me and my partner to make sure things were on the right track. They brought out the best of our group. They were simply amazing.

At the time, Mike and Jim had a combined 60+ years in the business. They knew exactly what they were doing. They walked our group down a similar but nuanced path as they had been doing with groups like ours for decades. The value was immeasurable.

For a few years we actually flirted with trying to do this programming ourselves. It was our way. Do it ourselves. We can learn how to do this work and save the money. We didn't. We stayed with Crux Move and started putting groups through the program. It has proven to be extremely valuable.

Today, looking back, this was one of the first times I didn't meddle too much with a highly priced item. I let it go, and I let Jim and Mike do their thing—mainly because I went into the relationship with a high degree of trust. They were pros and I knew it. The end result was powerful, and that was when I began to soften my "do everything ourselves" stance.

Getting a Fair Shake from Outside Partners

The lesson I learned from the Crux Move experience—and I have been adopting this theory ever since—is that the third parties are generally good at what they do. You have to get really clear with them about what you are looking for, pay them appropriately, and get out of their way. If you stay in the entrepreneurial mindset and continue to grind out every penny and meddle in the process because you think you are smarter, you won't create long-standing, healthy relationships that take advantage of other people's magic.

My old mindset—GRIND people down on price and meddle in every detail—is what led to the "abusive relationship" comment I mentioned earlier. I am certain that wasn't a one-off example with that one vendor. I know there were many other vendors during the BIGGBY start-up phase who felt the same way. At the time, I rationalized the behavior by believing I was just trying as hard as I could and expecting the highest value possible from others. In hindsight, this was unhealthy and counterproductive. People don't perform well when somebody is jumping up and down on their head and squeezing every penny out of their rectum.

Yes, during start-up, the GRIND phase, an "I know it all" approach may be necessary and appropriate, but as you transition into a stable, sustainable organization, you must mature in your thinking, you must grow. In order for people to work at the highest level, they have to feel good about their work, they have to feel valued. If you are sweating them for every penny, your company becomes a four-letter word. Again, are you getting their best efforts if they are mother#@*%ing you up and down when you aren't in the room?

As you transition out of GRIND and through GROW, one of the key roles of management and leadership is to make sure you are getting a fair shake from those you do business with. Vendors, like everyone in the organization, need to be managed and led. People get complacent; it is human nature. It is your job to stay engaged and keep the relationships with outside parties on the right track. Countless times we were shocked by a vendor who didn't perform in a given situation. How could they get so off track? They weren't paying attention, they weren't focused on our account, they got distracted. How does it happen? But really, if we are taking full responsibility for our organization, we understand that it was our job to make sure they stay on track. Just like dealing with a team member, you are responsible for a third party's performance as well. Everyone you touch needs to be managed. Is it frustrating at times? No doubt. Is it necessary? Undoubtedly.

As the manager you have to be paying attention and providing feedback to vendors in a very similar way you do internal people. You need to be constantly communicating about what is working and where things are bumpy. Tell them your needs. Make sure they have their finger on the pulse of your organization. Critique their work and make sure it is on point.

Let me give an example that had the potential to cost BIGGBY hundreds of thousands of dollars. We were working with our standard architect on a store in a certain county that required some absurdly large grease trap. Mind you, we don't produce grease in our restaurants. However, there was no getting around it for this one store. A few months later, a super pissed franchise owner who was building a store in a different locale questioned why he was being made to install a jumbo-sized grease trap for thousands of additional dollars. I was, of course, shocked. I called the architect and he explained that he thought we should just go ahead and put the heavier grease trap in as standard procedure so we never had to face such a significant delay down the road. I couldn't believe his thinking. Had we not caught this, we would have wasted hundreds and hundreds of thousands of dollars because the architect thought that four thousand dollars was no big deal—that instead of taking the risk of a one-off situation occurring again, we should burn enough cash to build three stores over five years. Insanity, right? I could tell 20 more stories just like this one. The architect took a valid position, just not in line with what mattered most to us, saving dollars in the build-out process.

Thus, professionals need to be managed too. They aren't bad people. They aren't dumb. They just don't know your business like you do. They don't know your risk profile. For example, I love my attorney. We hired him in 1998, and he is one of the main reasons we have been able to build our business the way we have. But there are still plenty of times, even after 24 years together, that I have had to engage and manage. I trust him to present me the situation, and he knows that though he will weigh in with his opinion, in the end I have to make the call. It is part of being a manager.

Lawyers & Accountants: Two Must-Have Outsiders

There are two things to pay top dollar for: accountants and lawyers. Someday, if I am staring down an IRS audit, I will definitely want a blue-chip firm rolling in with the truckload of information. I would not want to rely on my cousin, Vinny, who would likely have a half-tucked-in golf shirt and be annoyed about missing his tee time. I chose Vinny at the beginning because he was $250 a month cheaper. Valid then, risky now. As you progress in the development of your business, you will, over time, learn to appreciate the value of your accountant. They provide a critical service to you and your business as you progress. You want to have the very best at your disposal.

You would think, of all people, attorneys and accountants wouldn't need to be managed. They are getting paid well for their work, so shouldn't this be one place you can relax and trust that things will stay on course? That was my mindset, but over many years I was proven wrong.

I learned, for example, that accountants are not usually strong advisers when it comes to the day-to-day management of your business, although weak accountants will weigh in on all sorts of things outside of their wheelhouse. They have a very specific vantage point that you need but that doesn't take the entire set of circumstances into account. Keep your accountant's opinion and perspective near and dear but also relative to their area of work: keeping you organized and out of trouble with the tax authority.

It is not their fault. If you don't communicate with them and make sure they understand your intention, how could they know? The simple answer is, they can't. Their job is to go down rabbit holes. They are supposed to be uncovering the different nuances that might put you at risk. You as the manager must constantly be assessing and guiding their work. They don't decide whether a certain risk falls within your risk profile. That is up to you. If they bring something to your attention, it is your job to decide whether "we" need to address the risk or let it go.

Once upon a time, we were deep into the weeds on a technical part of our business. We had the accountants and attorneys hacking and slashing around with machetes trying to make the whole thing make sense. There was some gnarly legal code that needed to be defined and understood. It is the one aspect of franchising I don't like. The professionals were fully immersed. They kept talking about the ramifications and liability if we were to get audited.

At some point in the proceedings I asked, "How many times have you seen this part of the business audited?" The reply was that neither my accountants nor attorney had ever been a part of an audit where the topic we were discussing was engaged. My follow up question was, "Have you ever heard of this area of the business being audited?" The answer was no. I knew the activity we were researching was legitimate, maybe a little progressive in relation to how the code was written, but the code was simply behind the times in relation to technology. I overruled the concerns the professionals were presenting.

The preceding example is reasonable. Our professionals were presenting the reality of how the code was written. It was arcane and silly, but they were accurate. I had to decipher risk and make the decision. In the end everyone, including the accountants and lawyers, agreed we were making the right decision.

Listening to the Voice of Customers

Besides using outside experts for their specialized knowledge and perspectives, there is another outside group whose experiences and insights you need to bring into the fold: your customer.

We at BIGGBY lean heavily on our customers to provide us with insights we couldn't get otherwise. Understand that the customers we service are the people who have invested in a franchise within our system, the franchise owners. They are sophisticated people who have entered this endeavor with significant experience in some other area of life. We have franchise owners who were in banking . . . who have owned other businesses . . . who were in corporate America managing nine-figure budgets . . . who were in technology . . . who were teachers . . . who were in the military . . . who are significant franchise owners of other brands . . . who were hotel operators . . . who worked for the McDonald's corporate team . . . who worked in the county health department. The list goes on and on. Just imagine the diversity of knowledge, experience, and insights represented by this group!

We invite our franchisees to get involved in helping us manage the company through the formation of committees. It is amazing how committed they are to being involved with us, day in and day out. They are an incredibly valuable voice at our table.

Try to have the voice of the customer near and dear to you as you manage your business. They have insights that are powerful. Depending on your business, this can be complicated, but I strongly advise you have the voice of the customer consistently in your ear someway, somehow.

Walk through Your Own Front Door: Become Your Biggest Critic

I know most of this chapter has been about how to benefit from the perspectives of people who are technically outside your organization. But you must look at your business through the eyes of an outsider. My business partner, Bob, is a strong advocate of what he calls "walking through the front door." Remember, he was in the restaurant business for many years before getting into coffee. He expresses in amazement that restaurant owners would consistently come in through the back door (and some went so far as to sneak in the back door, trying to avoid contact with customers and employees alike). He has always promoted the idea of walking into your business through the front door, as if you are the customer, every time. It is common for managers to bury their head in the sand and not look at their business through the eyes of the customer.

Owner and Customer

When my wife and I would travel, my wife would sometimes ask me to stay in the car when we would stop for coffee. I was/am a control freak. I prided myself in knowing every procedural nuance in our business. I could stop in any store any time and see 20 or 30 different things that were outside of the system. Sometimes these stops ruin me for a few hours during a road trip. I have never stopped going in.

When I get frustrated as a customer, I am never frustrated with the employee behind the counter. I always look at it as a weakness within our internal systems. I am frustrated with myself and with the team for whom I am responsible that our systems aren't working. We need to improve, and therefore I need to be better as a manager and a leader. One of the only ways I know this is by being a customer in my own business.

Sometimes it is very difficult, but you need to know. As the manager you have to consider yourself one of your best outside resources. Of course, you are not technically outside, but you must pretend you are and look at your business from the perspective of the person with whom you are transacting.

My partner and I have always been some of our own harshest critics—it keeps us honest. As your business grows and becomes more successful, you will find that people start telling you how amazing you are doing, encouraging you to measure your success by outside sources. If you start believing them and stop being hypercritical, it will lead to a complacent culture. Your job as the manager is to never allow this to happen. Always remain your most critical customer.

Stay in Tune with the Appropriate Perspective

Generally speaking, I am still an advocate of having the lion's share of work done for my organization by internal people. I don't think anybody cares more about the end result or has the understanding of what we are trying to do more than the internal team. They understand the lay of the land, they know who to talk to get answers, and we as an organization are loyal to them. They are going to do a better job than an outside resource in almost every circumstance.

That being said, there are times when an outside resource has particular experience on a given topic and is highly effective, but don't abdicate your responsibility to oversee the results. The only way to make sure third parties don't unknowingly make decisions that will adversely affect your business is to be in the loop and monitoring the work.

Again, don't forget that the most valuable outside perspective is your customer. Keep them chirping in your ear and remain your most critical customer by using your company today, tomorrow, and every day.

CHAPTER 16

Learning from the Greatest Leaders of All Time

HOW DO I SAY IT ANY MORE BLUNTLY THAN THIS: The great managers/leaders I know are constantly reading. They are constantly trying to learn and improve. We all have access to the great thinkers of our day. Not only that, but we have access to the greatest thinkers of all time. It shocks me when I hear people say they don't read much. Where and how do they learn?

I network and talk with businesspeople all the time too, and I generally find it a waste of time. It's a harsh and probably slightly arrogant statement, but just because you have been successful in a business, it does not make you an expert in all business. At times I can pull a nugget or two from a conversation with one of my contemporaries, but generally, most of what I hear from business colleagues is complaining about one thing or another, or it is some topic du jour that is on everyone's mind. Frankly, I couldn't care less.

I want to hear from the greatest leaders of all time. I want to hear from people who have been doing research on a given topic for decades. I want to hear from people who have navigated extraordinary events. I want to hear from people who are different than me. I want to hear from people who manage a business similar to mine but also businesses that are wildly different. I want to get deep into their brains. I want to read from people who are committed enough to share their learning by sitting down and writing a book, by taking on the challenge of organizing their thoughts and sharing them in a cohesive way.

As somebody who has and is attempting to write more books, I know it is hard. When writing, I am constantly checking my thinking. Is this what I really believe? Is this the best example to illustrate my point? Am I wasting the readers' time? That is what authors do. We all know the best leaders of our time—Steve Jobs, Elon Musk, Oprah Winfrey, Warren Buffet, Ted Turner, Meg Whitman, Peter Thiel, Arianna Huffington, Richard Branson, Sheryl Sandberg, Bill Gates. What about the greatest business leaders of all time? The likes of John D. Rockefeller, J. P. Morgan, Andrew Carnegie, Estée Lauder, Walt Disney—and the list goes on. We should learn about lessons in leadership and business from people who are extraordinary leaders, no matter their field or arena. The amazing thing is, we can! Read, read, read.

Lessons from Nonbusiness Leaders

Let me also give you a few examples of vital things I learned from nonbusiness leaders to make my point:

From ***Long Walk to Freedom,*** Nelson Mandela's autobiography:

"A nation should not be judged by how it treats its highest citizens but how it treats its lowest ones." —Section 5 Treason

"Sometimes there is nothing one can do to save something that must die."—Section 9 Robben Island—Beginning to Hope

"A leader must also tend his garden; he, too, sows seeds, and then watches, cultivates and harvests the result. Like the gardener, a leader must take responsibility for what he cultivates; he must mind his work, try to repel enemies, preserve what can be preserved and eliminate what cannot succeed."—Section 9 Robben Island—Beginning to Hope[1]

From ***Picasso, Creator and Destroyer,*** a biography of Pablo Picasso by Arianna Stassinopoulos Huffington:

"He was loath to impede the freedom and spontaneity of child's drawing with expert direction. 'When I was their age,' he said after visiting a children's exhibit, 'I could draw like Raphael, but it took me a lifetime to learn to draw like them.'"

"'If I spit, they'll take my spit, frame it and sell it as great art,' he had once said."[2]

From ***Benjamin Franklin, an American Life,*** by Walter Isaacson:

". . . to be concerned in no affairs I should blush to have made public, and to do nothing but what spies may see and welcome. When a man's actions are just and honorable, the more they are known, the more his reputation is increased and established."

"There were even times when it was prudent to let an opponent retract a bad move: 'You may indeed happen to lose the game to your opponent, but you will win what is better, his esteem.'"[3]

From ***It's a Long Story: My Life,*** an autobiography of Willie Nelson:

"Power over my own thoughts—that's a helluva concept. It means that you don't ever have to fall into the trap so many people can't seem to avoid: victimhood. That's the worst feeling in the world 'cause it means that here ain't shit you can do about your current situation. I'd had my share of low moments, but I was learning that there's always something you can do. You can train your mind to look up, not down and not back."

"That's another big blessing, longevity—one I never expected. It's one thing to be eighty-two, but it's another to have the energy to keep touring the globe. That energy isn't fueled by anything I can generate on my own. The fuel is love—love of people, places, animals, plants, water. Love of sound, love of space, love of fireflies and star filled skies. Love is life. Love is home."[4]

These are just a few of the quotes I have pulled from nonbusiness leaders, and there are countless more. But my message isn't about these exact quotes; it is simply to make the point that we need to be reading broadly. There are lessons to be learned from many authors. Take a look at the reading lists of the great leaders of today and you will realize they are reading scientists, politicians, and academics.

Read Deep and Broad

In our culture today, I think a lot of people skim lightly through periodicals or posts on social media. There are "smart" people telling you to keep your posts light. Videos need to be under 25 seconds for anyone to pay attention. People want to get a quick message, and they certainly don't want to think deeply about what is being presented. They want the nugget, and they want to move on and keep scrolling.

This is fine if you are in it for entertainment and the ability to be charming at a cocktail party. If you truly want to find a deeper understanding, it takes effort. You have to be willing to immerse yourself in a topic and fumble around, and think, and argue in your brain. You have to let the author make their full, compelling case. It isn't for the faint of heart, because you are going to spend a ton of time in books that don't have impact. You get to the end and realize you don't agree. You will find flawed arguments that don't hold water. But you will find the passages deep in books that will rock your world. They will change the way you think or fully support you in some way that is powerful. This is the good stuff.

I hear from people that they get two or three chapters into a book and put it down because they understand the premise or maybe they disagree with the author and therefore don't want to waste their time. This is folly. First, it is as important to read books by people with whom we disagree as much as from those with whom we agree. We need to understand our world from as many perspectives as possible if we want to be powerful people. From my experience, authors leave their most powerful stuff until the end in the last chapter. Don't be arrogant enough to think that you can read the first few chapters of a work and have the author's position figured out. Don't think reading one or two articles, all the while skimming social media, will leave you with a well-rounded, reasonable position established. For the sake of everyone you manage, go deep, learn, and stay inquisitive. The pot of gold at the end of the rainbow is powerful.

Case in point with an example of how reading widely changed my perspective: I have been struggling with the Donald Trump phenomenon. I beg you to put politics aside for the next few paragraphs. I am not going to be taking a standard approach to this topic, I promise.

Politics and personal behavior aside, there is much about the man that is to be respected. He built a very powerful brand. Trump is, well, Trump, even before the presidency. He figured out how to harness the media and ride the hyperactive news cycle like his own personal thoroughbred. Somehow, he turned crazy into honesty. The fact that he was willing to say anything, no matter how impolite or rude, has made him seem authentic and genuine. He was therefore antiestablishment. He wasn't being handled by a PR machine and/or the politicos, and this was endearing to many. He figured out how to connect to a rural farmer in middle America from his private jumbo jet and penthouse suite in Manhattan. He is masterful in many ways.

What I have never been able to reconcile is the fact that from many accounts, his policies hurt the people who voted him into office. It doesn't take much digging to uncover that his presidency was very, very good for the 1 percent and was not fruitful for the bottom third of the income strata. When my accountants told me what my tax liability was going to be after the Trump policies went into effect, I thought they were joking. Seriously, I didn't believe them. I immediately worried that it wasn't sustainable. How could any government (yes, including the United States of America) give up such an incredible amount of revenue and continue to operate, let alone thrive?

My journey to read and learn more about Trump started for me when I was fortunate to be in the audience for a presentation by David Brooks, the conservative *New York Times* columnist, roughly 45 days prior to the 2016 election, and he predicted a Trump victory. At that point in the proceedings I was naïve, like most in my circle, and I brushed Brooks's argument aside. It was easy to do sitting in the catbird seat of a wealthy, liberal entrepreneur. What Mr. Brooks argued was the fact that if you were a middle-aged white man with a high school diploma, you were earning in the aggregate (meaning not inflationary adjusted) less money today than you were when you graduated from high school, and you were pissed.

Then, after President Trump won, I really got interested. There were a ton of explanations about the win. He mastered the 20-minute news cycle, he gave people a reprieve from the quagmire of political correctness, he was unabashedly patriotic and presented America as something to be proud of again. He took the conversations that were happening in every male locker room and union bar across America and aired them out for everybody to hear. It was refreshing for many. But none of these arguments held water for me. These were not the reasons Trump won.

What is the end result of all of this? The American worker, the hardworking, industrious employee that America has been built upon is, in one word, fucked. They can't compete with the lower labor rates around the world, and because of the pace of technology, they didn't have time to react. Again, they are furious. Their hearts ache for their children and grandchildren. They don't know what to do.

When Donald Trump stepped in, he gave an enormous swath of

America a voice that was being ignored by liberals and conservatives alike. He was able to point this anger and frustration at certain things that made sense to people. He captured lightning in a bottle, to the point that I think he even surprised himself.

Thank God he did. Before anyone loses their mind here, let me remind you I am a tax-and-spend liberal, who despises much about the Trump presidency. I have come to realize he has done our country a great service. How? We are all aware of this voice now. We need to fix this problem or our country could end up in an even more difficult spot. (This will be one of the primary purposes of my next book, but suffice it to say, the answer doesn't lie in the inane debate between Republicans and Democrats. The answer lies in the collective power and genius within the American corporation, private enterprise. Stay tuned!)

You are wondering, "Mike, you just went on a very long rant about Donald Trump. Please tie it together!" My point, and tying it back to this chapter, is that had I stayed on the surface level, had I read a few articles and scrolled my social media, I would most likely have one of the two standard positions on Trump. Because I have read deeply and broadly, I have a very different perspective on him, one that both disagrees with his policies and behavior but also appreciates him for what he was able to highlight as a deep, dark problem in America today.

The point here is to make the argument that reading broadly is critical. The Trump presidency is one of the great puzzles of my lifetime. At the surface level it is difficult to understand. Through spending time reading, thinking, and listening, I have been able to formulate my position on this incredibly complex topic. In our current state, with politicized sound bites being disseminated like lightning-quick sound waves rolling over our country as facts, in conjunction with the algorithms engineered by the social media companies to capture our attention, it is vitally important for our leaders to read deeply and consider all aspects of a situation before engaging.

Reading Is Our Most Powerful Antidote

We are facing untold risks in the coming years, let alone the coming generations. Whether it be climate change, AI, a new, fast-spreading virus, or political extremism, we need to find an antidote. We need leaders to step up and manage more effectively and help steer this vessel called Earth and all of its inhabitants in the healthiest direction possible. The most powerful leaders/managers anywhere are within our corporations, who are currently motivated by one thing and one thing only: profit. If we don't manage our resources more effectively, profit will seem like a silly, insignificant beacon when everything as we know it is decimated.

How do we equip ourselves as managers? What is the antidote to the scorched earth policies created by Milton Friedman in 1971? I am not sure yet. Discovery will happen through reading—not reading what is flashing on the screen of our phone, written by some hack who has an opinion deeply rooted in self-interest, but rather by reading experts in their field who have spent a lifetime researching and crafting arguments that have impact. Reading deeply and reading broadly is the start, and then we need to think heavily and set our course. I look forward to the discussions with people who see it as their responsibility to help find the antidote and move us in the right direction.

CHAPTER 17

Lessening Our Addiction to Financials

IN BUSINESS TODAY, THERE IS HYPER-FOCUS on being a good financial manager, to the point that being a good financial manager is almost synonymous with being a good business manager. I have even heard people say out loud that you should be able to run your business through the keyhole view of your financials. The expectation that your financials have to be spot-on in the early stages of your business is a huge burden on any manager who is traversing the early GROW phase. It screams at you because it seems like a prerequisite to running a good business. It isn't true.

Arguably the most successful franchise owner in the history of our company, who spent twenty years building her business and sold it to her daughters in 2022, used say to me, "Michael, you know I don't do numbers. Don't even try to make me go that direction. It's not gonna work." Back in my less-experienced days, I used to try to convince her she should be spending more time working with the numbers, financial statements, cash management, budgeting. Little did I know Deb would teach me in the end. What Deb was saying to me indirectly was, "I don't do numbers because they are not that important. I do people." She focused on building her team and providing an amazing experience for both her employees and therefore the customer. It worked; she built an amazing business and an incredible legacy without spending all but the minimum on the numbers.

Why in the heck would I start a section on finance and budgeting by basically saying they are not that important? Because . . . they are not that important. Keeping your financial records in order and your money organized is important, but that is simple bookkeeping. As you go, you must make sure you are staying square with the IRS and you must have the ability to document where the pennies went, but beyond that don't sweat it. In this chapter, I'll focus on the few financials that I think leaders should still pay attention to and explain why and how to use them.

Keep the Baby, Lose the Bathwater

Here is the thing about traditional financial statements: They are like driving your car by looking out the rearview mirror. Is it possible to drive the car looking out the rearview mirror? Sure, but you best be driving really, really slowly.

What financials am I referring to? The standards: income statement, balance sheet, and cash flow statement. Of course, there are a few things you are going to query monthly and keep track of to make sure they are staying in line—maybe four to six numbers, key performance indicators (KPIs) depending on what is occurring at the moment that you spent 20 minutes maximum on—but any more time spent in the financials is a waste of time.

That being said, you should be charting and graphing KPIs over time to see if there are any meaningful trends. These should be looked at quarterly. In a well-run company there shouldn't be much movement in these numbers month to month, but the graphs are useful for exposing trends that develop over the long haul. Again, just take a quick glance to make sure things are in the realm of reason. If nothing jumps off the page, get back to growing your business.

But there is one area of financial management I think is critically important to growing your company and reaching sustainability: revenue and cash flow forecasting. Create a crystal ball that allows you to project the future cash flow of the business 3 months, 12 months, 24 months into the future. This is the most critical component to financial management in any company. The comparative analysis between what you forecasted and what actually happened is the gold that we need to be focusing on. I think it is imperative to track and chart the variance monthly. The issue is not what actually happened; the important issue is how closely you were able to predict what was going to happen and what factors impacted your ability to get close.

It is really quite simple. You project the revenue you will be generating in 3 months, 6 months, and 12 months. You project the costs you will be incurring and net them from the revenue, and you have a projected income number. You layer in your balance sheet activity, and you have your cash projection. When you start, you will be really, really bad at this projection, but as you do it over and over, you will get better and better. At the beginning of the GROW phase you will be doing it sporadically, when you remember, and it will most likely be way off the mark. As you get closer to sustainability, this will become a regular part of your work. By the time you near completion of the GROW phase, this machine will be running well and provide you a clear look at what the company will be doing 12, 24, and 36 months out. This is freedom.

When you can get it to the point you are comfortable that you can trust your longer-term predictions, your business becomes more stable, and therefore it is easier to do the important work in the company that will propel you through the GROW phase. Short term, cash insecurity causes anxiety, and it is difficult to make the right decisions for the business when you are stressed. Strong and tight forecasting alleviates that stress and is a critical component to maturing out of the GROW phase.

Over the years, BIGGBY had a very strong relationship with our banker, and one of the reasons why was my ability to project my revenue and therefore cash flow inside of a tight radius. He was always amazed when I would present the quarterly and annual financials and they would be within 0.5 percent to 2 percent of what we projected. It gave him a whole bunch of comfort that we knew what the heck was going on with our business. When your banker feels secure, you feel secure.

This didn't happen overnight. The forecasting tool is something I worked on for the better part of a decade before I was really comfortable and confident in its performance. Early on, it was embarrassing how far I came in off the mark. But I stuck with it, because I knew building a strong forecasting model would be incredibly useful. Each time I went through the process, I learned something new about my business.

I find many managers spend their time looking at and reviewing past results, year-over-year comparisons, which to me seems like too much energy spent on old news. At times it feels good to see strong revenue and profit increases from the year before, but the more exciting game to play is trying to decrease the margin between projected and actual results in forward-looking, six-month increments. This is a sophisticated and fun game to play. Real world monopoly. When you start getting it tightened down, you will feel like the company can run itself financially and you can focus on other, more intangible aspects of the business.

Opening Every Bank Statement Once a Month

Another exercise that has proven to be critically important in the financial health of my company over the years is to do a deep dive on the bank statements every month. As you hand off the reins of managing the cash in the business, paying the bills, and receiving payment, you need to make sure everyone involved knows you are paying close attention. Still to this day I get the bank statements mailed to me at my home, and I go through them line by line. I ask questions about things that seemed to have changed or don't make sense. This is a laborious part of my month. It usually takes the better part of two hours (we have nine bank accounts), but this exercise will hopefully stop anyone down the road from trying any funny business. It certainly isn't a perfect science, but it is one of the last things I do at a micro-level that still feels important.

Surviving the Whiplash of Profitability

Turning profitable is a beautiful experience. Very few things are as professionally gratifying as when you start making real money. Early on, I remember having to pinch myself when I would look at the bottom of the P&L and find a lot of black numbers instead of red; it seemed like a fantasy. We were growing aggressively and had a pretty good handle on the cost side of the equation.

There is a moment when you cross the Rubicon of the tax collector. In my experience and that of many others leading up to profitability, you are stretching vendors and are slow-paying. As you start to generate excess cash, it feels great to pay down the vendors and start to get square with everyone. The problem is, by definition you are profitable, and you owe taxes on the income generated. If you have used all your cash to pay down the vendors who have been patient with you, there is no cash to pay the tax collector. This sounds so simple, but it sneaks up on you. Taxes are easy to deal with when you aren't making any money, but as soon as you start to generate income you have to stay all over the future liability of today's profits.

One of the most intense meetings of my career was with my accountant as he worked through my liability for the tax deadline the first year we were profitable. The company was doing great, and we were getting in good standing with everyone who had been good to us over the years. I remember having to come up with a check north of six figures to pay the tax collector. After all the hard work, getting the company profitable, and feeling good about paying down debts, the moment my accountant gave me the news was like a kick in the teeth.

This might seem like a small thing, but if I can prevent one person from having to get shocked by their accountant in that first year of profitability, it was well worth the ink spent. It was extremely painful for me.

Managing People, Not Numbers

Has your heart started beating again, or do we really need to get you the defibrillator? I figure my points in this chapter will be unpopular for many traditional managers who believe you can run a company via the financials. I hope this chapter has made a dent in that mentality. The reason goes back to the fundamental premise of this book: To lead your company through the GROW phase to sustainability, your role is more about making sure your people have everything they need to perform their jobs and less about you managing the details. I don't mean you should be ignorant of how your company is doing financially, but that you should lessen your addiction to studying the financial reports and use that time to pay more attention to the relationships within your organization and supporting people in being successful in their jobs and in their lives.

PART 4 CONCLUSION

Never Stop Learning

HAVE I OPENED YOUR EYES TO NEW POSSIBILITIES in terms of how you run your business? That was my intent in the preceding chapter. I want you to seriously consider EOS as a platform to run your company. Develop some routines and practices around encouraging reading within your organization—and make time for your own reading and study. Get many outside perspectives on your business. A fresh set of eyes can jolt the status quo and catapult you into a new way of thinking. And finally, start weaning yourself off of the need to know every single number related to your business. Pay more attention to people, and good numbers will follow.

These are concepts I feel strongly about. It is important as a leader to bring new thinking to the table. This is obviously not an exhaustive or comprehensive list, but I hope it is a reminder that there are important things you should be doing and perspectives to consider in order to evolve into a company of the future and reach sustainability—which I'll talk more about in part 5.

PART 5

ORGANIZATIONS OF TOMORROW

There once was a day when companies consisted of 99 percent white males in leadership positions. There once was a day when we communicated by pen and ink. There once was a day everyone showed up to the office to work. There once was a day when unions were formed to protect the employee. There once was a day when a handful of media companies governed our communications. There once was a day when organizational charts were drawn with ladders. There once was a day that the HR team represented the company's interest only. There once was a day when women could be harassed without repercussion. There once was a day when a manager lived by the rule that shareholder value reigned supreme. The list could go on and on.

My question is, what are we doing today that will be looked back upon in 50 years and scoffed at as arcane? We always need to be evolving. The world is changing at a furious pace; the expectations of leaders are growing dramatically.

The inevitability that the future will be different from today is why here in part 5 I'm continuing the theme of showing you different ways of thinking about your business. Part 4 addressed some pragmatic ways of learning and growing, and although I think the concepts covered in the part 4 chapters are critical, some might deem them simple. Part 5 is going to dive into what I think are large, powerful, and more complex ways we need to be thinking in the future. The concepts I am promoting in these closing chapters are progressive and I believe will be the expectation for all leaders in the coming decades:

- Chapter 18: Encouraging the Crazy—Creating a Workplace Where Innovation Is Inevitable busts myths around innovation and describes how you can make it a daily part of how your organization functions, even without your direct involvement. Make staying ahead of the curve a given in your business.

- Chapter 19: Becoming Deliberately Developmental—Fostering Constant Learning and Growth talks about the need to make your organization a petri dish for professional and personal development.
- Chapter 20: A Potpourri of Creativity—Creating a Melting Pot That Supports Justice, Equity, Diversity, and Inclusion explores the absolute need to increase not just diversity in its traditional definition (race, gender, sexual identity, etc.) but also in experience, background, and perspectives.
- Chapter 21: Replacing Profit with Purpose makes the case that the reason for a business to exist can no longer be tied solely to profit. You need a higher calling, a purpose all stakeholders—employees, customers, vendors, the environment, the community, and, yes, shareholders—can rally around and support.

These concepts are big and hairy and complex. Some of these concepts will be difficult to digest. My goal is to push you hard to conceptualize new ways of thinking. These chapters will advocate for new and different ways of thinking for the manager of tomorrow. We must evolve into a new paradigm. Business leaders need to become stewards of our communities and evolve into not just leaders of their organizations but leaders of society at large.

CHAPTER 18

Encouraging the Crazy—Creating a Workplace Where Innovation Is Inevitable

INNOVATION IS THE MYSTERIOUS, complex, beautiful process of taking something and making it better or improving what you are doing within the world. My guess is many leaders shudder at the word innovation. It is such a daunting part of being a leader. You have to stay current; you have to make bold leaps; and as the leader you must be wise, sage, and able to deftly guide your organization to the exciting future where everyone wears circular glasses and black turtlenecks. Of course, the fear is we won't be able to keep our organizations innovating and improving, and we will get left behind as a relic of our own incompetent leadership. There is a ton of pressure to innovate.

What most leaders fail to understand is that people are naturally innovative. It is the workplace environment and expectations that discourage creativity. In this chapter, I'll talk about how to remove those barriers so that innovation becomes natural and inevitable in your business.

Four Secrets of Innovation

I want to start this chapter out by becoming a myth buster. In the following section, I'll discuss four secrets of innovation.

- One, fear is the biggest impediment to innovation, so you need to inoculate your business against fear.
- Two, innovation doesn't have to be big, bold, and beautiful; more often it happens in bite-sized pieces.
- Three, you as the leader should be irrelevant to innovation—in fact, innovation will likely happen more often when you aren't involved.
- Four, you never check the box on innovation; it is a way of life.

Let me tell you a little more about these secrets.

Secret One: Inoculate Against Fear

What is the number one thing that gets in the way of innovation? Fear. People are afraid to run wild with their thoughts and emotions at work, as they might appear unstable and potentially untrustworthy. People are scared of their manager's impressions. Goodness, can you imagine if your manager thought your idea was dumb? What if your peers left the room and were snickering about your silly idea? We fear letting it all hang out and going for the unusual, interesting ideas because we may be ostracized by the group.

We all know being an outcast is dramatic and powerfully negative, as it revs up our survival instinct. As human beings we need to maintain our safety; we want to remain a cog in the wheel. Therefore, we don't take risks. We stay in our comfortable bubbles and only put ideas on the table if we are reasonably sure the group, and more specifically the group leaders, will accept them and validate our opinion. Hence my opening statement: Fear is the biggest impediment to innovation.

To have healthy, innovative teams, we must inoculate against fear. How do we do so as managers? It is much the same as I have presented earlier in the book. We must work hard every minute of every day to build trust within our teams. We need to be encouraging the crazy idea, the idea nobody else considered. When somebody brings something off the wall, we need to make sure we are accepting and enthusiastic as the leader, asking for clarification and then providing support. At the end of the meeting when you debrief, thank a few people specifically for going outside of their comfort zone and bringing in the crazy idea. Positive reinforcement related to specific boundary-pushing events is a great way to build trust so that tomorrow people will be willing to dig a little deeper and get a little crazier. When we inoculate against fear, we are enthusiastically encouraging people to push the group outside of its comfort zone and to look at things from a different perspective. This is how innovation occurs.

A few years ago a woman in our organization went to a conference that was focused on "conscious leadership." One speaker discussed the importance of teams centering before a meeting and coming together in the space before setting off to do work. Taking a few moments to do breathing/meditation at the beginning of a meeting is a powerful way to get started. She brought this idea home to our company and suggested adding it to our meeting norms. It was received with skepticism by many employees, but with support from leadership—in fact I remember one of the senior leaders in our group saying, "What can it hurt? Taking a minute to clear our heads must be a good thing."

So we tried it. The first few times there were a few giggles as silence enveloped the room. People were nervous at first because it felt weird. Relaxing and meditating in a meeting was akin to smoking a joint and burning incense. She launched it the following meeting. Now, years into the practice, people say things like, "I'm not sure how we did meetings without taking this moment."

This employee took a risk and brought a little crazy into a small company buried deep in the Midwest. She trusted that leadership—especially my partner and I—would back her, and she trusted it would be OK. In most companies, she probably wouldn't have brought the idea forward for fear that it would lack support and she would look a little silly. I feel lucky that we had an environment where that fear wasn't present, and she brought a really cool practice into our world.

Secret Two: Strive for Incremental, Bite-Sized Innovation

Was our centering practice a total game changer? Will it be talked about in a decade and credited with leading us to becoming an emotionally supportive environment where people show up as themselves, in the healthiest way?

Nope. It will be a small innovation, one of many in our organization over a long period of time that will lead to our goal of being a nurturing and supportive environment. Small, incremental steps are how most innovation occurs.

Innovation happens in hundreds and thousands of very small, seemingly inconsequential moves that over time add up to the kind of innovation and improvements everyone expects from a well-run organization. If you think of innovation as big, bold, beautiful strokes of genius, you will miss how real innovation happens.

Another simple, straightforward example of this type of innovation from my organization—one that has had a very positive impact—is centered around meeting schedules. At one point in our history, meetings had become daunting and unruly. Some leaders were good at sticking to the time allotment; others would treat the time parameters as mere suggestions and throw everyone's day into a tailspin. Of course, it was typically the senior leaders (i.e., me and my partner) who would run over because our work was important, don't you know? Meetings were scheduled for 30 minutes or 60 minutes, ending on the hour or the half hour. Meetings would launch into a specific subject matter and run the entire scheduled time until the ending minute, when people would rush out and on to their next appointment. From what I hear, this is standard practice within many organizations.

People were frustrated by how life was functioning day to day, hurrying from one meeting to the next, and were often embarrassed by tardiness. The daily experience went something like this: You walked into a meeting late and harried, scrambled to catch up, then the meeting ended with no time to regroup before you were on to the next meeting. There was no time to process previous events, and you carried baggage from earlier meetings into your current and future meetings (e.g., maybe Hank cut you off and changed the subject multiple times and you felt belittled, or maybe a coworker who always picks up his phone when you are talking triggered your insecurity about the importance of your work). Millions of dynamic interactions occur within one meeting, good and bad, but you have to blast into the next meeting and the cycle continues until finally, at the end of the day, the end of spinning on the hamster wheel, you go home exhausted and frustrated, dreading tomorrow.

We needed to innovate. We had to get better at running our meetings. A group was assembled to identify what would become our meeting norms. There's nothing too special about putting a committee together to consider a new way of doing things, but the difference (innovative component) was to develop a set of norms that looked at each meeting as an opportunity to infuse our teams with processes that encourage healthy team dynamics. The idea being to set up meetings for people to come together and support one another.

Based on the committee's decision, we ended up implementing several new practices. One was putting end-times that didn't run the full calendar appointment. If you had a 30-minute meeting, you end after 25 minutes, or an hour meeting would last 50 minutes. Those extra minutes allowed people to get coffee, stretch a little, use the restroom . . . normal things everyone should be able to do without stress and anxiety. Obvious, right?

We also built into the beginning of each meeting a moment for everyone to express their highs and lows, both personally and professionally. Knowing how somebody is walking into the room is critical to group health. Are they carrying a heavy load? Maybe a loved one was diagnosed with cancer, or the family dog passed away, or they had a terrible night's sleep; whatever it is, everyone needs to be aware. Or maybe a team member was able to buy their first house or booked an amazing vacation. What a great opportunity to connect and celebrate the victory. When somebody on the team has success, it should be partly attributed to the support they are getting from the team. Therefore, the team should know and be allowed to celebrate.

This practice of sharing was purposefully made both professional and personal, as we wanted to allow space for the whole person to show up. By sharing both personal and professional highs and lows, you are able to do so.

We now also build a debrief into each meeting. Debrief is a moment when each person gets to clear the air with the group. We make sure you aren't carrying anything forward into your day. If something happened in the meeting that will weigh on you throughout the rest of your day, you need the ability to let it out and share. In a healthy team, misunderstandings are rampant but solved very quickly. Debriefing often doesn't have much weight, but when something important happened in the meeting dynamics, it is critical to get it out and addressed. If there is not space to debrief, things fester and grow into large, overly meaningful, undiscussed elephants in the room that can become inhibitors to team health.

Meeting norms at the surface level seem dull as a doorknob, something that needs to be addressed but not of earth-shattering importance. Most likely you didn't think of meeting norms in your organization as ripe for innovation. I encourage you to consider that coming up with meeting norms that drive trust and cohesion within your group could be one of the more powerful innovations you could experience. Trust is the bedrock of accountability, and what traditional manager doesn't complain about increasing accountability within their "ranks"? Running healthy meetings is fundamental to healthy teams that have a high degree of trust. From trust we get accountability. This is innovation at its best.

I go into detail about our experience with meeting norms because I think it is important to note that the innovation wasn't about developing meeting norms. It was about creating space for our teams to be healthy, supportive, nurturing bodies where people walk out of a meeting in a better mental space than when they arrived. The things we did within meeting norms are innovative and interesting, and I am proud of our group for leading the way on this. Simple? Yes. Important and powerful? Doubly yes. This is not necessarily something most would consider a breakthrough innovation, but in the end our teams are becoming tight knit, supportive, and nurturing. They perform in beautiful, high-functioning ways. This work was one of the contributing factors.

Secret Three: Leaders Should Be Irrelevant to Innovation

This one is alarming for many leaders. You as the leader, irrelevant? Yes, I think you should always consider yourself to be inconsequential and the group should not depend on you to contribute to innovation.

Innovation doesn't come from one brain; it comes from a network of brains all engaged in the challenges at hand, working together and collaborating on how to improve. You as the leader should be just one of the brains in the network. I think many organizations depend on having leaders lead the charge, and the leaders have bought into that thinking. The leader should be out front, charging the hill, right? They should be the big brain bringing miraculous thoughts. Think Steve Jobs in his acid lounge.

In fact, this thinking is counterproductive when it comes to innovation. When you lead the charge, everyone is forced to line up and support your opinions because, well, you are the leader. When you engage, you are in fact stagnating the thinking and risk-taking over the group. People simply try to figure out how to go along and get along, as opposed to bringing their full brain to the table. Also, if everyone knows you are going to answer the question anyway, why should they bother going through the effort of trying to contribute?

There are many examples of how my partner and I have blocked innovation in our history. When we show up and engage, the group is automatically steered in the direction of our opinion. We own the company. We have been doing this for over 25 years. How could our involvement not sway the process and results? Even more insidious, though, is the stifling nature of our involvement. We approach every conversation with the mindset, "We have seen everything; everything is old hat. There are no new ideas, as we are informed by our experience/wisdom." This stifling bomb smothers the group. Many ideas are simply cut off because we know best or better, but who knows what some idea could have morphed into had we not cut it off at inception? There is genius in the fresh perspective on an old situation. Oftentimes experience and wisdom get in the way of letting it unfold.

The Group Is Smarter than You

I've said this before in the book: Most leaders think they are the smartest person in the room, and maybe you are fortunate for it to be so, but most likely not. You probably have the most experience, which can be good but also potentially detrimental to innovation, so be careful playing the experience card. Let me assure you of something that cannot be denied: The group is smarter than you! Let the group do its thing and be careful how you engage, because leaders get in the way more often than they add value when it comes to new and innovative thinking.

Secret Four: Don't Think You Can Check the Box on Innovation

The other important mentality of effective innovation is to eliminate the "check-the-box syndrome." You don't innovate, come up with something cool, check the box, and move on to the next cool innovation. Innovation is iterative and builds upon itself. The best method for change is to start with small improvements. Implement and let the ideas work, come back together to discuss the changes, make notes and improvements, and send it back into the wild. The process never stops. Remember, we shouldn't think about innovation as solitary big ideas that change the world, we should think about small improvements that stack on top of each other that add up to monumental advancements in our organizations. Innovation is never finished.

Revisiting the preceding example regarding meeting norms, at some point—in maybe two or three years—we are going to review the meeting changes we implemented.

We will discuss what has worked and what hasn't. Some of the stuff will stay, other things will be tweaked, and some others will be canceled altogether. As an example, there has been a cultural slide lately at BIGGBY, where meetings run right up until closing, leaving no time for debrief. Let's be honest: To most managers, debriefing a meeting and letting people share how they experienced the time together doesn't feel particularly useful, especially when there is work to get done!! I challenge this thinking and argue the 7 minutes of debrief after 40 minutes of meeting are critically important to the health of the team, and there is nothing more powerful than building trust and cohesion. The irony is that skipping the seven-minute debrief to get more work done means foregoing one of the best opportunities to create a highly productive and effective team. When we convene our review of the changes to the meeting norms, we will be reviewing how we "debrief" to figure out new and different ways to make sure debrief remains an integral part of our meetings.

The important point for this section is that we will be constantly reviewing and tweaking the work we did on meeting norms. We will learn as we implement and make tweaks to improve, and we will iterate in order to continue to innovate.

Becoming a Superorganism of Innovation

Innovation occurs when we bring in new and different perspectives to address our problems, challenges, or opportunities. This section will engage a concept I have found fascinating. I am by no means an expert, but broadly, biomimicry makes an enormous amount of sense as a concept that can be adopted to encourage innovation.

What is biomimicry? It is the design and production of materials, structures, and systems that are modeled on biological entities and processes. For millions of years, organisms the world over have been adapting and changing to their environments to improve their survivability. As Charles Darwin wrote, "It's not the strongest of the species that survive, nor the most intelligent, but the one most responsive to change."[1] (Please note this is the same quote from Keith McFarland's *The Breakthrough Company*, which I mentioned in chapter 1 in the section on adaptability—so this is obviously a concept I think is important.)

The pace of change in the world is staggering. We must begin to make change the only constant in our organizations. One powerful way we can do this is by observing and paying attention to the concepts of evolution. We need to be paying attention to how nature does it.

The concept of superorganism is aspirational for managers and leaders of human teams. Tamsin Woolley-Barker, in her amazing book, Teeming,[2] does a masterful job of taking a look at biomimicry and superorganisms. Here I will attempt to summarize her work enough to whet your appetite. (As a side note, I laughed out loud multiple times throughout her book. Where else can you learn that an orgy of same-sex dolphin behavior is known as a wuzzle?)

In nature, superorganisms are powerful and depend on the collective whole to make every individual within the organism increase the odds of their survival. Merriam-Webster defines the superorganism as "an organized society (as of a social insect) that functions as an organic whole."[3] In *Teeming*, Woolley-Barker defines a superorganism as "a group of genetically distinct individuals of the same species, where members take on different tasks, whole classes of non-sibling adults help others raise their young, and no one survives on their own for long. That, to me, is a superorganism." The important parts of this quote are "members take on different tasks" and "no one survives on their own." Superorganisms adapt more quickly because they tap into the collective wisdom of the group and focus on becoming regenerative.

Here are some attributes of superorganisms described in *Teeming*:

- Superorganisms cultivate collective intelligence—drawing on the intellectual resources of every member.
- Superorganisms nurture swarm creativity—making and breaking connections between members as needed.

- Superorganisms rely on distributed leadership—they don't rely on any single individual member for leadership; any member can step into a leadership position as needed.
- Superorganisms depend on reciprocity and sharing—all members of the group give and take equally.
- Superorganisms compound regenerative value—they feed the environment that provides their nourishment.

Even without knowing the biology, don't all these sound like attributes you want your teams to have if they are to be agile enough to innovate constantly and quickly?

Unfortunately, much of the philosophy of biomimicry and cultivation of superorganisms flies in the face of how traditional managers approach their organizations. Traditionally, in corporate America the structure of our groups is established on the framework of individualism. If I perform as an individual I will be promoted, and my work will contribute to the betterment of the entire team. The flipside is that if somebody else performs at a high level, it will limit my ability to "climb" within the organization.

> "Traditional environments are built on zero-sum thinking, where there can be no net gains: if I get something, someone else has to give up an equal amount; for me to win, you must lose. The individual is striving to climb the ladder and compete with colleagues for a few spots at the top, and therefore everyone is guarded in sharing information and insights because they worry success by anyone else on the team will limit their opportunity. The result

is that our organizations lose out on the benefits of being a superorganism. We lose out on collective intelligence, swarm creativity, and the value of regeneration because we are unwilling to distribute leadership that will encourage reciprocity and sharing. In this way, the traditional organization is flawed.

"Emulating other superorganisms may sound like a radically new way to do business and restructure society. It may sound vast and daunting—but I don't believe it is. Superorganisms operate on a dozen simple principles, and because we are superorganisms too, they feel natural to us. It's easy to reimagine our companies as platforms for collective value creation; nurtured and cared for by our tiny, distributed, self-organized and creative contributions. It's the way we ant-like apes like to work, and the way we work best. Everything is connected. If you can find the right leverage points, the whole thing may flip on a dime: Revolutions and tipping points often surprise us."[4]

Organizations of the Future Must Become Superorganisms

Nature has shown us that superorganisms are superior at survival. The organizations that can adopt the principles of the superorganisms will become the organizations of the future. They will adapt and innovate more naturally. They will become restorative. All managers of organizations should be highly focused on working to embed the principles of superorganisms into their environments if they want to become powerfully innovative.

The big question now is, How do we do it? We must reconsider how we think about the basic structure of our organizations. We must disassemble the archaic top-down, command-and-control model employed for decades—the model espoused by the military industrial complex.

If we were to take on the principles of the superorganism I just described, organizations would need to do things like the following:

- Cultivate and tap into collective intelligence. We would start to see our organizations evolve into powerful groups innovating at the highest level. We would aggregate "scattered scraps" into something greater by bringing as many people from as many diverse backgrounds as possible into the conversation and by considering the theory of design thinking (see p. 263).
- Facilitate swarm creativity through self-organized networks within our organizations (such as what BIGGBY has done with our concept of forums—see p. 96).
- Promote reciprocity and sharing. The only way that will happen is if we change our obsession with individualized, performance-based compensation. In *Out of Crisis*, Dr. Deming states the following as one of the seven deadly diseases: "Evaluation of performance, merit rating, or annual review. The idea of a merit rating is alluring. The sound of the words captivates the imagination: pay for what you get; get what you pay for; motivate people to do their best for their own good. The effect is exactly the opposite of what the words promise."[5] Anyone who has worked with an individual merit system knows that it's impossible to do it objectively and you end up demotivating

more people than you motivate. Group efforts should be rewarded collectively.

- Look at our organizations as regenerative. They will regenerate the people within and the community as a whole. (Much of this comes from establishing our organizations as "deliberately developmental," which I will address in the next chapter.)

Changes like these can only happen if we focus on cultivating diversity and independence by facilitating the distribution of leadership and ridding ourselves of the unhealthy and unproductive norms of the standard, up-down ladder mentality in the corporate world of today. With trusting and cohesive teams, we can open two-way, always-on conversations and trigger tipping-point decisions with simple rules and feedback loops.

Evolving into a Superorganism

Organizational structures modeled after the superorganism is next-level thinking. Organizations are doing it today, and they will thrive. Thinking about your group as a biological formation that is constantly morphing, evolving, and improving is one of the most powerful ways to innovate and grow. It is simple: We are collections of human beings coming together to accomplish work. Is there anything more biological?

A BIGGBY example: In a scotch-fueled conversation between my partner and I at the Ritz-Carlton bar in Toronto, we birthed a new concept that is now our organizational structure. We wanted/needed to change from a company that was structured as a rigid, top-down departmental structure with everyone climbing up and down ladders to one of spheres that are amorphous and constantly flowing. The idea of top-down always rubbed us the wrong way. We talked about being on a ladder and looking up and all you got was a view of the rump attached to the person who was higher than you on the ladder. Ladders also, by design, emphasize a silo effect where you are only working with and communicating with people within your department, on your ladder. The leader is at the top and the minions are below doing all the heavy lifting.

So, we dismantled the traditional organizational chart and spheres were designed. There is a leader at the center of the sphere with everyone in the sphere surrounding and supporting each other dynamically. Sphere size fluctuates and spheres can overlap to different degrees at any given moment in time. People can be involved in two spheres at once if something they are involved in creates more overlap. When one project is complete, they morph back into their home sphere and the overlap shrinks. We have been working hard to root our world of the top-down vernacular and replace it with "in and out" vernacular. The concept is that of a microorganism morphing and changing as the company grows and evolves. It is flexible and malleable. There is no longer a need to run things up the chain of command. We think it is a new and innovative way to consider organizational structure.

Spheres are a natural formation that look and feel more like a superorganism and reflect the power and genius of how nature might assemble a group of people to work together. I believe there is a lot to learn from nature and how nature promotes organisms that evolve, innovate, and adapt, also known as the concept of biomimicry.

Collective Decision-Making Using Design Thinking

One last concept I feel compelled to land with you before moving on from innovation is the concept of design thinking. It is a powerful way to think about decision-making and innovation. The premise at its core is based on the idea that diverse perspectives allowed to cocreate will end up at a significantly more powerful place than one brain or a bunch of similar brains spinning around a problem in a similar fashion. Design thinking is primarily focused on product development and creating products the marketplace will embrace enthusiastically. In my opinion, though, the concept of design thinking can be broadened out to all creative endeavors.

This is from "What is Design Thinking and Why Is It So Popular?" on the Interaction Design Foundation website:

> "Design Thinking is an iterative process in which we seek to understand the user, challenge assumptions, and redefine problems in an attempt to identify alternative strategies and solutions that might not be instantly apparent with our initial level of understanding. At the same time, Design Thinking provides a solution-based approach to solving problems. It is a way of thinking and working as well as a collection of hands-on methods.
>
> "Design Thinking revolves around a deep interest in developing an understanding of the people for whom we're designing the products or services. It helps us observe and develop empathy with the target user. Design Thinking helps us in the process of questioning: questioning the problem, questioning the assumptions, and questioning the implications."[6]

The only way we can question the problem, assumptions, and implications is to bring as many different minds to the table as possible and let them run free. Seriously, free!! You don't firmly frame the problem. When there is an issue needing attention, assemble a diverse body and present the issue, which could be a problem, an opportunity, or an external event that originally presents as a threat, but from a different perspective might appear as a huge opportunity.

An example of a threat that turns into an opportunity: In the early days of our company, we developed a couple of strong markets in Michigan but had yet to crack into the major market—Detroit and its surrounding suburbs. We had built a nice company, but we were by no means a strong brand. We had a few stores in the Detroit market, and they were struggling when in rolled Caribou Coffee, a well-heeled company with a strong presence in Minneapolis, MN, that quickly built 22 beautiful stores, some of the nicest ever. The investment per unit was astronomical.

Everyone told us we were doomed, that Caribou was going to eat our lunch. But in our souls we knew differently. We were taking our business model down a diametrically opposed path; we were boiling out every last dollar from the initial investment per store. Our innovation, our opportunity, was to make sure every one of our stores would generate positive cash flow quickly. Our initial investment was already less than half what Caribou was putting into each of their stores, and I was on a quest to carve out another $100K, which represented 33 percent of our existing total. The outside threat, Caribou Coffee, made me work harder, dive in deeper, and innovate more aggressively. Our innovation was to keep our concept simple, with initial investment costs as low as possible. This was in the face of Caribou building gorgeous, log cabin–style stores with sky high capital expenditure. We prevailed. We now have north of 75 stores in Detroit Metro, and Caribou has closed all 22 stores. The outside threat proved to be the most amazing opportunity for us to continue to innovate and get better by doing the hard work, and most importantly to prove out our business model.

Today we believe wholeheartedly in what we are doing and in our business model because we have road-tested it against the "best" and prevailed. What everyone else perceived as a threat, we saw as a beautiful opportunity. Had the threat not existed, I don't know if we would have gone throttle down to innovate and compete. Many would have gotten shaky and probably gone conservative. We were all in like Captain Dan of *Forrest Gump* fame, strapped to the mast of his fishing boat during the hurricane. It was a gift for us in that stage of the development of our business. We moved forward, after our face-off with Caribou, knowing we could compete and win.

Critical Impact of an Outside Perspective

As I talked about in part 4, bringing in outside vantage points is one way to infuse new thinking into your organization. In BIGGBY's fight against Caribou, we had an outside influence that compelled our thinking. It happened to be none other than the founder of Subway, Fred DeLuca. He made us think from a different and critically important perspective. He made us think about our jobs, our responsibility as managers of our business, as the bastions of our franchise owners' capital. First and foremost, we must protect, and then second, we must grow their capital. His perspective was critically important,

continued

> and we were fortunate to have it at our table. We took it and ran as hard as we could with this way of thinking. Different perspectives may come from many different places, maybe even a billionaire.

Diversity of Thought Is Essential

Did you think that in my dive into design thinking I forgot about the "diverse perspectives" part of the description? Not so. When assessing issues, threats, weaknesses, etc., it is critically important to have a diverse group of people around the table bringing their life experience to the conversation. Let them free flow, wax poetic, and riff upon the subject from every possible angle and experience. For real, bring people from everywhere and cut them loose, no limits, no boundaries, just creative expression around a given concept. Steve Jobs used to add hallucinogens to the mix to try to squeeze every ounce of creative juice from the moment. It worked for him. Maybe you are not comfortable with illicit drugs, and so be it, but you get the point. Let people "unlock and roll" if you want true innovation.

An example would probably be useful. How about what has become a classic business success story known as "the bear and the honey pot":

Many years ago, Pacific Power and Light (PP&L), now Pacific Power, had a problem with ice building up on the power cables that supplied their customers in the Cascade Mountains. During the autumn and spring, the buildup of ice could overstress the lines, causing them to break. The normal solution was for a linesman to climb the towers and shake the power line—extremely dangerous for the linesman!

There had been many attempts to come up with a solution, but the company was struggling to find an answer, so they turned to a professional facilitator who suggested that a diverse group be assembled to look at the problem. A group was assembled that included the linesmen, supervisors, accountants, and people from the mail room.

Over a coffee break, one of the linesmen recounted the story of how he came across a black bear who was not happy about his trespassing and ended up chasing him for over a mile. To try and stimulate the group, the facilitator retold the story. One person suggested training the bears to climb the poles to shake the ice off the lines. Ideas followed about how they could be tempted with pots of honey placed on top of the poles. Elaine Camper picks up the story:[7]

> " . . . one of the more senior, more sarcastic linesmen said, 'You know all those fancy helicopters those fat cats in the front office fly around in all the time? Why don't we grab one of those and fly from pole to pole placing the honey pots on top just after an ice storm. That way the honey will be there when we need it, and, besides, it will do those fat executives some good to walk for a change.'
>
> Another period of laughter followed. Then one of the secretaries spoke for the first time. 'I was a nurse's aide in Vietnam. I saw many injured soldiers arrive at the field hospital by helicopter. The downwash from the helicopter blades was amazing. Dust would fly everywhere. It was almost blinding. I wonder if we just flew the helicopter over the power lines at low altitude, would the downwash from those blades be sufficient to shake the lines and knock the ice off?'
>
> This time there was no laughter—just silence. She had come up with an answer. In most environments a secretary

wouldn't have been invited into the conversation. By valuing diversity and by encouraging divergent thinking, the resource had enabled the group to come up with a possible solution to an important problem that everyone wanted solved."

There are lessons from this story that can be applied to any group session for developing solutions to business problems. The first step is to design the group session with an aim in mind. In the case of PP&L, the aim was to find a way to knock ice off the power lines without risking linesmen and at a tolerable cost. Step two is to pull together people with different backgrounds, with enough people to provide a range of perspectives but not so many that the group becomes cumbersome. A diverse group will produce different perspectives on the problem and could result in a radically different solution. The final part of the design must include enough time for people to relax, have fun, and allow the ideas to flow.

The problem to be solved must be described in simple terms so that it is easily understood by a diverse group of people, and therefore it needs to be devoid of technical jargon. The importance of the problem needs to be emphasized. In this case, ice forming on power lines was a fundamental issue. It involved getting the core product to the customer. The current solution, linesmen risking their lives, wasn't acceptable, ever. The problem was clear, so everyone understood.

Now the tricky bit. Managing diverse people in a meeting can be difficult. For example, people with a technical background will often start work on designing solutions, which will leave the rest of the group wondering. Finance people will automatically start doing cost analysis. Marketing people will be focused on the story to be told. And so on. For the session to be successful, many voices need to be heard; therefore those on the periphery must always be brought into the discussion. The facilitator must be skilled at working within all groups, formally and informally. They must always pay attention to mining the golden nuggets and presenting them for consideration. All participants must be encouraged to throw off their inhibitions and be creative in their contributions to the session. Ultimately, the leader must give strong, positive reinforcement to the crazy, outlandish, insane ideas.

This story epitomizes the concept of having broad and diverse experiences at the table supporting mission-critical creativity and innovation. Had they not had the secretary's voice at the table, they wouldn't have had the experience learned in Vietnam about the downdraft of helicopters. She lived downdraft and understood its power. Bingo!

I challenge you: When was the last time you invited your administrator or intern to a high-level creative session attempting to solve a strategic issue for the organization?

Ready to Innovate

In summary, I hope you will consider the following as we close this chapter on innovation:

- First, innovation doesn't happen in a vacuum, and you never check the box on an innovative process.
- Second, look around you everywhere for inspiration on different ways to view an issue. Biomimicry and nature is one example, but you can also look at different industries, different business models, different cultures, different times of day, different moments in history. Look and think deeply.

- Finally, keep your circle broad and diverse when looking at issues. With just a few similar perspectives around the table, you will continue to look at the problem from small variants of your current reality. When you bring in broad perspectives, you will surely get different views of the same issue. Cut people loose and let them run naked through the fields of tall grass. I am quite sure you will end up with magical results, whether you choose to take the Steve Jobs approach and add hallucinogens or not.

CHAPTER 19

Becoming Deliberately Developmental–Fostering Constant Learning and Growth

WHEN MOST FOLKS LEAVE HIGH SCHOOL OR COLLEGE, it seems their learning journey comes to an abrupt halt. It's as if when people turn 18 or 22, they act as if they have learned everything they need to grow into a mature, healthy adult. They stumble forward, continuing to learn and grow in a haphazard, half-cocked, aimless journey. They learn by hook or crook and by experience. Some do it better than others, but I dare say most get complacent and the learning journey eventually sputters out.

Another part of the picture is that the workplace today is typically uninspiring and transactional. The employee does acceptable work and gets paid a wage; the organization agrees to do no harm. And when both parties live up to their obligations, everyone is content and expected to remain engaged and inspired. The organization of the past 20 years has been focused on doing no harm and maybe even trying to promote health.

> "It is pretty commonplace today that the workplace is focused upon people's well-being, meaning it won't harm them. Meaning it is safe and relatively supportive."
>
> —*An Everyone Culture,*
> Robert Kegan and Lisa Laskow Lahey[1]

Safe and relatively supportive is not enough. It doesn't need to be this way anymore. In fact, it had better not stay this way for much longer.

The workplace of tomorrow will be a place where people go to be nurtured and supported, where they go to grow and develop. A place where they are encouraged and challenged to become better people. It will be deliberately developmental.

> "A deliberately developmental workplace is not in the business of having a workplace that supports well-being but encourages and even demands people to flourish."
>
> —*An Everyone Culture*[2]

Let's imagine this deliberately developmental organization for a moment. Imagine the company you work for . . .

- Is invested in providing you opportunities to keep growing and learning, not simply providing a safe environment.
- Has tools and resources to support you in doing your work to better understand your own strengths and weaknesses and identify opportunities for personal growth.
- Sets up support groups for you in your quest toward living a fulfilling and powerful life.
- Works to get you out onto your leading edge, constantly pushing you to evaluate your position in the world.
- Not only offers up the opportunity to do this learning but also makes it a condition for employment—personal growth and development is a job requirement.
- Expects you to determine the two or three powerful self-improvements to tackle each year and then makes these as important as meeting your job duties and responsibilities.

In short, the company treats personal development as a critical component of the job. Not only to become more proficient, more efficient, more productive, and therefore a better employee. They do it to encourage you to develop your own position in the world, to explore your passions on your terms, and to make you a more powerful person. If organizations are full of powerful people, people who are deeply engaged in an ongoing trajectory of lifelong learning and self-improvement, just think about how these deliberately developmental organizations will thrive.

A Supportive Environment, Not a Cult

I expect some readers will be uncomfortable with a discussion about required learning. It may sound akin to a cult (e.g., forcing people to engage in self-development as a job requirement when "self-development" feels like stuff people would work on in church or as part of personal therapy). However, it is important to understand that in a deliberately developmental organization, the direction and topic of the learning is not prescribed or dogmatic. It is simply about bringing principles to the table and encouraging people to engage in ways and around topics they are comfortable with. It is best said by the authors of *An Everyone Culture*: "A deliberately developmental organization, through its community and its practices, slips its hand under its people, wherever they may be in their developmental journey, and supports their forward movement when they are ready."[3]

By the way, this stuff isn't new. Great managers have been supporting employees in their learning journeys forever; it's just no one pinpointed it as the reason they are great leaders. They simply know and understand intuitively that investing in their people, taking care of their people, treating people like the beautiful, precious beings they are is how people want to be led. When you are engaged in healthy ways supporting people in their development, building a community on this premise, there is no limit to what people can do together.

The million-dollar question is, How do we make this happen? Let's first approach it from a theoretical standpoint and then we can move into practical applications.

A Petri Dish of Self-Improvement

In many ways I think the workplace is the perfect place to do important work on yourself.

When we are on personal development journeys it is important to do self-assessment and consider areas you would like to work on and improve. We have to be deliberate. In my mind, self-improvement is about increasing your self-awareness, which means acknowledging, managing, and shaping how the world perceives you and your actions.

In its simplest form, self-awareness is about controlling and tempering your behavior to maintain a healthy relationship with others. Running a filter on your thoughts so as not to negatively impact the relationship. This is fundamental, elementary self-awareness.

Next level self-awareness is understanding the impact you are having on others. How do other people feel when they interact with you? From my experience most people have little idea how they make others feel and therefore they lack awareness. The outlier in all of this lies in the fact that most people feel like they do know, and this is a poignant example of a lack of awareness. This disconnect is what we need to improve.

To become more self-aware, we must fight our hard-wired biology because the brain acts as a mechanism to limit our ability to increase our self-awareness. The main culprit is our limbic system, which is a set of components in the brain that process emotions and behavior (among other functions). With any perceived threat, the limbic system acts to protect us at all costs. The more anxious we are, the more the limbic system digs in, and we are powerless to stop it. "Because these areas of your brain are not accessible to your conscious awareness, it is virtually impossible for you to understand what they want and how they control you. They oversimplify things and react instinctively," writes Ray Dalio in *Principles*.[4]

Since we aren't consciously aware of these responses, it is impossible to monitor this behavior ourselves. That's why we need other people to shine a light on behavior driven by our unconscious; their observations are critical to bring us information—give us feedback—on how we are being perceived in the world. Without that outside input, we are living in our own imaginary fantasy bubbles.

To grow and develop you need to be immersed with people whom you trust and who are willing to bring you feedback. The stuff can hurt a little, or even a lot, but it is gold. It is important that your people, your tribe, bring you feedback from a place of love and understanding so you are able to appreciate and absorb the feedback as a generous gift. Loving feedback in relation to your behavior is one of the most valuable gifts you can receive from others.

With great enthusiasm I submit to you the corporate entity is the perfect environment for obtaining that kind of input. A business is a petri dish for self-improvement. You need to create the perfect conditions for growth inside that petri dish.

One critical factor in individual development is having challenging work. If you are home making yourself a peanut butter and jelly sandwich, ready to enjoy an afternoon of Netflix, there is little challenge and room for growth. In contrast, work can be a place that is offering up new and different challenges every day that provide you the opportunity to learn and grow. The possibilities are endless:

Having to deliver a presentation to a group of 600 people (a moment the butt will pucker!) . . . working on a complex mathematical model to improve the efficiency of the supply chain . . . managing a new team that is from disparate corners of your organization on a journey to solve an issue with a strategic partner . . . supporting a colleague who is going through cancer treatment . . . dealing with foreign currency fluctuations, or . . . There is also the opportunity to establish methods and processes for important conversations to occur.

It is when you are stretching and growing through the challenges you face that you will have the opportunity for feedback on your behavior. This allows you to understand specifics on where you may need improvement. Significant challenges like those we encounter every day in the workplace test us and allow for growth. So let's all take advantage of the opportunity the workplace presents to learn, grow, and become better human beings.

A second critical factor for learning, as I discussed, is feedback. Most of us have very few opportunities in our adult lives to be in an environment where feedback can flow. If you coach a little league team, most likely the players or parents aren't going to bring you any real inputs around your performance. At church, you show up on your best behavior—and unless you are challenging yourself by taking a leadership position, there is going to be little opportunity to stretch and grow. In your family, there are far too many competing dynamics and vested interests for anyone to be objective; everyone has a dog in the hunt. The workplace is the perfect environment for creating conditions where honest and open feedback can occur. There isn't a ton of baggage people bring to the relationship. People take, at face value, the things you present as your leading edge, the two or three things you are working on to be better.

Beyond providing challenging work and making feedback a constant, there are many methods and processes you can use if you are willing to go on the journey and explore innovative things to create a deliberately developmental organization. Following are a few that BIGGBY is implementing, and there are many more.

1. Support Groups

As I talked about in chapter 7, in college I was fortunate to have stumbled into a project that would forever change my thinking. I researched the power and impact of Alcoholics Anonymous (AA). I threw myself into studying AA with the enthusiasm of my four-year-old watching T. rex battle seven velociraptors. I was fascinated by the organization but truly mesmerized by the stories of the people within AA, heroic stories of people changing their lives, going from rock bottom to a newfound place of health and stability. To the letter, each member I talked with credited AA for their transformation.

I got interested in the subject because my best friend's father was in AA. He had lost his wife, my friend's mom, to cancer. This was the first person I ever knew well to pass. After her death, my friend's father sunk into a difficult place, and at the bottom he was drinking a fifth of scotch every evening and using illicit drugs sporadically. He managed to keep his life together, all things considered. When we connected, I was a high school senior, and he was in recovery and committed to the regular routine of meetings. But more importantly, he was also willing to talk freely about his experience. I would do odd jobs around the house, and we would inevitably get spun up in some tale. Often we would talk until after midnight. It was a magical relationship, as I was just a kid and he actually treated me like an adult giving me the real story with all of the gory details. I could ask anything, and he would tell me the truth. For me, engaging the inner workings of an adult in recovery and learning about the importance of AA was powerful.

A few years later when I was in college, I approached him about my research project, and he was happy to engage. He guided me into the depths of the organization. He told me beautiful stories of transformation, tales of woe, and everything in between. He connected me with people to interview and gave me reading material that I devoured. I dove in like a pig at a trough. In the end I produced good work. My conclusion after many hours of researching and thinking about AA was that people in AA were fortunate, very fortunate. They had a tribe. It was not forced on them by geography, religion, ethnicity, or history, but a true tribe bonded together by experience in the world, by the common goal of sobriety. They meet regularly, for some even daily, in order to support each other through the trials and tribulations of life and sobriety. The conclusion of my paper was that everyone, I mean everyone, needs a group like AA. I joked that I was inspired to become an alcoholic so I could have the opportunity to immerse myself into AA and have a support group for life. I have never forgotten the power of AA and the love and support the members showed for each other.

My experience with the power of being a member of a tribe was reinforced when I joined the Young Presidents Organization (YPO), as I also talked about in chapter 7. YPO was a great support group for CEOs, allowing us to discuss any issue with a nonjudgmental, supporting group. As I explained earlier, the YPO forum takes on the whole person, not just the business issues, because the personal issues when impacting your world become business issues just like business issues that have you jacked-up impact your ability to parent or be a loving spouse. The web between personal and professional is complex, and that is why strong support groups in a professional setting take on the whole person.

After my experiences studying AA and in YPO, I realized that everyone in any organization would benefit from having the support of a group structured like the YPO forum. It isn't just CEOs that need support—everyone does. We all need a place to go to air our issues in a loving environment and get support, a perfect place to learn from others' experiences and to be unconditionally loved. Sometimes the relationships in properly structured support groups can feel more supportive on certain issues than those we have with our spouse. The folks in your support group don't have a horse in your race or a dog in your hunt. They want what is best for you and for you only.

It may be a new and different concept, but I advocate putting together a structure within your organization that assembles small intimate groups to support each member. Remember, this is not specifically to make them a better employee but to support them in their life, to provide them a place to take their complex issues and have a sounding board. A place to facilitate growth and learning, to let them connect with their colleagues in a way that everyone dreams to be connected, genuine and authentic.

Building Loyalty

Traditionally, leaders expect loyalty from their people and are offended when an employee doesn't demonstrate such.

Expecting loyalty within the construct of the traditional employee/employer relationship is a fool's errand. I ask the question: What are you doing to earn the loyalty of your people?

Trust me, if you decide to provide support groups or forums for your employees, you will not only end up with a more well-rounded and stable environment for your people, but they will also see that you are investing in them in a meaningful way. That builds loyalty between you, the organization, and your employee. Forums and support groups in general are a healthy way to invest in people and build loyalty. It does cost time, maybe a few hours a month, but the result will go a long way to developing meaningful relationships for the people within your organization. Meaningful relationships are why any of us commit and fully show up for anything.

Five Ground Rules for Support Groups

There are a few fundamentals I advocate as ground rules for the establishment of these groups. I will go through some of the major constructs here, but if you want to get a copy of our forum playbook, please reach out to me and I will make sure you get a copy.

First, limit the size. The more people in the room, the more diversity of thought will add up to better outcomes for everybody involved, but if you have too many people, the logistics become onerous and cumbersome, and the group members won't see as much benefit. With bigger groups it also takes longer to build the bonds within the group and therefore it takes longer to find safety. I advocate that groups should be between six to nine people. When you send out the invite list make sure to invite more than 9, maybe 11 to 12, as you will surely end up with a few people who don't accept. As the group moves forward, people will exit, so I advocate adding members when the group size gets to six or seven. Smaller works too, but you just don't want to be in a spot of getting down to three or four members.

Second, have a strong governance document that outlines the structure of the group. Insist that everyone commits, in writing, that they will live by the structure outlined in the agreement. It should outline how attendance-related infractions are managed. It should explain how a new member is added. It should deal with who will lead the group and for how long, with each individual's length of engagement, and so on. The important roles you and the organization play are to provide structure for the group. The key is to allow the group flexibility in relation to the dynamics within the "room" but give them enough structure to provide safety within the process.

Third, put a trained facilitator in the room for the first year; then let the group decide when they are ready to be cut loose and manage their own time together. The first couple of groups will need an outside (professional) facilitator, but over time you can ask experienced members from older groups to facilitate the launch of a new forum. Most people who are in healthy, productive, loving forums are happy to make the commitment to facilitate a group for 12 months. They have gotten a ton of benefit and they want to pass the opportunity along to others within the organization.

Fourth, require some kind of learning mechanism be built into the meeting rhythm. I think it is important for groups to commit to reading and reporting to each other. This takes some effort and energy outside of the forum meeting time, but the benefit is massive. Adults, especially ones that are working within dynamic high-growth environments, typically slow active learning because their job is too demanding. As leaders we need people to continue to grow.

We have a reading list for every new forum, and we strongly encourage them to engage. When I have actively led forums, I always used reading as an indicator of people's commitment to the group. If people showed up unprepared, it was an early indication they were losing commitment to the group, and that was my opportunity to start a conversation about whether people were "in."

Fifth, have the groups take an annual retreat together off-site and spend additional time together in a relaxed environment. These are great opportunities to reset. At this annual retreat you can provide an outside resource on a meaningful topic. At the end of the annual retreat, you have everyone recommit and sign a new agreement that has been updated and reflects the current thinking of the group. Annual retreats are also a wonderful way to immerse a new member into the group.

2. Provide Individualized Coaching

Forum structures are a great place to build cohesive, healthy environments that allow people to bring their authentic selves to work and get support. One downside can be a few people's "stuff" taking up most of the meeting time, and some members may go three or four months without getting their own airtime. Therefore, we created a different methodology in our world for people to get specific and real-time feedback through individualized coaching.

Each employee of our company is provided an individual coach. The coach is committed to assisting and supporting the employee on their own personal growth journey. The coaching may have to do with work, but by design the coaching is meant to be much broader in scope. The work is to support the individual on their path to building a life that they love. Each person who is a member of our team should be on a quest to pursue their passions and explore the opportunities in life that upon their deathbed are powerful memories that provide feelings of fulfillment, meaning, and pride.

Let me clarify a few things. One, the coach is not the employee's manager nor has anything to say about nor has any influence over the mentee's day job. In fact, there is confidentiality in place so the coaches can't take anything they learn in coaching to the organization. By design there is no interaction between an employee's coach and their manager directly. Coaching is more about engaging the mentee in a conversation about how to engage their coworkers and manager in a healthy and productive way to get rewarding results. Second, the coach is not a therapist. At times the conversations may veer in that direction, and coaches need to be comfortable with moving the engagement back into the realm of coaching and mentoring. This can at times be complicated and risky, but if the conversation remains authentic, the discussion will navigate back to a healthy place.

As I discussed with other developmental topics, coaching can mean a person explores other options and opts to leave our organization to pursue another dream. It happens, and we fully support and celebrate the person who makes that choice.

The Benefits of Having People Explore Other Life Options

Still wondering how in the world we can be OK with encouraging people to look at and consider options outside of our organization? We invest hundreds of hours and many dollars in someone only to have them take their learning and apply it elsewhere? Yes!

Two things are important here. First, those who leave will be your biggest fans. They will tell everyone about your amazing organization. Second, and most importantly, the people who actively decide they want to stay with your team have realized that your company is the place they will thrive within on their journey. Your organization is the home base for their self-development work, and staying will provide them the ability to pursue their passions. These people will be superheroes.

In the end you are creating superfans by spinning people off who are going to do remarkable things and be huge advocates of your company. You will be connected to these people forever. Also, those that stay will be passionate about their lives and the work they do for you; people who have made a deliberate decision that you are with whom and where they want to be doing meaningful work. I don't think it gets any better as a manager.

Individualized coaching is about creating a safe place for people to get direct one-on-one feedback, encouraging them along their self-improvement journey. It is a powerful force in our world and is a massive investment in living up to our company's purpose of supporting you in building a life that you love. Remember, you make the investment in people first and in the end, they will make a massive investment in you. It starts with you.

3. BIGGBY's "Life You Love" Curriculum

One other major project we are deeply committed to is a curriculum we developed to support people in building lives that they love. We believe there are four foundational elements that need to be in place for anyone to build a life they love: knowing who we want to be, having a sense of vitality, having a sense of belonging, and exceeding your basic needs. This is the kind of stuff that isn't taught anywhere else. Where in your schooling did you learn about the importance of visioning or managing personal finances? How about thinking about your vitality or having a sense of belonging? This is the stuff that makes life meaningful. My guess is you were never taught any of this. What a shame! Learning in these areas is fundamental and powerful—I would suggest more powerful than learning geometry or Russian literature.

Below is a brief description of each course and what we are attempting to accomplish:

1. Knowing who you want to be: In this guided experience, people discover their personal core values through the life-changing power of visioning. They imagine what they want their life to look like and take the first steps toward realizing their dreams.

2. Discovering personal vitality: Here, people invest in how they feel—mentally, emotionally, physically, and spiritually—and find that the smallest actions can create the big rewards.
3. Sense of belonging: People explore where they fit into the groups in their lives and find a place where it is safe to be their truest self, where they are the most honest, vulnerable, open, and loved.
4. The ability to exceed basic needs: People create the ability to look beyond the boring budget by exploring relationships with money, crafting an inspiring vision for financial future, and beginning to build a life you love!

These four courses meet once a week for six weeks. They have a facilitator in each group guiding everyone through the content. The work is meaningful and has proven to have powerful results for the people attending. No matter in what stage of life, people gain value from the courses, which are free for anyone employed within BIGGBY Nation. Again, these are the life skills nobody is teaching anywhere. By providing this content we are hoping to encourage everyone in their personal journey on self-improvement.

4. Sabbaticals: Real Time Off . . . Way Off!

A fourth method we have deployed for supporting those in building a life they love is by providing a three-month paid sabbatical to any employee for every five years of service. There are no requirements other than one will not engage in BIGGBY work. Each employee must turn in their phones and hand over their computers. They are expected to spend the time in a meaningful way, whatever that means to them. It has proven to be powerful.

Yes, a few people have opted to resign and move on to other endeavors post-sabbatical. This is a natural consequence when you have three months to contemplate your life. I support this occurring for the same reasons as stated previously. We love them and wish them the best!

There are other benefits of the sabbatical to the organization. First, the sabbatical-taker's team must absorb the additional work. Everyone must prioritize their world and consider what they are handling to deemphasize certain items and make room for additional work. We should be doing this anyway, but when a sabbatical lands on a team, they are forced to prune and evaluate each member's workload. Second, every person on the team realizes that the group is bigger than any one individual. Anyone could be hit by the proverbial bus tomorrow, and we must be mentally prepared to absorb all their responsibilities. Finally, team members get charged with new duties and responsibilities when a member leaves for three months, which opens up new and different opportunities for all by working on new projects and different work that inspires people to imagine their role differently.

One thing we didn't consider at the outset of the program was that our most senior people would likely be eligible first. This was an important component to success because these people went on sabbatical, returned . . . and found everything copacetic; the world hadn't fallen apart in their absence. That meant a senior person had a relatively clean slate upon return, which allowed them to explore dynamic and compelling new work to propel the business forward. Meanwhile, junior people gained valuable experience during the senior person's absence. Additionally, people trust that the sabbatical is real.

I would encourage you to consider adopting some version of a sabbatical, as it has been a powerful program in our culture.

Being Deliberate about Personal Development

The four methods I discussed in this chapter—support groups, individual coaching, "Life You Love" curriculum, and sabbaticals—are ways that BIGGBY is working to create open space and encourage people who are on a personal development journey. There are many small things we are doing in addition to the four big ones, and the list of other possibilities is long. Maybe our ideas and methods won't work for you, but I would encourage you to look at ways of supporting people in their development. It is an active process and feels unsettling at first when approaching it from the traditional mindset of people as an asset, as a cog in the wheel of production. When you transition to thinking about people as beautiful human beings, when you start thinking about your people as someone's beautiful, precious child, and you commit yourself to their personal growth, the payoff is immense.

Investing in people, nurturing people, and supporting people in their own growth is the future of managing. We as managers need to be taking into consideration the whole human being and supporting them in living a healthy and fulfilling life. Having healthy, well-adjusted people active in your organization is the magic sauce of building high-functioning, high-performing teams.

CHAPTER 20

A Potpourri of Creativity—Creating a Melting Pot That Supports Justice, Equity, Diversity, and Inclusion

I DON'T CARE ABOUT your persuasion: put aside all politics, do your best to embrace your biases, and maybe we can have a meaningful conversation about JEDI: Justice, Equity, Diversity, and Inclusion. I don't care if you are a Black American living in a large urban area, a Christian conservative, a transgender gay Latina, a Caucasian liberal from the suburbs, or a female farmer who has never been outside of your state lines. Again, I come back to the statement that your truth (or my truth) is not the truth. It is only the truth from your experience and context.

There is risk for me to present my perspective on JEDI and the importance of uncovering restraints of unconscious bias because I am a 50-year-old white male who has benefited from being part of the white male power structure his whole life. I have bias, as we all do. All of that being said, I am going to give it a shot. Frequently people are too intimidated to talk about bias out of fear of offending. This fear impedes our ability to have healthy conversations and move in a healthier direction.

The subject is near and dear to my heart if for no other reason than the challenge it has presented in building BIGGBY. We have always been aware of our lack of diversity, and we suffer from the comfortable and complacent position of status quo. It has never been a make-or-break issue for us, and we always kicked the can down the path as it fell into the important but not urgent category ("JEDI, next quarter" was our mantra). But at last we have taken on JEDI, though our progress has been agonizingly slow. However, in this chapter I want to talk about why I am so committed to improving JEDI at BIGGBY and the world over.

Flocking with Birds of Many Feathers

Why is this important? Why is having as many diverse perspectives and as many different biases as possible around the table important? Whatever your opinion regarding JEDI initiatives, you need to be aware of the power of diversity on decision-making. If you are surrounded by white folk who all grew up in the suburbs, who are partnered with heterosexuals who went to the local university for 4.5 years, and save all year to vacation in Florida, and spend their weekends chasing their kids around to sporting events, the diversity of thinking in your group is going to be staggeringly limited.

The fact of the matter is that people like to hire, work with, and generally spend time with people like themselves. The heterosexual male is going to feel some discomfort being the only person working on a project where everyone else is gay (or vice versa). A Black female is likely going to feel uncomfortable if everyone else in a room is male and white. The one Ohio State fan who walks into a tailgate with a big gray "O" on his red sweatshirt and is surrounded by a sea of University of Michigan fans—each wearing a dark blue shirt bearing a large yellow ("maize") M—is going to feel awkward. My point is that when you are the one that feels different, it is uncomfortable. And I think, as a general rule, if we are left to our own devices, we are going to self-select into groups of people who look, act, and think like we do.

This mentality easily filters into hiring. When 85 percent of your company is white and hails from central Indiana, you are going to attract people who are comfortable with that population, and the people in charge of hiring are going to select others who fit well within that bubble. Your company will look like it has always looked.

Let me be clear what I am talking about in relation to diversity. It isn't simply about race, gender, and sexual preference. There are all kinds of other biases that we must focus on to make sure we are keeping diverse perspectives around our table. For a lighter example, the average height of a male Fortune 500 CEO is two and half inches taller than the average American male. (My partner and I will bring that average down when we reach that status.) We can make an argument that there is a bias against short people in roles of leadership. It might seem banal, but there is a distinct difference in the height of American CEOs. Does it make a difference in terms of decision-making or strategy or profits? I certainly don't think so, but frankly, we won't know for sure until more shorter men make it to that status.

Height is an innocuous example, but I hope it demonstrates that there are hundreds and even thousands of biases, and until leadership is diversified and all CEOs aren't tall white men, we won't know the positive impact.

There are other examples of bias that receive less attention but are still acutely painful, and I want to make sure we are reaching into those, like the impact of bias on trans people. I have recently befriended a trans man with an incredibly sharp mind who is always bringing me new and different business ideas. He has opened my eyes to a truckload of issues he has to tackle that a cisgender man like me doesn't consider. Also, there are the issues facing people with disabilities and how they struggle to find gainful employment. Or how about the convicted felon who has served their time but still must check that box on every employment application? Or how about age? Is a 19-year-old manager of a coffee shop going to be comfortable hiring a 68-year-old retiree? As progressive organizations of the future, we need to take into account everyone and accommodate all people having an opportunity to be successful on our teams.

JEDI Starts at the Top

Management must make active decisions to change and convince people of the importance of diversity and then ensure it is happening. Until each manager in your organization is committed to improving diversity, it won't happen. JEDI starts at the top, from the person with the keys to the kingdom expressing the importance of diversity and laying it down as a mandate. It is the CEOs who must make conscious decisions to bring in strong people with perspectives who will alter our truths.

Today, the "top" is typically a white male, and I recognize that asking anyone to give up power is an enormous request. One of my truths is that the white man at the top needs to step aside and make room for others. The privileged white male has a set of biases getting in the way of the strong leadership as defined in this book.

We need to apply the principle that our organizations have the power to be utilized to make the world a better place. I think people who have been dragged through the shitter for centuries are going to be better at understanding the communal perspective. We won't know until we have done it. We need to take every opportunity to put people from diverse backgrounds in positions of leadership and end the era of the white male.

Wait a minute, isn't that just reverse discrimination? Yes, it is. Everyone other than the white hetero male has had the deck stacked against them for, well, ever. Let's try changing up the power structure and see how things turn out. I think the era of the white man has been good for the rich white man. Let's instill the era of the non-white, female, non-hetero person and give them a bite at the apple. They will do a good if not better job than the white male, in my opinion.

Some organizations are doing this work, and for them I am grateful. Just this year I was on the slate of candidates for an interesting and prestigious board position. Many thought I was a shoo-in for the role, given the fact that I had been a "good friend" ($$) for decades. The organization turned me down and voted in three others. I was disappointed, of course, but I also understood. A friend who has a leadership role in the organization called me and said, "There is no doubt the era of the fat rich white dude is coming to an end." We both laughed, and the decision the board made was impressive. I feel better about the organization now than I would have if they had made the standard decision and put me on the board. These are the decisions every organization needs to make, and over time we will begin to see progress.

A Tangent on Women Judges

Another strong opinion I live with is that I have always considered it critical to get as many female judges elected as possible. I have never voted to put a male into a judgeship if there was a female option. This may sound way too simplistic, and maybe some male judges were more qualified, but we need to get more and more female perspectives in real positions of power, such as judges. First, I want as many moms as possible making the decisions on how best to treat teenage criminals. Second, any woman today who has been able to put herself in a position to become a judge is impressive. The cards were stacked against her, and she made it happen anyway. That is somebody I would be proud to put on the bench. (My position on women as judges goes deeper than this, but that is the topic for a chapter in another book.)

Creating a Diverse Web of Connections

There is another way in which JEDI starts at the top, and it has to do with your role as leader and what kinds of talent you attract and keep.

In my inner circle I am very fortunate to have a great leader, a strong CEO who I learn from constantly. Just a few months back we were talking about labor issues. He went on a rant and explained that any good leader should be spending 80 percent of their time hiring and developing people. Your job as the CEO is to assemble the team and build an environment for people to thrive (80 percent!). How much of your time goes into attracting, supporting, and nurturing talent from all walks of life?

He referenced an amazing book called *Who* by Geoff Smart and Randy Street[1] as he explained his rationale that a CEO should be constantly networking and engaging talented people. Essentially, being a CEO is a lifestyle. You are always talking to people and building an organism (my term) that is attracting people. You start by having a healthy culture that people within the organism are proud of and enjoy working within (what GROW! will help you do).

Once you have a strong culture, you move into a role of head scout and recruiter. How? You build healthy, strong relationships everywhere in the world, with people who are similar to and very different from yourself. Engage everyone in your circle and ask for connections. You want to get to know the three highest-performing people in their circle. Not necessarily the three best people in a particular discipline, but just the three highest-performing people they know. Ask permission to use your contact's name and reach out to those high performers. Set up coffee with the elite three and meet them, not to hire them but to get to know them and be of service and bring value. When you are being of service, you have started a relationship.

As you go in your career you will build up a powerful web of people with whom you relate, and this will make you a more powerful leader in the world. Connectivity with high-performing people is one of the ingredients to having the world work in your favor. Not only are you connected to everyone in your web, but the amazingly powerful part is that those in your web are connected to each other as well through you. You work hard to be of service to those in your community, and the community will give back to you tenfold stronger. The secret to being effective in the world is to give first, give often, give always.

At each meeting with the elite three, walk away committed to supporting that person. Make a connection for them, send them a book you referenced, invite them to an event that could be helpful. Live up to your commitment by following through and, bingo, you are in a relationship.

Follow this advice and build strong relationships with high-performing people. You will be in an ongoing conversation with talented people, many of whom will have an interest in coming to work for you or will be such a fan of you and your organization they will be endorsing you aggressively. When you need somebody, you won't have to go out and hire a headhunter and do a cold search, as you will have a massive network of people that are interested in supporting you. You send a quick note out to your network about an opening, and my guess is you will get a handful of people who are interested themselves or you are gonna get a strong list of candidates from disparate arenas who are one degree separated and come with a strong recommendation from somebody you trust. It isn't about recruiting and finding good talent; it is about building a company that is a magnet for powerful, talented people. They want to be a part of what you are up to, and they want to become part of your organism that is filled with heart and soul and is doing powerful things in the world. This works in a diverse community that is open and safe to everyone. It all starts with you.

Diversity at the Table Doesn't Assure Equitable Influence

The challenge is deeper than diversity. Having diverse people around the table doesn't guarantee wisdom. We can't just bring the right people to the table and assume the rest will take care of itself; we have to nurture an environment where each piece of a diverse puzzle is able to bring their authentic self and present their true and pure opinions and emotions. This is why leaders with diverse backgrounds are going to be better than the tall hetero athletic white male. They understand what it feels like to be the odd one out and they approach the environment with empathy and are able to extract genuine authentic engagement from everybody.

Let me try an example. When the white male is still in charge, or somebody who has been reared in the context of the white male power structure, they are rooted in traditional ways. Today, the white male power structure is still in place in most organizations, and people who get a seat at the table are those that can adapt and conform to that structure. If you rock the boat too much or bring opinions that fly in the face of convention or don't act how you are supposed to, you won't last long.

My assumption, in all of its political incorrectness, is that women tend to cry more easily than men. I am not working with statistical evidence that supports my theory; my statement is anecdotal from my experience in the world. If you can ride with me on this gross assumption and overlook the juvenile, elementary school playground nature of my assertion, I think this story will help make my point.

For 20 years, one of our key male managers and I had an understanding that if either of us cried at work, we would summarily resign. We joked about it and it was meant to be funny, but it was a thing. Our inside joke communicated to everyone in the organization that there was something wrong with crying. We have a strong contingent of female leaders in our company, which I am proud of, and there have been a number of occasions when emotions rose to the surface, and they would apologize for crying.

So what is the matter with crying? Emotion is important and we were stifling it. By being stereotypical male jerks, we were saying that to be an important figure at BIGGBY, a woman leader couldn't be herself. Instead, she had to act like a stoic, white, emotionally repressed man. This limited important behavior and natural reactions that should have existed around the table, and it required people to behave in ways that weren't authentic. Leadership capacity is naturally limited anyway, and bias—such as semiserious statements that tears are bad—impacts the group's functionality and decision-making and ultimately makes certain people uncomfortable. If you want people to perform at a high level, they must be comfortable and never feel like they need to act in a certain way to fit with the group. You be you, bring you unabashedly, and then we can start having the real conversation.

We Don't Know What We Don't Know

The most daunting aspect of bias is that, like self-awareness, we don't know what we don't know. There is no way to figure it out alone. Hence, teams need to be made up of many different perspectives so a group can see deeply into the abyss of subconscious bias. When you face an issue that involves things you don't know that you don't know, you can't even ask questions to uncover truths because you don't know what to ask!

Example: Some years ago, I was in one of our stores and enthusiastic to meet everyone. I work hard to engage with eye contact, shaking hands, and asking for names. The owner of the store, who is Muslim, was present with two of his children. I had the opportunity to introduce myself to his daughter, who was 20 years old. I stuck out my hand to greet her, but she didn't reciprocate and looked away, embarrassed. Her brother took my arm and simply stated it isn't customary for his sister to shake hands with men. The owner of the store was watching the exchange, and I was supremely embarrassed. I apologized to the children and their father. They accepted my ignorance graciously, but I can't help but think of how it must have made them feel.

I wasn't aware and I didn't know what to ask to be sensitive. Had I had more Muslim women or Muslim people in general working with me day to day, I would have known it is common to ask a Muslim woman if she shakes hands before extending your hand. I didn't know what I didn't know. In this incident I was made aware and I learned, but how many times do I commit a similar faux pas and have no idea? I am unaware, I offend, and it impacts my relationships. It was a gift the brother gave me, but most people wouldn't have spoken up to a perceived power figure out of either politeness or fear.

Where is bias getting in your way? Do you have people around you who are strong enough and willing to call you on our bias? How would you know?

Allowing Biases to Collide

What I hope is clear from this chapter is that I'm not arguing that we should focus on getting rid of bias, per se, but rather we should bring as many different biases together and make sure they all have an equal voice. Biases will collide and smart people will empathize, understand, analyze, and bring forth strong options that encompass each person's experience and viewpoint to bring the best solutions forward.

A Black lesbian who grew up in the Deep South is going to run her bias headlong into the Asian hetero male from NYC. Add to the mix a white male gay football player, a Latino transgender man from a small town in eastern Minnesota, a white female heterosexual mom of three who was captain of her cheerleading team, and bingo—you have a recipe for a potpourri of genius. Compare and contrast the action around this table to what would be occurring around a leadership table with seven white, heterosexual, gender-conforming males (about 80 percent of leadership teams in America). The conversations, the thinking, the decisions, the expectations, the compromises, and the empathy within the multidimensionally diverse group would be so much deeper and broader. I shudder from excitement to think what companies will be like when this is a reality, and it will be a reality. Remember there was a day when Black people were property, women couldn't vote, and gay people could be "cured." Someday leadership teams will be filled by everybody. The white male power structure will be dismantled and the people leading our teams will be bold and beautiful people from every walk of life and every corner of our glorious planet. The sooner the better.

CHAPTER 21

Replacing Profit with Purpose

IF YOUR MINDSET IS STILL ALIGNED with Milton Friedman (circa 1971) when he declared that the purpose of business was to maximize profits and shareholder value, you are living in a bubble birthed out of the security of your own wealth creation. You are living unaware of everyone else. You have been able to live in this place because you, the owner, held the power. But times have changed.

People are demanding more. They want to know how you intend, based on your position of wealth and privilege, to contribute to improving the human condition, how you intend to lead. You need to be able to provide a guiding light for yourself, everyone in your organization, and the world as a whole. And that guiding light is your purpose.

There is a lack of understanding of the word "purpose" in the world. Purpose is not about what you are going to do, or how you are going to do it, but about why you exist—and for most strong leaders, why is about having a powerful impact on the world and ultimately improving the human condition. Phew! I know. Here's the rub (and the premise of my next book): To be a powerful leader, it can't be about profit and making people rich; that is management, specifically the management of finite resources to maximize one's take. It has to be about improving the world for your fellow human—that is, leadership. Purpose communicates how you are going to do so.

Purpose is a critical component to creating a healthy environment in your workspace. It is why people choose to show up for work with you rather than somewhere else. Have you defined your purpose? Does everyone in the organization know what they are showing up to do? If so, your people will show up ready to take on whatever is in front of them to support you and your defined purpose.

Your business's purpose must let people within the organization know what their hard work is meant to accomplish. A well-articulated purpose will communicate to employees, customers, vendors, the community, and, yes, the shareholders why supporting your business is a powerfully positive endeavor.

In short, purpose has replaced profit as the reason for being in business. This does not mean the shareholder doesn't receive a sufficient return on their capital and isn't treated with the utmost respect; it just means there are other stakeholders whose interests, needs, and concerns must be considered as you manage your business. These other stakeholders are not more important than the shareholder, but they are equally important.

So if someone asks, "Why would I want to come work for you?" and your answer is, "To provide employment, growth opportunities, and a paycheck," you will soon find yourself an anachronism in a world that is moving beyond you at light speed. Your answer needs to be different and powerful.

Some would argue this multi-stakeholder approach is a more complicated construct for business. At times that is true, no doubt, but I would argue when you are operating a business and everyone wins, there is synergy, and that, in one word, is magical. Let me use the BIGGBY story to illustrate how and why finding a purpose can help companies take that final step into sustainability.

The Malaise of Success

The moment entrepreneurs/managers of businesses realize their company is either well along the journey to sustainability or perhaps has even gotten there is the moment they start to navel-gaze. They begin to look inward and wonder what the whole thing is about. They are likely making an extraordinary living, and adding one more zero to their tax returns or another comma on a balance sheet is not inspiring. Some increment of millions beyond where they are now is not going to bring joy and fulfillment. "As such companies reach maturity, they often find themselves in a sort of existential crisis, much in the same way that many adults start asking questions about meaning and purpose when they reach midlife."—*Conscious Capitalism*, by John Mackey and Raj Sisodia.[1]

My partner and I spent three or four years in the malaise of "What comes next?", navel-gazing, and wondering where our passion, our fire, had gone. We were still doing "it." We were still showing up to work trying to grow our retail network of coffee shops. We talked and talked ad nauseum about how we were going to proceed. We talked about doing acquisitions. We talked about starting new companies. We talked about new and different directions we could move the business. We talked about moving our headquarters. We talked about whether it was time to sell, step down, and move on to other endeavors.

In the end, most everything we talked about was in the effort to grow our business. For what? To make more money or cash out and live the good life. We instinctively knew these answers didn't work. We kept talking. We knew there needed to be more.

Then, like a fairy tale, it happened. If I hadn't lived it, I wouldn't believe it. What follows is a true story.

My Shaman in the Woods

In the fall of 2015—20 years after the founding of the first coffee shop that eventually grew into the BIGGBY phenomenon—my brother, Curt, and I took my nine-year-old son on a camping expedition. We planned a trip to South Manitou Island, off the west coast of Michigan. It was fall, the last weekend the ferry service was going to be available for transport. It was a grand adventure. On Saturday afternoon we went on an 11-mile hike around the island. At the farthest point from our campsite, on the beach, I looked over and there was a couple huddled around a camp stove. There wasn't another human being within miles. I found great peace and serenity looking at these two. What an amazing way to spend an afternoon.

South Manitou is set up with communal campsites, four sites to one fire pit. Later in the evening we were wrapping up dinner when the couple from the beach joined us at the communal firepit. My brother and I were sipping whiskey, and they were enjoying green tea. My brother and the husband got engaged in a wonderful, spirited conversation. Our new friend was talking about his work in what he called "conscious capitalism." I was engaged with my son and didn't contribute much to the conversation, but I was intrigued enough to give our new friend my card the next day while we were returning on the last boat of the year off the island.

Enter Nathan Havey into the realm of BIGGBY. He called me the next week and passionately challenged me to think about how I and BIGGBY could embrace taking on something powerful in the world. How could we positively impact the thousands of baristas who flow in and out of our company annually? We were seven minutes into the conversation when I interrupted, as I wanted to bring my partner into the conversation. The next week, Nathan came to our offices and presented the opportunity as he saw it. We shook hands and agreed to work together. The following week, we accepted his proposal as written and started on our journey of finding our purpose. It wasn't a straight path, but the end result has been truly powerful.

Hard Truths Create a Pivot Point for BIGGBY

Nathan's proposal was to start with an audit of our stakeholders. In a traditional company there was one master the company served, the shareholder. In conscious capitalism, there are six equal stakeholders: employees, customers, community, environment, vendors, and shareholders. We were interested in moving in the direction of the responsibility espoused by conscious capitalism. The audit would take the pulse of each stakeholder. We agreed, and Nathan went to work. Months later, he delivered his report. I printed it and set it on my desk at home to read the following morning. The gist was that we were performing very well for some stakeholders, reasonably well for others, and dramatically underperforming for one stakeholder group: our employees.

The summary paragraph reporting out on our relationship with our own employees was dreadful. It was the hardest thing I have ever read. By the time I was finished, I had tears running down my cheeks. This was another moment where the specter of creating abusive relationships reared its head, just as it did in our work with suppliers. I couldn't believe I was running a company where it was common for coworkers to simply ghost their position, leaving nothing more than a clean desk behind. A company where people showed up to work wondering if today was going to be the day they got fired, even if they had 10+ years of service. I felt like a failure, even though we had built a strong company that was growing rapidly and was quite profitable.

Nathan's recommendation in the closing paragraph was to read the report out loud, word for word, to the entire company. Bob and I talked and knew we faced a crossroads. We could remain all-in with Nathan and take his recommendation, or we could throw the report in the circular file. We both knew the right answer.

We had a staff meeting that day and we did exactly what Nathan recommended: read his report, word for word. It was very difficult, as there were anonymous scathing quotes from people in the organization. It was hard for everyone to sit and listen to the words, but it was the truth. We closed the meeting by saying thank you for the honest feedback, and we committed to getting better.

The Journey to Purpose

Nathan's report set us off on our journey. We went into a two-year process of finding our purpose and vision. Nathan led the charge, and the entire company was invited to be involved, starting with a kick-off meeting that replaced our regular company business meeting that happened every Tuesday at 1:00 p.m. for an hour. For this kick-off meeting, we invited everyone (about 50 to 60 people at the time), and since some didn't show, everyone else conveniently fit into our meeting room, which holds 40 to 50 people. As with our regular meeting, the leadership team was in the middle of the room at a U-shaped table. Everyone else sat around the outside of the inner table. All were invited to provide input.

In these meetings, we explored many worthy causes that could provide a clear purpose: solving hunger and malnutrition in each community where we had stores, lowering the suicide rate, improving literacy, tackling substance abuse. None of these rang true for the group.

Early in the process, prior to the audit, Nathan had spent a couple of days with Bob and me to get to know our philosophy. When we talked about our individual purposes, the theme of personal individuality kept emerging. Bob and I talked about how we both took unconventional paths to get to today. We talked about bucking conventional wisdom. Doing it our own way. Actively creating our own lives exactly by design. Not bowing to the powers that be. Individualism was a huge theme. We believe in people being themselves, pursuing their passions, and letting the world unfold. As Bob is quoted in a video we did on our purpose, "You be YOU!" Nathan wrote down that phrase on a piece of paper and tucked it away in his briefcase.

Then, after many weeks of discussion, the "You be YOU!" phrase was brought up to the group. It resonated. After much deliberation, we settled on our quest: Our purpose was to support you in building a life you love. No matter who you are, if you come into contact with our organization, we exist to support you in pursuing your passion and building a life you love. Not a life others think you should have, but truly a life you love for the one and only you.

Our business model fits perfectly and is about helping others build successful businesses so they can use that asset as a springboard to building a powerful life, a life they love. The customer walking in our stores looks to us to provide them a little joy and energy in a cup as they go about their day. The key is a life YOU love, by your design.

Boom! We had it. It felt great, and we were ready to dive in.

Vision, Then Reality

As in any theoretical endeavor, we were left sitting with the question of how to execute it in the real world. How were we going to adapt our company to live out this purpose? Nathan stepped in and said we were only partly done. He explained that along with purpose, there is a need for a target, something you are aiming to accomplish. This is where your vision enters the picture. The vision needs to be items that, if completed, you can confidently say you are fulfilling your purpose.

The whole company continued to meet every Tuesday at 1:00 p.m. Open to everyone in the company, we wrestled with the theoretical, we questioned the premise of our purpose. We felt lost most of the journey, exploring the multitude of options. In the end we arrived at the dire need to improve workplace culture. We wanted to be an example of a company that could go from horrible to exemplary and demonstrate it was possible to make this important transition.

Indulge me in a story. Each company should be on a quest, some way of improving the human condition, their purpose capped by a vision that acts like a beacon you are aiming for. Our purpose is to support you in building a life you love. Our vision is to improve workplace culture in America. We are going to do so by aggressively growing a big company, and when we get asked, How did you do it?, we now have the opportunity to tell our story. We talk about how a loving, supportive, nurturing environment produces a kick-ass culture and a high-growth company.

How were we going to measure the results to know if we were accomplishing this objective? Developing metrics was as hard as coming up with our purpose. Again, we did it in the same format as our purpose and vision conversations. Tuesdays at 1:00 p.m. Following are the metrics attached to our 2028 vision:

1. Ninety percent of our people who have been with us for one year or more will rate us a nine or a ten when asked the question, "Is BIGGBY COFFEE supporting you in building a life you love?" Ten being the highest possible affirmation.
2. We will be doing $1B in revenue at retail by 2028.

These metrics are daunting and at times feel impossible. We are trying to do something unprecedented, something no other leadership team has ever done before. Imagine if we can get 90 percent of people who work for BIGGBY COFFEE—baristas, store managers, store owners, and our internal team (which adds up to thousands of people)—rating us a nine or a ten on the quest of supporting them in building a life they love. Our environment will be magical to enter each day as you show up to work. Something like this has never been done to my knowledge in corporate America. If we can do it and grow a huge company and prove out that taking care of people, loving people, and supporting people can become a more productive workplace than the Milton Friedman's zero-sum environment focused on profit alone, then we will meet our quest of improving workplace culture in America.

Why is it important? In a sentence, chronic disease is the leading cause of death in the United States, the leading factor in chronic disease is stress and anxiety, and the leading cause of stress and anxiety is the workplace and financial pressure. Therefore, we are taking on the leading cause of death in America. It is powerful. It is why our work is important. We are on a quest together; we are on a journey. Something of this magnitude has never been pulled off before.

We liken our group to a team locked in a spaceship being launched into outer space and subsequently figuring out how to fly to Mars. Nobody has ever done it before. No company has ever attempted to build a culture where love is as important as profit, where the primary goal is to have a loving and supportive environment where people's growth and development is the primary focus of the organization.

Ready to Grow and Succeed

Today, BIGGBY employees show up to work understanding our purpose, ready to grow and succeed. We're working hard to make the workplace a healthy environment where people are nurtured and supported, where they go home after work more invigorated than when they came.

We firmly believe you can build a loving, caring, supportive environment within a company and grow an amazingly successful business. We are going to prove it out, and when people ask how we did it, we get to share our story. We get to inspire others to consider a purpose worthy of everyone's time, attention, effort, and energy. A purpose worth committing your life to. That is the power of purpose.

What is your purpose? What are you up to? Why should anyone care what you are doing?

Please write me and tell me. There is nothing more powerful on the planet than business and the leaders of those businesses. This is why this book is so important to me, because I believe we, leaders of private enterprise, can and need to take on the most significant challenges of our time. We need to and we can change the world in powerfully positives ways. Tell me how you are doing it. Get me fired up to share your story too; together we can solve any issue, problem, or dilemma we face. The world will be a better place when we take our seat on the rocking chair surrounded by all the love we have created in the world.

PART 5 CONCLUSION

GRIND, GROW, and Everyone Prospers

WE CAN NOW ENGAGE A COLLECTIVE SIGH, led by me, the author. You have honored me by climbing into my capsule and allowing me to describe my thoughts on leadership and management. If in six months you are telling somebody about my book GROW! and you can recite three or four messages from the book, I will deem it a success.

What are the things I hope you'll remember?

- First, your self-awareness, defined as understanding how you impact others in your organization, is critical to your success as a leader. It allows you to meet your organization where it needs you.
- Second, love is what makes our world work. We need to embrace it as a powerful part of our teams and facilitate love as an anecdote to many of our travails in leadership.

- Third, communication is our relationships. How we communicate with others is how we relate to them, and how we relate to them is the bedrock of our relationship.
- Fourth, tomorrow will look different than today, and we need to be creating organizations of the future. We need to become deliberately developmental, inclusive organizations where innovation is natural and that everything we do is aligned with a powerful purpose.

If you remember those four things, I will consider this book a huge success. We need as many people as possible in this conversation, so I hope you will share my book with another leader who you think can step forward and GROW.

The Next Mountain to Climb

This book was written to help you reach the promised land of sustainability in your business, a day when you are no longer relevant to the future success of your organization. At that moment, you will sense a powerful feeling of relief; you will be guiding your ship with a deft touch, involved in inspiring projects, only doing the things that fire you up. You will have an amazing asset that you control that is flexible and supporting you in pursuing your perfect life. This was the point of GROW!, to provide you this opportunity. I predict you will now face a moment of deep reflection. What is it all about? What has it all been for?

Your position in the world comes with great responsibility. You have reached the pinnacle of business success. When you started, the goal was to survive (the GRIND phase), and then it became about sustainability (the GROW phase). Congratulations—you have traversed treacherous terrain. You have been on this powerful journey, presumably for decades. You have learned a ton, you have a strong leadership team in place, and you have vast resources available to you. Now what?

You need to stay in the game, but now the game has changed. You need your next challenge, your next mountain to climb. You have, we all have, the responsibility to engage the world and contribute to improving the human condition. That is the game you now need to be playing. Don't be content with simply writing checks to charity and letting them do the hard work. Take your experience, take your team, take your vast resources and commit to some powerful way of contributing to a better world. In short, build your legacy.

How are we doing so at BIGGBY? How are we creating our legacy? My business partner is deep in the throes of building farm-direct relationships for our business. He is engaging farmers around the world, setting up arrangements to benefit the farmer and their communities and provide us direct access to the supply of the most important ingredient for our business: coffee. We are only working with farmers who have a progressive mindset and have developed programs to support the local community and who are farming in a sustainable way. His work is next level, and we hope to lead by example and get many more companies engaged in building healthy relationships with farmers no matter what product/commodity they are buying. This work will be my partner's legacy.

My book series is my legacy. I want to change the way people think about private enterprise. I want to redefine capitalism. Private enterprise (i.e., capitalism) is the most powerful force on the planet. Capitalism is people providing products and services to other people.

If consumers demand more from companies, and leaders of private enterprise take on the responsibility of being stewards of our future, we can all have dramatic impact on the direction of our planet. We can and need to improve the conditions for our fellow travelers on this "One Bigg Island in Space"—the title under which my business partner is doing all his work. We go for a short ride on this big island in space, and we all have a responsibility to leave it a better place than we found it. You as a successful entrepreneur have a greater responsibility than most. Live up to that responsibility, take on a worthy cause with your vast resources, and build your legacy. How? That is the subject of my next book, GRACE. (Teaser alert!)

Thank you for going on this ride with me. If you are reading this line, you have honored me with your time, energy, and attention. I am deeply grateful, and I look forward to seeing the positive impact we can have together as we march forward and change the paradigm of business.

Godspeed!!

Endnotes

Chapter 1

1. W.E. Deming, *The New Economics for Industry, Government, Education* (Cambridge, MA: MIT Press,1994), 45.
2. Deming, *The New Economics for Industry, Government, Education*, 73.
3. Liz Wiseman, *Multipliers* (New York: Harper Collins Publishers, 2010).
4. Keith McFarland, *The Breakthrough Company* (New York: Crown Business, 2008), 201.

Chapter 4

1. Brené Brown, *Braving the Wilderness* (London: Penguin Random House UK, 2017), 39.
2. Richard Sheridan, *Joy Inc.* (New York: Penguin Group, 2013), 139.
3. Kim Scott, *Radical Candor* (New York: St. Martin's Press, 2017), 36.

Part 2

1. Keith McFarland, *The Breakthrough Company* (New York: Crown Business, 2008), 201.

Chapter 5

1. Danny Meyer, *Setting the Table* (New York: Harper Collins, 2006), 206.
2. Meyer, *Setting the Table,* 195.

Chapter 6

1. Kim Scott, *Radical Candor* (New York: St. Martin's Press, 2017), 21.
2. Susan Scott, *Fierce Conversations* (New York, Viking, 2002), xix, 18.

Chapter 7

1. "The Path to Prosperity – Craig [Episode 2]," TRU Colors TV, YouTube video, 2:34, https://www.youtube.com/watch?v=634Ewso-kcc&list=PLwfZv1zlpQuzZ6xXfhLsJgj14gaBZbP-3&index=2.

Chapter 8

1. Louis Kahn, *On the Thoughtful Making of Spaces* (Baden, Switzerland; Lars Muller, 2010).
2. Richard Sheridan, *Joy Inc.* (New York: Penguin Group, 2013), 41.

3. John Mackey and Raj Sisodia, *Conscious Capitalism* (Harvard Business School Publishing Corp., 2013), 249.

Chapter 9

1. Dan and Chip Heath, Switch: *How to Change Things When Change Is Hard* (Chicago: Random House Business Books, 2011), 127.
2. Francesca Gino, "Managing Yourself: Are You Too Stressed to Be Productive? Or Not Stressed Enough?" *Harvard Business Review* (April 14, 2016).
3. Sheldon Cohen, *Perceived Stress Scale* (Menlo Park, CA: Mind Garden Inc, 1994).

Chapter 10

1. Karen Weintraub, "'Stress Hormone' Cortisol Linked to Early Toll on Thinking Ability," *Scientific American* (October 25, 2018).
2. Kim Scott, *Radical Candor* (New York: St. Martin's Press, 2017).

Chapter 11

1. Kim Scott, *Radical Candor* (New York: St. Martin's Press, 2017), 4.

Chapter 12

1. Kim Scott, *Radical Candor* (New York: St. Martin's Press, 2017).
2. Scott, *Radical Candor*, xvi.

Part 4

1. Entrepreneurial Operating System, EOS, and Traction: registered trademarks of EOS Worldwide, LLC.

Chapter 14

1. Gino Wickman, *Traction* (Dallas, TX: BenBella Books, 2012).
2. "Waze." Waze.com, Wave Mobile Limited in Israel (2009).
3. Phone interview with author, June 23, 2021.

Chapter 16

1. Nelson Mandela, *Long Walk to Freedom* (Randburg, South Africa: Macdonal Purnell, 1994), 187, 477, 476.
2. Arianna Stassinopoulos Huffington, *Picasso: Creator and Destroyer* (New York: Simon and Schuster, 1988), 368, 462.
3. Walter Isaacson, *Benjamin Franklin, an American Life*, (New York: Simon and Schuster, 2003), 372.
4. Willie Nelson, *It's a Long Story: My Life* (Boston, MA: Little, Brown and Company, 2015), 201, 374.

Chapter 18

1. Keith McFarland, *The Breakthrough Company* (New York: Crown Business, 2008), 201.
2. Tamsin Woolley-Barker, PhD, *Teeming* (Ashland, OR: White Cloud Press, 2017), 31.
3. Merriam-Webster.com Dictionary, s.v. "superorganism," accessed October 2, 2022, https://www.merriam-webster.com/dictionary/superorganism.

4. Baker, *Teeming*, 29.
5. W.E. Deming, *Out of Crisis* (Cambridge, Mass: MIT Press, 2018), 101.
6. Rikke Friis Dam and Teo Yu Siang, "What Is Design Thinking and Why Is It So Popular?," Interaction Design Foundation, https://www.interaction-design.org/literature/article/what-is-design-thinking-and-why-is-it-so-popular.
7. Elaine Camper, "The Honey Pot: A Lesson in Creativity and Diversity," Insulators Glass & Porcelain, April 2, 1993, https://www.insulators.info/articles/ppl.htm.

Chapter 19

1. Robert Kegan and Lisa Laskow Lahey, *An Everyone Culture: Becoming a Deliberately Developmental Organization* (Boston: Harvard Business Review Press, 2016), 10.
2. Kegan and Lahey, *An Everyone Culture: Becoming a Deliberately Developmental Organization*, 10.
3. Kegan and Lahey, *An Everyone Culture: Becoming a Deliberately Developmental Organization*, 71.
4. Ray Dalio, *Principles* (New York: Simon & Schuster, 2017), 184.

Chapter 20

1. Geoff Smart and Randy Street, *Who* (New York: Ballantine Books, 2008).

Chapter 21

1. John Mackey and Raj Sisodia, *Conscious Capitalism* (Harvard Business School Publishing Corp., 2013), 57.

Index

A

B

C

F

G

H

I

J

K

L

M

N

O

R

S

Introducing Max St. Bernard

THE LEGEND OF THE BARRY DOG: These dogs are large, powerful, and dedicated to their work. They are revered for their sagacity and fidelity, meaning they strictly observe their promises and duties and have acute mental discernment, sound judgement, and a calm, patient, and sweet demeanor. Legend has it that, when they used to assist travelers who were trapped in winter storms and avalanches in the Swiss Alps, they were brilliant at passing along detailed protocol and strategy from generation to generation, which kept them alive in the treacherous surroundings in which they worked. Little if any guidance was provided by the monks they served. Sounds like the kind of leader we all pine for; sound judgement, a sweet demeanor, strong mentoring capability, dependability, and a sip of brandy go a long way when leading others in the world.

About the Author

MICHAEL J. MCFALL spent his formative years in Highland, Michigan, living on Dunham Lake. He graduated from Milford High School in 1989. His junior year, he was a member of the Canadian Class Afloat program, sailing on a square-rigged barkentine tall ship called Pogoria. The ship left Louisbourg, Nova Scotia, and sailed to Singapore, stopping at thirteen countries; Mike had dynamic experiences in each of them.

During his senior year, he captained both his hockey team and golf teams to two of their best seasons to date. He then attended Kalamazoo College, a small liberal arts school that is a shining star for diversity and inclusion, which solidified Mike's commitment to the cause of justice, equity, and opportunity for all. In his junior year of college, he studied in Sierra Leone in West Africa. At the time, Mike was studying there (1991) Sierra Leone was the poorest and least developed country on the planet, according to the world bank, and amid civil war that would continue to rage for more than a decade after he returned home. This experience guided Mike's thoughts, teaching him that no matter where we live, or what circumstances we live within, we are all searching for the same thing: love.

Mike saw a lot of the world at a young age and learned early that similarities in people far outweigh the differences by a factor of one hundred to one. He loves the Arthur Miller quote from Death of a Salesman: "We are all searching for the right way to live so we can call the world a home."

Mike graduated and took a job as a straight-commission sales representative in Houston, Texas. He often credits his success in business to the foundation this sales job provided. There are no more valuable lessons in business than waking up in the morning and trying to sell a ton of products. If we do that as businesspeople, we stand a much better chance of being successful. He enjoyed his work in Houston but wanted to be closer to friends and family in Michigan.

Mike moved home and, after a couple of meaningless jobs, landed in Lansing, Michigan, working at a coffee shop called BIGGBY COFFEE as a minimum wage barista. The owner of the original store, Bob Fish, supported him in getting deeply involved in the business, and they eventually struck up a mutually beneficial partnership to grow and expand the brand and concept of BIGGBY COFFEE. Today Mike is the co-CEO with Bob, and BIGGBY has over 320+ stores open in 12+ states. After twenty-seven years, the company is in high growth mode, and the future looks bright.

In 2018, Mike, Bob and the team at BIGGBY COFFEE, after two years of struggle, settled on the purpose of their organization. The purpose of BIGGBY COFFEE is to support you in building a life you love. They also penned their 2028 vision of improving workplace culture in America. There are two sides to the vision metrics. The first is that 90% of our employees who have worked at BIGGBY COFFEE for a year or more will rate us a 9 or 10 on the question, "Is BIGGBY COFFEE supporting you in building a life you love?" The other is that we will be a billion-dollar company at retail. The goal for the organization is to build a world class culture that encourages everyone within the company to thrive. Not just in their jobs but as people in the world. The idea is to create one of the highest growth brands in America and have people ask the question, how? Then everyone associated with BIGGBY COFFEE will be able to tell the story, we did it through building a loving, caring, nurturing environment where everyone left work at the end of the day more invigorated than when they arrived. Love is the magic elixir to many of the struggles for organizations today.

The book GRIND was published in fall of 2019 and is focused on documenting the experience of business start-up. It is not a how-to manual but sets the attitudinal tone needed for success in a new venture. Mike is not an academic studying entrepreneurship or an uber successful billionaire looking down on start-up from a private plane with rose colored glasses. He is still in the trenches and wanted to bring a real-world perspective to the experience of entrepreneurship. GRIND captures the essence and mindset it takes to be a successful entrepreneur. GRIND and GROW are books one and two in a three-book series.

In the same year he joined BIGGBY COFFEE, Mike tried out for and made a beer league hockey team that would eventually become the BIGGBY Bomber's. These guys have been his posse, his best friends for twenty-six years. They have quite literally grown up together. Never has there been a better group of people assembled to play beer-league sports.

Mike lives in Ann Arbor, Michigan, with his wife, Elizaveta, and their four children. Liam, Klava, Oscar, and Lorenzo. They are fortunate to have a wonderful community of love that starts with their families and extends to their school community and beyond with many beautiful and interesting friends. Life can be a dream, a fairytale. Mike wakes up every day amazed at how much of his life is exactly how he dreamt it would be.